The Upgrade Day

The Upgrade Day

Quarterly Rituals to Reset Money, Health, and Goals

Talia Wrenford

Mindful Pages

Published in 2026

ISBN: 9789376556021 (PB)
ISBN: 9789376556045 (eBook)

Published by

Mindful Pages
Imprint of Alpha Editions LLC
312 W. 2nd St #1834
Casper, WY 82601, USA

This book was developed using advanced writing tools to support the drafting and ideation process. All content has been thoughtfully curated, refined, and reviewed to ensure quality and relevance.

Content

Introduction

On 26 January 2016, Apple Inc. held its first-quarter earnings call from Cupertino, California. Analysts joined from everywhere, hearing that flat, papery conference-line audio, the faint clicks of headsets, the little pauses where a finger finds the mute button. There is something almost monastic about those calls: numbers are read, questions are asked, guidance is revised. No one pretends the previous quarter can be wished away by positive thinking. The past ninety days are treated as a known terrain, with receipts. What changes is the next ninety days, by increments, by decisions, by small adjustments that add up. A business does not romanticise it. It simply turns the dial a quarter-turn and watches what happens.

Time is a poor accountant.

And yet, outside corporate life, January arrives and people behave as though time is best handled in a single annual performance: grand vows, fresh notebooks, new routines purchased like talismans. A gym smells of rubber and disinfectant; a bank app shows a number that feels accusatory; a calendar is repainted with good intentions. The strange part is not that these rituals fail. The strange part is that we persist with a rhythm that does not match the way drift happens in real life. Drift does not announce itself. It is quiet.

The problem is not laziness; it is timing. Annual resolutions create distance. They make the "real change" feel safely far away, like a mountain that can be admired without being climbed. Daily tweaks, at the other extreme, encourage panic. They make life feel like a cockpit in turbulence—constantly adjusting levers without a clear horizon, mistaking motion for direction. Somewhere between the heroic year and the frantic day sits a more humane unit of change: long enough to be meaningful, short enough to be corrigible. A quarter.

Drift is the more interesting enemy because it is rarely dramatic. It looks like a subscription renewed without thought, and another, and another, until a monthly total becomes a quiet tax on the future. It looks like sleep shaved by fifteen minutes to "get ahead", repeated until tiredness becomes a personality trait. It looks like a friendship that survives on affectionate messages but no shared time, until the first serious conversation feels awkward, then postponed, then lost. These are not moral failures. They are the default behaviour of any life lived at speed, with incomplete attention. When the mind is busy, the world continues to alter the terms of the deal. Costs creep, bodies adapt, relationships respond, opportunities narrow. A person wakes up to find that the dial has been turning all along—just not by choice.

The advantage of a ninety-day window is not mystical. It is practical. It is close enough to be remembered with texture: what work felt like on those Mondays, how often the late-night scrolling happened, when the stomach tightened at that particular bank notification, how the shoulders felt after sitting too long. It is also long enough for consequences to appear. A week is too small; most decisions have not had time to reveal their shape. A year is too large; it invites fiction. By the time the year has passed, drift has hardened into circumstance. Ninety days is an interval where evidence still feels near, where habits have had time to leave a trace, where quiet regrets can be converted into small tests rather than grand confessions. The quarter makes drift visible early enough to correct gently rather than dramatically.

Cadence is the more reliable engine than motivation, and it is worth being blunt about why. Motivation is an emotion. Emotions are weather: real, informative, and not remotely guaranteed to cooperate. Cadence is infrastructure. It does not ask for charisma, or for a new identity, or for constant self-surveillance. It asks for a repeated appointment with reality, an interval so ordinary it becomes almost boring. In boringness lies mercy. When a reset is scheduled, it stops being a referendum on character. It becomes a maintenance ritual, like changing a filter or clearing a drain before it floods. Cadence beats enthusiasm, reliably. This is not a protest against ambition; it is a refusal to stake a life's direction on moods.

Modern institutions already know this. They audit, close, review, and revise on a cadence because they assume the world will change and errors will creep in. The fact that individuals often reserve review for New Year's Day is less a sign of personal inadequacy than a sign of inherited cultural theatre: we are trained to treat January as a moral turning point. There is a reason many organisations run on quarters even when the calendar year remains the formal ledger. It is not because they enjoy bureaucracy. It is because the world delivers consequences on its own schedule. If costs rise, if a project stalls, if a team burns out, the year does not pause politely until December. The quarter provides an interval in which reality can be faced without melodrama.

A telling example came from the United Kingdom's energy regulator, Ofgem. In February 2022, in London, it announced that the energy price cap would move to quarterly updates rather than the previous six-month cycle, a response to the speed at which wholesale markets were shifting. The detail matters less than the logic: when volatility increases, a slower cadence becomes hazardous because it forces larger corrections. With longer intervals, changes pile up; the adjustment arrives as a shock. A shorter cadence turns shocks into smaller turns of the dial. It is a sober acknowledgement that timing is a form of risk management. The same principle applies to a person's money, health, relationships, and work. When drift and volatility are allowed to accumulate unnoticed, the eventual correction is harsher: the sudden budget crisis, the abrupt injury, the friendship break, the panicked career pivot. A quarterly rhythm does not prevent shocks, but it changes the size of the corrections life demands.

Still, cadence is not a universal solvent. There are lives in which the quarter is too slow: acute illness, sudden unemployment, crisis caregiving, the kind of unstable housing or precarious work where every week is a new negotiation. There are also lives where the quarter is too fast, where a long-term creative project or recovery process needs months of steadiness before judgement becomes meaningful. The quarter is not a moral law. It is a tool, and tools have grain. Used against the grain, they splinter. Used with it, they make clean cuts. The honest reconciliation is this: a quarterly reset is not for emergencies, and it is not a substitute for day-to-day responsibility. It is a discipline of noticing, a regular return to the question of direction, carried out at an interval that fits most ordinary lives—busy, imperfect, and still steerable.

What makes this kind of reset psychologically tolerable is that it shrinks the scope from everything to something. A year tempts totalising narratives: "This is who I am now." A quarter encourages narrower, more testable statements: "This is what happened." Abstractions like trust, efficiency, and risk stop being vague ideals and become visible behaviours. Trust becomes the decision to look at bank balances without flinching, to admit what is happening rather than what should be happening. Efficiency becomes the act of comparing a calendar against claimed priorities and noticing the mismatch. Risk becomes the small gamble of changing one habit or commitment for ninety days and watching for second-order effects. The quarter turns virtue into evidence. It also creates a boundary that is psychologically clean. If something is tried and disliked, it ends. If it works, it can be repeated. The future is approached as a sequence of experiments rather than a single audition.

The architecture of an Upgrade Day—four times a year, brief, deliberate—rests on an insistence: the reset must be small enough to be repeated. Repetition is the point. Consider the difference between a sprawling annual "life audit" and a lean quarterly ritual. The audit is alluring because it flatters the mind's love of grand plans. It is also fragile. It breaks under ordinary interruptions: a child's illness, a deadline, a bleak month, an unexpected trip. The lean ritual survives because it has a script. A person sits down with a handful of data and a notebook, compares snapshots across time, and makes a few decisions. Nothing is perfect. Nothing is total. The aim is not control; it is course correction.

Money is the easiest domain to misunderstand because numbers feel like judgement. Yet the most useful approach is not obsessiveness but a periodic snapshot—direction over precision. The point of a simple net worth picture, taken quarterly, is not to predict markets or perform virtuosity with spreadsheets. It is to make "I think I'm doing fine" and "I feel anxious" answerable to reality. When the snapshot is repeated, patterns appear without drama: debt that is shrinking, savings that are flat, spending that has migrated from one category to another. Behaviour becomes visible. A quarter offers enough distance for honesty and enough proximity for changes to be reversible. It is the same with spending patterns. The meaningful question is not whether a person bought a coffee on a Tuesday; it is what clusters have formed, what the money is actually supporting, and whether that support aligns with what matters. The dial moves either way. The quarter-turn makes it legible.

Health is similarly distorted by the culture of extremes. A year encourages fantasies of reinvention; a day encourages guilt. A quarter allows for a scorecard that is neither punitive nor vague. Sleep can be treated as hours rather than moral virtue. Movement can be measured as consistency rather than intensity. Training can be assessed through trends—what has improved, what has stalled, what has quietly become painful—without forcing a person to live inside a fitness app. The most adult act, in health, is often the simplest: to notice what has actually been happening, and to acknowledge recovery as part of the system rather than a reward for suffering. Rest, maintenance, and check-ups are not indulgences. They are the cost of having a body that must last through many quarters.

Relationships resist quantification, which is precisely why they drift. The calendar fills with obligations because saying yes is easier than renegotiating the social story attached to a recurring commitment. A quarter is long enough for neglect to become visible and short enough to repair it without theatrical apology. Mapping relationship circles does something subtle: it converts the fog of "I should keep in touch" into a picture of where attention has actually gone. It also reveals overcommitment. Many people do not lack friends; they lack space. A quarterly check-in can be gentle and unsentimental: which ties energise, which drain, which are strained by avoidance. The behaviour-level corollary of trust appears again here. Trust is not an abstract warmth; it is a specific act—making a call, planning a visit, stepping back respectfully from a commitment that has become performative. When the quarter is the unit, these acts can be planned without turning them into vows about being a "better person".

Work and projects are where drift often masquerades as busyness. A project pipeline spreads. Meetings replicate. Email becomes a low-level fog that blurs the edges of the day. A calendar review exposes reality with an almost comic clarity. If a person claims that health matters, but the diary shows twelve-hour days and no slack, the mismatch is not solved by self-reproach. It is solved by design: cancelling, shortening, delegating, or simply admitting that the current season is not one where certain goals are possible. This is where quarterly thinking becomes a form of integrity. Integrity is not purity. It is alignment. A quarter makes it possible to plan sprints and slack in the same breath, to accept that intense effort without recovery is not dedication but erosion.

Learning, in adult life, is particularly vulnerable to fantasy. A new skill promises a new self, and the internet sells that promise in tidy units: courses purchased, apps installed, books stacked. A quarter is long enough to make learning real, and the way it does so is wonderfully unromantic. It forces specificity. Instead of "become fluent", the quarter insists on smaller, verifiable outputs: practice projects completed, conversations attempted, pages written, problems solved. The questions become practical rather than aspirational. Which learning vehicle fits the actual texture of a life—time, energy, obligations? Which tracking method supports engagement without turning it into a contest? The quarter transforms learning from consumption into application, without requiring an identity makeover.

The environment—spaces, gear, systems—sits behind all these domains like an invisible stagehand. People underestimate how much behaviour is negotiated with friction. A cluttered desk is not merely untidy; it is a cue to avoid the work. A phone screen crowded with icons is not merely busy; it is an invitation to distraction. Worn-out shoes are not merely shabby; they are a low-grade deterrent to movement. Small repairs prevent large irritations. A quarterly walk-through of spaces, physical and digital, makes friction points speak. It also prevents accumulation disguised as "preparation". The question is not whether a person owns the perfect tools. It is whether the tools and systems in use are making the chosen habits easier or harder. This is the quiet power of a quarter-turn: it suggests that a life can be improved not only by effort, but by making effort less necessary.

Then there is the domain that modern culture treats as optional: rest, travel, play. A year can swallow these whole. Days can postpone them indefinitely. A quarter is a rhythm that allows recovery to be planned with seriousness and without guilt. Energy can be assessed as honestly as finances: where exhaustion clustered, where flow appeared, where boredom acted as a warning rather than a sin. Trips and retreats need not be extravagant to matter; they are interruptions that restore perspective, especially when the calendar has become a machine for producing obligations. Hobbies, too, are diagnostic. The loss of play is often the earliest sign that life has become over-instrumental, that everything must justify itself by output. A quarterly reset treats enjoyment as legitimate data: not a reward for a life well-managed, but a component of a life worth managing at all.

What holds all this together is not self-improvement as a personality. It is a cadence that becomes part of the year's texture, anchored to seasons and cues. Humans are seasonal creatures whether we admit it or not. Terms begin. Holidays end. Weather shifts. Work cycles tighten and loosen. A quarterly ritual can borrow these natural anchors and become less a task than a familiar turn in the year, like changing the bedding when the temperature drops. Over time, the script evolves because the person evolves. Some prompts stop being useful. New ones appear. The ritual remains lean by shedding what no longer serves. It can also, used wisely, involve others: not as a confessional theatre, but as parallel reflection, shared planning, or a respectful exchange of intentions where privacy is protected and support is real.

The deeper claim beneath all of this is almost unfashionable: that a good life is not built by intensity, but by revision. Revision is a craft mindset. It assumes the first draft of a quarter will contain errors and omissions, and that this is not shameful but expected. Revision is how a person stays in relationship with reality rather than in relationship with a fantasy of themselves. It is also how ambition becomes sustainable. The Upgrade Day does not ask for dramatic change. It asks for measured change: compare, test, adjust, repeat. The quarter-turn appears again, not as a slogan but as a method. A tiny turn, done often, outperforms a grand turn, done rarely.

The forward tension is simple and uncomfortable. Every quarter presents a trade-off between what is easy now and what is easier later; between the comfort of drift and the discomfort of looking; between the illusion that time will sort things out and the quieter truth that time only amplifies what is repeated. A person can live by hope alone for surprisingly long, and then one day the calendar, the body, the bank balance, or the strained conversation makes the bill come due. The ritual equips a different decision: to treat the next ninety days as steerable, to accept that not everything can be changed at once, and to choose which dial deserves the next quarter-turn.

Chapter 1
Why Quarterly Resets Work

On 15 September 2008, employees at Lehman Brothers arrived at 745 Seventh Avenue in Manhattan to find a kind of quiet that felt wrong. Security was tighter. Conversations were shorter. The building—so often a machine for momentum—had acquired the stillness of something waiting to be emptied. In the days before, the headlines had caught up to what insiders already knew: the firm had run out of room to improvise. The story is often told as sudden collapse, a cliff-edge moment. Yet the cliff was approached by inches: assumptions left unchallenged, exposures tolerated because they were manageable in the short term, small decisions accumulating into a position that could no longer be adjusted gently. Catastrophe has a talent for arriving with theatre, but it is usually rehearsed in private.

Most personal derailments are less dramatic and more intimate. No one gathers outside your flat with a camera when your bank balance tightens, your sleep frays, or your friendships become a handful of apologetic messages. Your life does not file for bankruptcy in a courthouse. It simply becomes narrower. The remarkable thing is how rarely this narrowing is chosen. It happens through slow drift: the quiet movement of money, habits, and commitments when they are not examined. Drift is not a villain. It is physics. Left alone, systems slide towards the path of least resistance.

Drift is almost never announced.

That is why quarterly resets work. They are not a personality test. They are not a promise of a new self. They are an interval designed to interrupt drift while the adjustments are still small enough to be kind. If that sounds oddly mechanistic—treating a life like a system—it is worth noticing how often modern life already behaves like one. Subscriptions renew automatically. Apps learn your patterns. Work expands to fill the available hours. Social obligations become recurring events with no clear author. Time is not neutral here; it is an amplifier. Without a cadence of review, the defaults quietly win.

The first task of this chapter is to make drift visible without turning it into melodrama. A person rarely wakes up one morning having "become bad with money" or "lost fitness" or "neglected friendships" as though a switch has flipped. What happens is smaller and stranger: a few pounds more on the weekly shop because you started buying convenience; a few evenings lost because work spilled over; a few minor aches ignored until movement becomes something you bargain with rather than enjoy. These are not dramatic decisions. They are micro-compromises, often made under fatigue. They feel rational in the moment. They are also cumulative.

Consider spending, because it offers a clean illustration. A single subscription is trivial. Two are manageable. Twelve are an ecosystem you never consciously built. Each one arrives with its own justification: it helps with work, it helps you relax, it is "only" a small monthly cost. The drift happens not in the subscription itself, but in the absence of a moment where the whole pattern is seen at once. Without that moment, spending becomes a set of unconnected anecdotes rather than a system. The same is true of health habits. A single late night is nothing; a season of late nights becomes a baseline. The same is true of commitments. A small favour becomes a routine; a routine becomes an obligation; an obligation becomes resentment. Drift does not feel like change. It feels like normal.

This chapter treats a ninety-day window as a practical lens for catching that normal before it calcifies. Ninety days is short enough that memory still has texture. You can still recall the week when you ate badly because of deadlines, the stretch when you moved less because the weather turned, the moment you agreed to something you did not want because it was easier to say yes than to explain no. Yet ninety days is long enough for consequences to show their outlines: a financial trend rather than a single expense; a shift in energy rather than a single tired day; a thinning of connection rather than one missed call. The quarter is where patterns begin to reveal themselves, but where they have not yet become destiny. It is the difference between noticing a small crack and waiting for the wall to split.

The modern world intensifies drift because it industrialises distraction. Attention is chopped into fragments and sold back to us in alluring forms, and the cost is not only time. It is coherence. When attention is fragmented, reflection becomes harder. When reflection becomes harder, defaults take over. That is how a person ends up optimising for what is urgent rather than what is important, for what is loud rather than what is meaningful, for what is instantly gratifying rather than what compounds quietly. The quarterly reset is a small rebellion against that industrial rhythm. It is a commitment to stepping out of the stream long enough to see where it is carrying you.

If drift is the mechanism, cadence is the antidote. The culture loves motivation because it makes a good story. It is cinematic: a surge of inspiration, a decisive turning point, a montage of effort. Cadence is less glamorous. It is a calendar entry. It is repetition. It is the unsexy discipline of showing up when you do not feel particularly inspired. Yet cadence is the only method that respects how humans actually behave. Motivation rises and falls. Energy fluctuates. Confidence is fickle. A scheduled ritual does not demand that these variables behave. It simply requires that you return, at a predictable interval, and compare what you thought would happen with what happened.

This distinction matters because the motivational approach quietly turns every lapse into an indictment. If change depends on willpower, then any failure becomes evidence of personal deficiency. People internalise that narrative easily. They say they are "undisciplined" or "bad with money" or "never stick to things". Cadence offers a different story: the system was not designed to support the behaviour. This is not an excuse. It is a diagnosis. When the diagnosis changes, the solution changes. Instead of seeking more grit, you build better timing. Instead of waiting for the mood to strike, you create an appointment with reality. Instead of treating the year as a single heroic project, you treat it as four manageable drafts.

Infrastructure is not cold. It is compassionate.

The quarter is the sweet spot in that infrastructure because it sits between two familiar failures: the annual review and the weekly plan. Annual reviews are inspiring and, for many people, pointless. They are inspiring because the horizon is wide enough to hold dreams. They are pointless because the interval is so long that memory becomes unreliable and procrastination becomes plausible. A year is spacious enough for self-deception. You can tell yourself a story in January and forget it by March. You can postpone discomfort for months and still feel as though you have "time". Weekly planning has the opposite problem. It is intimate with reality but often too reactive. It can become a ritual of managing the urgent, a treadmill of small fixes and endless optimisation. Weekly plans are excellent for logistics. They are less effective for steering life's deeper currents.

Quarters allow both evidence and intention to meet without either dominating. They are long enough to generate meaningful data: how much you saved, how consistently you moved, what projects actually advanced, which relationships received attention. They are short enough that a correction is plausible. If a quarter goes badly, it does not become a moral crisis. It becomes information. If a quarter goes well, it does not require grand celebration. It becomes a pattern worth repeating. This is why organisations use quarters, but it is also why human beings can. A life is not a corporation, but it is still a set of systems interacting under constraints. The quarter is a humane way to hold those systems lightly, without pretending they will self-correct if left alone.

Of course, there are counter-examples worth respecting. Some pursuits do not show their value in ninety days. Learning a language, recovering from a serious injury, building a meaningful body of creative work—these often resist quarterly judgement. A quarter can tempt a person into premature evaluation, mistaking slow growth for failure. The reconciliation is not to abandon cadence, but to adjust what is measured. The quarter need not be a verdict; it can be a check-in on inputs rather than outputs. Did practice happen? Did recovery remain protected? Did the work continue in the small, stubborn way it must? The quarter remains useful even when the results are slow, because it keeps the process from dissolving into vague hope. It prevents drift in the long projects too, but it demands humility about what can be seen.

Once the cadence is accepted, a second risk appears: the ritual can swell. People are talented at turning a helpful practice into a punishing audit. They add more metrics, more categories, more rules, until the reset becomes an annual review in miniature—heavy, anxious, avoided. The final movement of this chapter therefore narrows the scope to something workable: choosing focus domains. The world offers infinite possible improvements. A quarter does not. A quarter is finite. It has weekends, evenings, obligations, tired days, good days. The power of an Upgrade Day comes from treating that finitude seriously.

Choosing domains is not about pretending every area of life can be optimised simultaneously. It is about deciding which areas deserve attention because they have leverage—because small changes there ripple into other areas. Money might be the domain that reduces background stress and buys time. Health might be the domain that makes every other domain easier to carry. Relationships might be the domain that improves resilience, because a supportive network changes how setbacks land. Learning might be the domain that expands options, making future quarters more flexible. Work might be the domain that protects time and energy. Environment might be the domain that removes friction, making good habits less effortful. The choice is personal, but the logic is structural: pick the few that matter most *this quarter*, not the many that matter in theory.

The image to keep in mind is not a dramatic reinvention but a dial—small turns, repeated, with attention paid to what changes. A quarterly reset is not a promise that life will become controlled. It is an agreement to stop being surprised by the predictable. It is a way of noticing that certain stresses recur, that certain temptations reliably win, that certain parts of life are quietly starved of attention, and that these patterns are not fate. They are feedback. The quarter gives you a rhythm for listening.

Today, the appeal of such a rhythm is not merely personal; it is cultural. When news cycles are rapid, work can be boundaryless, and social comparison is constant, the mind is pushed towards short-termism. Everything feels immediate. Everything demands response. A quarterly cadence reintroduces a slower, steadier layer of time—one that can hold priorities without being bulldozed by the latest urgency. It does not deny the chaos. It simply refuses to let chaos decide everything. The quarter is a container in which you can make decisions that are not reactive, that are not driven solely by the mood of a particular week, and that respect the reality that small patterns compound.

There is also something quietly dignified about quarters. They acknowledge that life is lived in seasons. Energy rises and falls. Work intensifies and relaxes. Relationships have phases. Bodies respond to weather, stress, and rest. A quarterly reset aligns with that seasonal truth. It makes room for the idea that not all quarters should look the same. Some will be focused and productive; others will be restorative; others will be messy. The cadence survives because it does not demand uniformity. It demands return.

By the end of this chapter, the reader should feel a shift from self-judgement to design-minded curiosity. Not the brittle curiosity of optimisation, but the sturdy curiosity of someone willing to compare, test, and revise. The promise is not that the next quarter will be perfect. The promise is that it will be chosen more deliberately. Drift will still exist; it always will. The difference is that drift will have less time to accumulate unnoticed, and less power to decide outcomes by default.

The page-turning question is simple, and it is sharper than it first appears: which parts of life are currently being run by your intentions, and which are being run by inertia? The quarter is where that question stops being philosophical and becomes measurable—through calendar traces, spending clusters, consistency patterns, and the quiet emotional signals that appear when you look honestly at what you keep postponing. There is an unmistakable moment, once you start working in quarters, when you realise that the year is not a single mountain but four hills. Hills can be climbed. Hills can be re-climbed. Hills can be approached with strategy rather than bravado. The next step is to understand why that rhythm is not merely convenient, but structurally powerful.

Understanding slow drift

On 28 January 1986, the Space Shuttle *Challenger* broke apart seventy-three seconds after launch from Kennedy Space Center in Florida.

The images—white exhaust against a bright blue sky—became instant shorthand for catastrophe, as if the event had erupted from nowhere. Yet in Diane Vaughan's later account of the disaster, published in 1996, the most unsettling detail is not the violence of the end but the banality of the lead-up: prior anomalies were discussed, reclassified, tolerated, and gradually absorbed into the definition of "acceptable" performance. The system did not snap from safe to unsafe in a single moment; it slid. Engineers and managers did not wake up intending harm. They adjusted to small deviations until deviation felt normal.

Drift hides in plain sight.

That is the first fact worth facing: the outcomes that feel "sudden" are often the final frame of a longer, quieter film. In organisations, drift shows up as standards that soften, exceptions that become routine, and risks that are renamed until they sound manageable. In personal life, drift is less formal but no less real. A spending pattern shifts by a few decisions a week. Sleep erodes by minutes. Commitments multiply by polite assent. The result can be the same structural surprise: a person looks up and realises the life they are living is not the life they meant to build.

Slow drift is not simply "change over time". It is a particular kind of change: unexamined, incremental, and propelled by defaults. It thrives where attention is scarce and friction is low. A person does not need to choose drift. Drift is what happens when choice is never reactivated. The everyday machinery of modern life is optimised for this. Payments renew automatically. Notifications nudge behaviour continuously. Work expands through invisible channels—messages, "quick" calls, minor crises that become permanent. Social expectation rewards responsiveness more than reflection. None of this is malicious. It is efficient. But efficiency without periodic inspection turns into a kind of silent governance: the calendar, the bank statement, and the body begin to express priorities that were never consciously endorsed.

The mechanism is easy to miss because each step is rational in isolation. A streaming subscription is taken out because it offers relief at the end of a tiring day. A takeaway meal is ordered because time is tight and energy is low. A late reply to a friend becomes normal because work is "just busy right now". A small ache is ignored because it seems too minor to warrant attention. Each action is defensible. The drift emerges from aggregation. When a person never looks at the pattern as a pattern, the pattern becomes the plan.

In sociological terms, Vaughan gave the organisational version of this a name: "normalisation of deviance". The phrase matters because it captures something more precise than "people made mistakes". The deviance was not a one-off breach; it was a deviation from expected performance that, over time, became treated as routine. The important step is not the first anomaly but the second: the moment the system learns that nothing awful happened last time, so the same deviation feels safer now. Familiarity dulls risk perception. In personal life, familiarity performs the same anaesthetic. Overspending can become familiar. Exhaustion can become familiar. Resentment can become familiar. Familiarity is not consent, but the nervous system can confuse the two.

It is tempting to treat money, health, and relationships as separate compartments—one governed by spreadsheets, one by biology, one by emotion. Drift does not respect those boundaries. It moves across them like silt in a river, settling where the current slows. A slight increase in work intensity creates less time to cook, which nudges spending up and health down. Poor sleep reduces patience, which changes the tone of conversations, which makes relationships feel heavier, which encourages escapist spending or screen time, which further erodes sleep. The system reinforces itself. The problem is not that any one decision is catastrophic. The problem is that small decisions can align into a direction.

The mind has predictable blind spots here. Behavioural economists have spent decades documenting how humans handle future costs poorly, especially when immediate rewards are easy and delayed consequences are vague. Kahneman and Tversky's work on judgement under uncertainty (1979) shows how people weigh outcomes in ways that are not purely rational; Thaler and Sunstein's later work on "choice architecture" (2008) popularised the idea that defaults and framing shape behaviour at scale. These are not academic curiosities. They explain why drift flourishes. The future is abstract; the present is tactile. The present offers comfort you can feel in your hands: a warm meal, a quick purchase, a "yes" that avoids awkwardness, a late night that feels like reclaimed time. The future offers only a story—until it becomes a bill, a symptom, or a silence between two people who used to speak freely.

Take spending as a visible example because it leaves traces. A person rarely intends to build a life dominated by fixed monthly outgoings; it is assembled gradually through "small" recurring choices. A gym membership that is not used becomes a kind of donation to guilt. A digital service that is kept "just in case" becomes a quiet subscription to indecision. A convenience habit becomes a budget line. The drift is often not extravagance but repetition. Risk, in this domain, is not the dramatic gamble. It is the slow acceptance of a new baseline. The behaviour-level signal is simple: when the monthly total is predictable but never consciously re-chosen, drift is already at work.

Health drift works the same way, with different metrics. The body is adaptive. It adjusts to the rhythms it is given, often without complaint until a threshold is crossed. The modern trap is that the threshold feels moralised: people speak as if fatigue proves weakness, as if aches prove age, as if lack of fitness proves poor character. That story is seductive and useless. The more accurate story is mechanical. Repetition accumulates. Posture becomes habit. Sleep debt accumulates. Movement patterns narrow. The implication is not judgement; it is inevitability. If small changes can quietly degrade health, small changes can also quietly stabilise it. But the stabilisation requires noticing. Without noticing, the body becomes the place where drift invoices you.

Relationships drift in a subtler register because they are governed by narrative as much as by time. People often say a relationship "faded", as though it were a photograph left in the sun. The fading usually has a schedule: fewer conversations, shorter messages, less shared experience, more assumptions. A relationship can survive long gaps if the underlying sense of mutual regard remains strong; it can also be damaged by small, repeated absences that communicate, unintentionally, "You are optional." Trust, here, is not a lofty abstraction. It is visible behaviour: who is called when something good happens, who is called when something hard happens, who is repeatedly postponed. Drift thrives in the gap between affection and action.

High-stakes industries offer another stark illustration of how drift becomes invisible. On 20 April 2010, the Deepwater Horizon drilling rig exploded in the Gulf of Mexico, killing eleven people and triggering a massive oil spill. The U.S. National Commission's 2011 report described a complex chain of technical failures, but it also pointed to deeper issues: judgement calls, risk tolerance, and safety practices shaped by routine pressures. Again, the point is not that one person "caused" the disaster by waking up reckless. The point is that a system can become accustomed to operating near the edge. When nothing goes wrong for long enough, the edge feels like the centre.

Personal life is not an offshore rig, and it should not be dramatised as one. Yet the analogy is useful because it shows how the absence of catastrophe can be misread as proof of safety. A person can overspend slightly for months without disaster; the credit line absorbs it. A person can run on insufficient sleep for years; the body compensates. A person can neglect friendships and still receive polite replies; the relationship masks the damage. In each case, the system is buffering the drift. Buffers are not endless. When a buffer fails, the moment feels abrupt. But the drift has been charging interest.

This is where the ninety-day window becomes more than a neat calendar unit. It functions as a perceptual tool. Most drift is invisible at the scale of days because the signal is noisy. A single week of spending can be distorted by travel, birthdays, unexpected repairs. A single week of health can be distorted by illness or deadlines. A single week of relationships can be distorted by competing obligations. Daily inspection can therefore produce anxiety without insight: people stare at fluctuations and mistake them for trends. The quarter, by contrast, reduces noise. It does not remove complexity, but it makes patterns legible enough to be named.

Naming matters. A pattern that is unnamed cannot be negotiated. It can only be endured. When a person sees, over a quarter, that certain costs recur, that sleep has been shaved consistently, that a recurring commitment generates dread, the pattern stops being a mood and becomes information. Information creates agency. The implication is not that a person must "fix" everything; it is that they can *choose* what to adjust rather than being adjusted by default. The quarter makes the dial visible: it shows what has turned, in which direction, and by how much.

There is a further psychological advantage to the ninety-day lens: it restores proportionality. A common failure mode of self-assessment is either catastrophising ("Everything is falling apart") or minimising ("It's fine"). Both are distortions. The quarter invites a calmer question: what changed enough to matter? In finance, the relevant behaviour might be whether a surplus has quietly vanished, or whether recurring payments have multiplied. In health, it might be whether energy has been consistently low, or whether movement has become less frequent. In relationships, it might be whether certain people have become absent from the calendar. These are not grand narratives. They are measurable shifts. They are the kind of shifts that can be corrected gently precisely because they are caught early.

A limitation deserves to be stated plainly: not all outcomes are drift. Some outcomes are shocks. A sudden redundancy, an acute illness, a family crisis—these are not the result of slow accumulation, and it would be cruel to imply they are. Even in domains where drift exists, causality is messy. People can do "everything right" and still face bad luck. A quarter cannot protect against the randomness of life, and it cannot make every outcome controllable. The reconciliation is this: drift is not the only source of trouble, but it is one of the few that is *regularly negotiable*. Where shocks demand resilience, drift rewards attention. Treating them as distinct prevents both self-blame and magical thinking.

There is also a subtler counter-example: sometimes drift is positive. People mature. Tastes refine. Relationships deepen quietly without formal effort. A person can slowly become more frugal, more patient, more curious, almost without noticing, because the environment and routines support it. Drift, in this sense, is not inherently harmful; it is simply directional. The danger lies in unconscious drift that contradicts stated values, or that erodes buffers without consent. The opportunity lies in recognising that the same mechanism can work in your favour if the direction is chosen and then allowed to compound.

That word—compound—often appears in financial contexts, but the principle is broader. Time magnifies repetition. Repetition magnifies identity. This is why drift is so consequential: it is not merely about outcomes; it is about the person a life is training you to become. If the quarter reveals that evenings are consistently consumed by low-grade distraction, that is not just a time-management issue; it is a claim about attention, about what the mind is learning to seek when tired. If the quarter reveals that certain relationships are always postponed, that is not just scheduling; it is a claim about what kind of friend or colleague one is being shaped into by habit. The visible metrics—bank totals, sleep hours, meeting counts—are proxies for something more intimate: the formation of a life.

The motif of silt is useful here because drift rarely arrives as a boulder. It arrives as tiny particles. Each one seems harmless. But over time, silt can change a river's course. It can clog, slow, and redirect. A quarter is not a dredging operation. It is a walk along the bank with enough distance to see where the water is going and whether the current still serves the destination. The power lies in the timing. If the observation happens once a year, the river may have already carved a new channel. If it happens every day, the observer may go mad trying to measure every ripple. The quarter is a workable compromise between negligence and obsession.

Notice, too, the emotional signature of drift. People often experience a vague sense of being "behind" that does not match any single failure. The sensation is real. It comes from misalignment between what is being lived and what is being valued. A person can be productive and still feel behind if productivity is displacing something essential—sleep, friendship, learning, play. The quarterly lens does not solve that tension by offering comforting slogans; it makes the tension specific. It ties feeling to evidence. It turns existential unease into concrete discrepancies: time spent versus time claimed, money flowing versus money intended, energy used versus energy restored. That specificity is not cold. It is clarifying. It reduces the need for self-deception.

It also changes the nature of risk. Risk is often imagined as a dramatic leap: quitting a job, moving cities, making a big investment. Slow drift introduces a different kind of risk: the risk of never deciding. The risk of allowing the defaults to write the story. The behaviour-level sign of this risk is quiet: recurring costs never reconsidered, recurring meetings never questioned, recurring fatigue never investigated, recurring irritations never resolved. The quarter makes these recurrences visible enough to be treated as decisions rather than weather.

And yet the most important implication is not simply that drift can be seen. It is that drift can be corrected without humiliation when it is seen early. People delay reflection because they assume it will require dramatic change: harsh restriction, grand confrontations, sweeping redesign. That assumption makes avoidance feel protective. The quarter undermines it. When the discrepancy is small, the correction can be small. Small is repeatable. Small is survivable. Small respects the fact that adult life contains obligations that do not vanish because someone has discovered a new system. The quarter does not demand purity. It demands attention.

By the time a person notices drift through pain—an overdraft panic, a sustained exhaustion, a friendship that feels brittle—the correction tends to be dramatic because buffers have thinned. Dramatic corrections often provoke backlash: rigid budgets that collapse, overtraining followed by injury, performative relationship gestures that do not repair underlying neglect. The quarter is valuable precisely because it keeps the corrections in the realm of proportion. It catches the silt before the course changes.

A final tension remains, and it is the one that makes this work intellectually serious rather than merely practical. Attention has a cost. To look closely at one's own patterns is to risk discomfort, because the patterns may contradict the story one tells about oneself. Some people prefer not to look, not because they are lazy, but because they are protecting an identity: "I'm responsible", "I'm healthy", "I'm a good friend", "I have things under control". Quarterly noticing threatens the comfort of these labels. It replaces them with evidence. Evidence can bruise. It can also liberate, because it turns identity from a claim into a craft.

So the forward test is not whether drift exists—it does, as surely as gravity. The test is whether the discomfort of noticing is smaller than the eventual discomfort of surprise. That trade-off is rarely faced directly. The quarter brings it forward. When the ninety-day window is held up to a life, a question forms naturally, sharp enough to matter: which small, repeated defaults are quietly steering the outcome, and which of them are still worth consenting to?

Cadence versus motivation

In October 2008, at the World Health Organization headquarters in Geneva, a deceptively small document was released into a very large machine: the Surgical Safety Checklist. It was not a new drug. It was not a new scanner. It was, essentially, a script—nineteen items to be confirmed at defined moments before and after an operation. The idea travelled fast because it addressed an old problem with an unglamorous tool: complex work performed under pressure is vulnerable to omission. In 2009, a study led by Alex B. Haynes and colleagues, published in *The New England Journal of Medicine*, reported that introducing the checklist across a set of international hospitals was associated with reduced complications and deaths (Haynes et al., 2009). It was not inspiration that produced that outcome. It was timing.

The checklist does not care.

This is the hidden argument beneath every durable change: the world is shaped less by how intensely one feels on a given day than by what reliably happens when feeling is absent. Motivation makes wonderful openings. It makes poor scaffolding. A surge of resolve can launch a project, a diet, a saving plan, a new learning habit. It rarely sustains it, because resolve is not an asset you hold; it is a state you visit. Cadence—scheduled repetition—acts differently. It is the metronome beneath the performance, the quiet ticking that keeps the piece together even when the performer is tired, distracted, or uncertain. When people say they "can't stick to things", they are often blaming the performer when the missing part is the metronome.

The motivational model flatters a particular story about human agency: that the decisive factor is will, that success belongs to those who want it enough, that lapses signal weakness. It is a story that sells well because it is simple and moral. It is also a story that collapses under inspection. Human beings do not live in controlled environments. They live among interruptions, temptations, obligations, and shifting energy. The person who manages to act consistently is rarely the person who feels consistently inspired; it is the person whose environment and timing make the desired action the path of least resistance. The moral language of willpower turns what is often a design problem into a character problem. That is a subtle cruelty. It adds shame to an already difficult task.

The research landscape reflects this tension. The popular idea that willpower is like a muscle that becomes "depleted" after use was associated with Roy Baumeister and colleagues' work on ego depletion (Baumeister et al., 1998). The notion seeped into common sense: resist temptation now, become weaker later. Yet the evidence base has been contested. A large multi-lab replication led by Martin Hagger and colleagues in 2016 reported difficulty reproducing classic ego depletion effects under certain conditions (Hagger et al., 2016). Other analyses and debates have argued about publication bias and heterogeneity (Carter & McCullough, 2014). The honest take is not that willpower is irrelevant, nor that it is a myth, but that relying on it as the main engine is risky. A person can make a serious change and still have a depleted Tuesday. A system that requires heroic Tuesday discipline is not robust. A cadence that survives Tuesday is.

The more reliable lever is scheduling: not in the sterile sense of filling a diary with obligations, but in the specific sense of assigning decision points to time. This shifts a task from the realm of "should" to the realm of "when". A "should" can be delayed indefinitely because it never meets the resistance of reality. A "when" collides with the calendar. The collision is useful. It forces choice: do it now, move it, or admit it is not being prioritised. That forced clarity is why cadence is infrastructure. Infrastructure does not guarantee beauty, but it reliably carries weight.

One of the strongest psychological tools for turning intentions into actions is the idea of implementation intentions—"if-then" plans—

associated with Peter Gollwitzer's work (Gollwitzer, 1999). The core insight is that people are more likely to follow through when they specify the situational cue that will trigger the action, rather than holding a vague intention in the mind. This is not motivational poetry; it is cognitive engineering. It reduces the need for a fresh act of will at the moment of action. It makes the cue do some of the work. Cadence, at its best, is implementation intention expanded to a seasonal scale: a repeated cue embedded in time itself. When the quarter turns, the ritual turns with it. The metronome ticks.

The point becomes clearer when you look at how people actually fail. They do not usually fail because they do not know what they want. They fail because the moment arrives and something else is louder. The inbox is louder. The child is louder. The exhaustion is louder. The phone is louder. In that moment, motivation is a fragile voice, easily drowned. Scheduling does not silence the world, but it changes the battleground. It moves some decisions out of the heat of the moment and into a calmer context. That is not laziness; it is judgement. It is the decision to decide under better conditions.

Consider money, because it has a grim honesty. A person may be highly motivated to save, invest, reduce debt, or simply feel less anxious. Yet motivation tends to express itself as episodic austerity followed by a rebound: a week of strictness, a weekend of spending as relief. Scheduling, by contrast, builds a pattern of attention. The most effective financial interventions at scale often rely on defaults and regularity rather than exhortation. The "Save More Tomorrow" programme proposed by Richard Thaler and Shlomo Benartzi in 2004, for example, centred on committing in advance to allocate future pay rises towards retirement saving (Thaler & Benartzi, 2004). The mechanism is not "feel motivated forever". The mechanism is "decide once, then let the system execute". That is cadence in institutional form.

A more concrete national example sits in the United Kingdom. In October 2012, automatic enrolment into workplace pensions began rolling out, requiring employers to enrol eligible workers into a pension scheme while allowing opt-out (The Pensions Regulator, 2012). Whatever one thinks of pension policy, the behavioural logic is unmistakable: participation rises when the default is enrolment and the action required is opting out, not signing up. The system does not plead with people to be responsible. It schedules responsibility into the baseline. It shifts the burden from motivation to structure. The implication for personal practice is not to mimic government policy, but to recognise the principle: where actions are repeated, make the default do as much of the work as possible.

Health and learning tell the same story, albeit with more cultural noise. People often imagine that health improvements require continuous enthusiasm, when what they actually require is consistent exposure to certain behaviours and consistent protection from others. Habit formation research supports this. In 2010, Phillippa Lally and colleagues published a study in the *European Journal of Social Psychology* showing that habit formation time varies widely depending on behaviour and person; the popular myth of a tidy, universal timeline does not hold (Lally et al., 2010). The significant point is not the headline number. It is the variability and the implication: if a habit takes longer than expected, motivation will not last. Only a system that expects boredom can survive boredom.

Cadence expects boredom.

This is where the motivational narrative becomes subtly dangerous. It implies that if you do not feel driven, you are failing. Cadence implies something more psychologically sane: if you do not feel driven, you are human. The work is to keep the metronome ticking anyway, at a tempo you can sustain. That is not a call to grind. It is the opposite. It is an argument for designing a rhythm that respects fluctuation, and for creating check-in points that allow course correction before a lapse becomes a collapse.

The quarterly reset is one such check-in point, but its power is best understood by contrast with more familiar rhythms. Weekly planning is excellent for managing logistics—meetings, errands, deadlines—but it is too close to the noise of daily life to detect the slow shifts that matter. It can become a kind of reactive bookkeeping: rearranging commitments without questioning whether the commitments should exist. Annual reviews are spacious enough to invite big thinking, but so spacious they invite fantasy. A quarter occupies an unusual middle ground. It is long enough to generate evidence and short enough to keep embarrassment low. If you decide in January that you will change something, and you check again in April, you have a story with a beginning and a visible trajectory. If you wait until the next January, you have a mythology.

This distinction matters because human beings are storytellers. We constantly narrate ourselves. The motivational approach encourages identity slogans: "I'm the kind of person who…" Slogans are seductive because they sound like certainty. They are also brittle. Cadence encourages a different kind of narrative—less heroic, more empirical: "Over the last quarter, this pattern appeared." It shifts the story from personality to practice. It trades self-image for evidence.

Evidence can sting. It can also free.

The first obvious benefit is reduced self-blame. When a person stops treating inconsistency as a moral failure, they can start asking more productive questions. Which cues triggered the unwanted behaviour? Which constraints made the desired behaviour unrealistic? Which commitments crowded out the rest? These are design questions. They are the questions engineers, researchers, and good managers ask when a system underperforms. The same posture can be applied to a life without turning it into an optimisation project. It is simply a shift in where you locate the problem. Instead of "Why am I like this?", the question becomes "What conditions produced this result?" The difference is not semantic. It changes what you do next.

A second benefit is better management of risk. In the motivational model, risk is often underestimated because a person assumes that future willpower will rescue them. "I'll get serious later" is a risk assumption disguised as optimism. Cadence is more conservative. It assumes the future will contain tired days, unforeseen expenses, and emotional weather. It therefore builds check-ins before problems become expensive. In money, that means catching creeping outgoings before they swallow margin. In work, it means noticing when commitments have exceeded capacity. In relationships, it means noticing when contact has become thin and perfunctory. In health, it means noticing when recovery has been treated as optional until the body insists.

Yet cadence has a limitation worth treating with respect: it can become ritual without thought. People can schedule a review and still avoid reality by going through motions. They can turn the metronome into background noise, a tick heard but ignored. This is why cadence alone is not enough; it must be paired with attention. The ritual must contain a moment of honest comparison: what was intended versus what happened. Without that comparison, scheduling becomes bureaucratic theatre.

There is a second limitation, almost the opposite. For some people, especially those working in unpredictable environments—clinical shifts, fieldwork, crisis response, precarious employment—a fixed cadence can feel like another burden. The calendar is already a battlefield. Here, the reconciliation is not to abandon cadence but to adjust its form. Cadence is not synonymous with rigidity. It can be a bounded window rather than a fixed hour; it can be a protected interval that moves within a week rather than a precise date; it can be shorter when life is volatile and longer when stability returns. The principle remains: allocate decision points to time so that life is steered, not merely endured. The metronome may need a different tempo. It still matters that it exists.

A deeper philosophical point sits underneath all this: motivation is internal, cadence is relational. Motivation depends on the state of a mind. Cadence depends on the design of a life in context—work cycles, seasons, responsibilities, relationships, energy. This is why cadence is not a personality trait. It is a negotiation between intention and reality. A person who thrives on cadence is not necessarily more disciplined; they may simply have constructed a better interface between themselves and time. They have made room for decisions to recur. They have put guardrails where drift would otherwise take the wheel.

Guardrails are not glamorous either. They are the reason the road is survivable.

The metaphor matters because it suggests what cadence is *for*. It is not for squeezing maximum output from a human being. It is for preventing small deviations from accumulating into expensive corrections. It is for keeping values connected to behaviour. Trust, in this frame, becomes the willingness to consult evidence at scheduled intervals. Efficiency becomes reducing decision load by reusing a script rather than reinventing the process each time. Risk becomes recognising where you have been relying on future motivation as a bailout plan. These abstractions become measurable when attached to visible behaviours: did you keep the scheduled review, did you compare actual patterns against intended ones, did you make one or two deliberate adjustments rather than none?

The most countercultural aspect of cadence is that it treats steadiness as an achievement. Contemporary culture rewards intensity: the dramatic transformation, the heroic streak, the public declaration. Cadence rewards a quieter competence: the ability to return, to revise, to continue without spectacle. It is closer to how serious work is done in laboratories and studios. Researchers do not rely on a burst of motivation to replicate results; they rely on protocols and schedules, on routines that make work possible even when they are unsure. Artists do not wait for inspiration every day; they show up at a time and work until something appears. Cadence, in this sense, is a respect for craft—craft of living, not merely craft of producing.

The metronome returns here, not as a cute image but as a diagnostic. In a life built on motivation, the tempo changes constantly: frantic weeks, then collapse; dramatic vows, then drift. In a life built on cadence, the tempo may still vary—seasons are real—but there is an underlying beat that keeps decisions from being postponed indefinitely. That beat is what makes the quarterly reset useful. It is not magic. It is the simple power of recurrence: the assurance that you will look again soon, which changes what you tolerate now.

The unresolved tension is the one every thoughtful person eventually faces. If motivation is unreliable and cadence can become mechanical, what does it take to keep the metronome meaningful rather than merely dutiful? The answer is not a slogan. It is a choice repeated over time: whether to treat the calendar as a place where reality is faced, or as a place where reality is deferred. The quarter puts the question into a practical form. When the next scheduled check-in arrives, will it be used to confirm a story you prefer, or to compare the evidence you have?

Why quarters beat years

On 30 July 2002, President George W. Bush signed the Sarbanes–Oxley Act in Washington, D.C., a legislative response to corporate collapses that had made "trust" feel suddenly fragile. One of its concrete effects was procedural rather than poetic: senior executives were required to certify the accuracy of their companies' periodic reports, including quarterly filings, tightening accountability around a rhythm that already structured modern commerce (U.S. Congress, 2002). It is a dry detail with an important lesson. When the stakes are high, serious systems do not rely on annual confessions. They build shorter loops of evidence and correction.

Quarters change what you notice.

The year has prestige. It sounds complete. It also gives drift a long leash. A week, by contrast, is immediate and noisy. It captures what happened, but not what it meant. A quarter sits between these scales with an almost unfair advantage: it is long enough for the consequences of small decisions to become legible, and short enough that those consequences can still be nudged. The power is not motivational. It is temporal. It comes from placing attention at an interval that matches how habits, spending, fatigue, and commitments actually accumulate.

To see why, it helps to watch what annual thinking does to the human mind. Annual reviews invite grand narratives: a person tells themselves they are "turning things around" or "starting fresh", as if January were a cleansing fire. That story can be psychologically comforting because it converts messy complexity into a single turning point. It also invites a subtle form of dishonesty. A year is spacious enough to postpone discomfort without admitting postponement. "I'll sort it later" sounds plausible when "later" can mean September. The cost is that time continues to pass while attention is deferred. By the time the year's story is revisited, the evidence is blurred. Memory becomes selective. The mind fills gaps with intention: *I meant well*, therefore *I probably did well.* Annual review becomes less like measurement and more like mythology.

Weekly planning has the opposite pathology. It is brilliant at managing logistics and terrible at judging direction. A week is a flurry of contingencies: meetings, unexpected tasks, illness, travel, family obligations, moods. The signal-to-noise ratio is poor. You can "win" a week by getting many things done and still lose ground in the domains that matter, because the week rewards urgency. It is too easy to confuse busyness with progress. Weekly planning can become a ritual of rearranging pressure rather than reducing it.

Quarters, by comparison, offer evidence with edges. Ninety days is long enough that patterns have time to repeat. Repetition is the key. A single overspend can be explained away. Three months of overspending becomes a trend. One week of poor sleep might be a deadline. A quarter of poor sleep suggests a baseline shift. One missed call might be coincidence. A quarter of missed calls becomes a relationship pattern. The quarter makes repetition visible without requiring obsessive monitoring. It is a humane form of measurement: infrequent enough to be bearable, frequent enough to be useful.

The practical virtue here is proportionality. When people wait a year to look, the correction often needs to be dramatic because buffers have thinned. In money, that can mean sudden austerity. In work, it can mean burnout and abrupt withdrawal. In relationships, it can mean apologies that feel theatrical because the neglect has lasted so long. Quarters reduce the drama because they catch drift earlier. A correction made in April is often gentler than a correction made in December, for the same underlying issue. The quarter does not remove consequence; it changes its shape. It turns cliffs into slopes.

Organisations use quarters not because they are obsessed with spreadsheets, but because quarters allow mid-course correction while a course still exists. The language of "accountability" often sounds moral, yet in practice it is behavioural: a calendar forces someone to compare what was promised with what happened. The U.S. Securities and Exchange Commission's quarterly reporting regime, anchored in 10-Q filings, institutionalises that comparison (SEC, n.d.). A company that drifts cannot drift invisibly for long. The quarter is a spotlight that returns on schedule. Importantly, the spotlight is not daily. Daily scrutiny would paralyse. Quarterly scrutiny keeps the system steerable.

The same logic shows up in public policy where volatility makes slower rhythms dangerous. In February 2022, Ofgem announced that the UK's energy price cap would shift to quarterly updates, explicitly because market conditions were changing too rapidly for the prior cadence (Ofgem, 2022). The energy market is not a personal finance problem, but the time-design principle transfers cleanly: when conditions shift quickly, long intervals force harsher corrections. Shorter intervals distribute pain and information in smaller doses. That is risk management, not motivation. It is also a reminder that cadence is not aesthetic. It is a response to how reality behaves.

A quarter also respects the way human beings learn. If a person tries a change—spending less in one category, moving more consistently, protecting one relationship, reducing one recurring time leak—three months is long enough to see whether the change is viable. Does it persist beyond the novelty phase? Does it collide with predictable obstacles? Does it create unintended side-effects? Does it alter energy, time, or mood in ways that matter? A week is too short to answer these questions honestly, because the body and the calendar have not yet had time to push back. A year is too long, because if the change is misguided, the cost of learning is high. The quarter makes learning cheaper. It turns life into a sequence of low-stakes experiments rather than a single high-stakes vow.

This is where "trust" becomes a visible behaviour. Trust is not self-belief. Trust is a willingness to compare assumptions against evidence at an interval that prevents self-deception. A quarter supplies enough evidence to be persuasive without being overwhelming. A person can look at their bank activity without drowning in receipts, notice clusters without litigating every transaction, and still have time to adjust the next ninety days. Similarly, a person can look at their calendar and see whether their week-to-week story about priorities matches the actual use of hours. The abstraction resolves into a decision: keep a commitment, renegotiate it, or admit it is shaping the quarter in a way you do not want.

Quarters also align better with the lived architecture of the year than people admit. Many modern lives already run on seasonal pulses: school terms, financial quarters, project cycles, weather shifts, holiday clusters, conference seasons. Even in workplaces that pretend time is uniform, the rhythms show up: autumn intensity, end-of-year deadlines, spring renewals, summer disruptions. Annual planning often ignores these pulses and therefore fails at the point of contact with reality. Weekly planning is too fine-grained to hold them. A quarterly rhythm can incorporate them without being enslaved to them. It can accept that winter quarters may require a different balance than summer quarters, that one season demands more work while another allows more recovery. Quarters are big enough to hold a season's character.

The quiet motif worth keeping in mind is the quarter-turn. Not a reinvention, not a wheel spun wildly, but a dial moved a small amount and then observed. A quarter-turn is meaningful precisely because it is not dramatic. Dramatic turns are hard to repeat. Small turns can compound. The question a quarter invites is not "Who will I become this year?" but "What direction did the dial move?" That is a more adult question. It assumes imperfection. It also assumes agency.

There is, however, a credible limitation that deserves respect: quarters can distort pursuits that mature slowly. Some work does not reveal its value in three months. Academic research projects can take years to ripen; the quarterly lens may tempt premature judgement based on superficial outputs. Creative work can look stagnant for long periods and then suddenly cohere. Recovery from serious illness or injury can be nonlinear. In these contexts, quarters can become an impatient auditor, pressuring a person to produce visible results rather than to protect the conditions that eventually make results possible. The quarter-turn, applied crudely, can become a jerk on the dial.

The reconciliation is to shift what is being compared. When outputs are slow, compare inputs and constraints instead. Instead of asking whether the project "advanced", notice whether time was protected, whether attention was sustained, whether unnecessary commitments were trimmed, whether recovery was honoured, whether practice occurred. This is not a trick. It is a recognition that the right metrics depend on the nature of the work. Quarters remain useful, but they must be used with intellectual humility. A good cadence does not demand the wrong evidence.

Once that humility is granted, the comparison with annual review and weekly planning becomes clearer. Annual review is useful for identity-level decisions: values, long arcs, major commitments, the kind of changes that require a broad horizon. It is less useful for operational correction. Weekly planning is useful for coordination: keeping promises, managing tasks, ensuring that life does not collapse into chaos. It is less useful for diagnosing drift. The quarter is the bridge. It is where the operational meets the existential without either dominating. It is where a person can notice whether the week-by-week pattern is serving the year-level intention.

This bridge function matters most in the domains where drift is quiet and compounding: money, health, relationships, learning, work, environment. These domains do not usually fail through one decision. They fail through hundreds of small decisions made without review. A quarter introduces review at an interval that catches accumulation. Efficiency, here, is not about doing more. It is about reducing the cost of steering. Steering once a year is inefficient because the corrections are large and emotionally expensive. Steering every day is inefficient because the monitoring load becomes oppressive. Steering quarterly is efficient because it minimises both types of waste: the waste of late correction and the waste of constant vigilance.

The next question is less philosophical and more practical: where should the four quarterly days sit? Many people default to conventional quarters—January, April, July, October—because business calendars do. That is a reasonable starting rhythm, but it is not sacred. Real lives have their own seasons. For a teacher, a quarter anchored to school terms may feel more natural. For someone working in finance, the intensity of certain reporting periods may make some weeks unsuitable. For parents, the start and end of school holidays may be the moments when drift is most likely, and therefore when review is most useful. For researchers, the cadence of grant deadlines and conference seasons may dictate when reflection is realistic. The point is not to obey a calendar template. The point is to place the quarter-turn where it will actually happen.

Timing is not an aesthetic preference; it is a constraint problem. A cadence survives when it is scheduled into the least fragile parts of the year, not the most aspirational. If an Upgrade Day is placed in the same week as a predictable work peak or a recurring family obligation, it will be postponed, and then postponed again, until the rhythm breaks. That is not a failure of character. It is a mismatch between ritual and reality. The more honest approach is to inspect the year's pattern and anchor the four days to calmer edges—after major deadlines rather than during them, before predictable disruptions rather than after they have scattered attention.

There is also a subtler timing consideration: some quarters need different kinds of reflection. A quarter that begins in late winter may call for attention to energy and recovery; a quarter that begins in early autumn may call for attention to commitments and time. The ritual is the same, but the emphasis shifts with the season. This is one reason quarters beat years: they allow seasonal intelligence. A year-level plan often assumes consistency across months. The quarter recognises that a human being is not consistent across months. The body responds to light and weather. Social life responds to holidays. Work responds to cycles. A quarterly cadence makes room for that variation without letting variation become drift.

The quarter-turn returns here as a discipline of honesty. It asks for a particular kind of courage: not the courage to make a grand vow, but the quieter courage to look again soon. A year invites a performative confidence—declare the goal, announce the identity, promise the transformation. A quarter invites something more grounded: compare, notice, adjust. It is less romantic. It is more reliable.

That reliability becomes especially valuable when life is unsettled. Volatility does not only occur in markets and energy prices; it occurs in careers, families, bodies, and social worlds. In volatile periods, the temptation is to abandon planning altogether or to plan obsessively. The quarter offers a third stance: plan in a way that expects change and therefore schedules revision. This is not prediction. It is preparedness. It is the decision to keep a feedback loop open.

The unresolved tension is the one that keeps the whole practice honest. A quarterly cadence can become a form of comfort—an assurance that reflection is "handled"—while a person continues to avoid the hardest truths. Or it can become a tool for genuine course correction, which sometimes requires admitting trade-offs: that a season of career intensity will reduce social availability; that a financial goal will constrain certain pleasures; that a learning ambition will displace some leisure. The quarter does not remove these trade-offs. It forces them into view. When the next quarter-turn arrives, will the dial be moved deliberately, or will it be allowed to move itself again?

Choosing focus domains

In September 1997, back at Apple's headquarters in Cupertino, Steve Jobs stood in front of a company that had become busy in the most dangerous way: busy without a coherent centre. Apple was selling a sprawl of machines and variations, each with its own rationale, each consuming engineering, marketing, support, and executive attention. Jobs' response was not to demand more effort from exhausted teams. It was to narrow the field. He used a simple product matrix—consumer and professional, desktop and portable—and began killing projects that did not fit. The outcome, recorded in any straightforward history of the period, was a brutal simplification that made the company legible to itself again.

Scope is kindness, not weakness.

That moment matters here because it reveals a practical truth about human systems, whether corporate or personal: attention is finite, and therefore selection is inevitable. The only question is whether selection happens deliberately or by default. Without deliberate selection, the loudest domain wins. Work expands. Admin multiplies. Screens colonise the gaps. The calendar fills with other people's priorities, and the rest of life becomes whatever can be squeezed into the leftover minutes. When that happens, "balance" becomes a fantasy, and the quarterly ritual risks swelling into a punishing audit—everything examined, nothing changed, because the mind cannot hold it all at once.

The act of choosing focus domains is not self-improvement theatre. It is a method for deciding where to place a limited resource—attention—so that the next ninety days are steerable. A well-designed quarterly reset does not attempt to oversee an entire life in one sitting. It establishes a control panel with a small number of dials and a commitment to turn only a few of them at a time. This is not a retreat from ambition. It is what makes ambition sustainable. Systems fail when they are overloaded; people do too. The most consistent error among highly capable professionals and students is not a lack of intelligence or drive. It is an excess of simultaneous aims.

The reason simultaneous aims feel so tempting is that life does not arrive in neat categories. Money is entangled with work. Health is entangled with stress and time. Relationships are entangled with energy and geography. Learning is entangled with confidence and schedule. Environment is entangled with habits, which are entangled with everything. The mind therefore tries to fix the whole knot at once, and then—because the knot is complex—either freezes or thrashes. Drift, which thrives on unattended complexity, loves this moment. The person tells themselves they will "sort things out properly" when there is more time, more energy, fewer obligations. Meanwhile the quarter passes, and selection still happens, just invisibly: the urgent wins.

A better approach begins with a sober acknowledgement of cognitive limits. Herbert A. Simon's work on bounded rationality, developed in the mid-twentieth century, argued that human decision-making is constrained by limited information, limited time, and limited computational capacity; people therefore "satisfice" rather than optimise (Simon, 1955). In plain terms, the mind cannot evaluate every possible action against every possible outcome. It chooses a workable option and moves on. This is not a flaw. It is how a brain survives. The failure comes when a person tries to behave as though they can optimise everything simultaneously—every domain, every metric, every commitment—while living in a world designed to demand continuous response. The quarterly ritual works because it is a deliberate satisfice: a chosen subset of reality examined with enough depth to matter.

The selection problem shows up vividly when stakes are high and information floods in. On 13 April 1970, in Houston, Texas, NASA's Mission Control faced a situation that could not be solved by paying attention to everything. After an oxygen tank explosion crippled Apollo 13, engineers and flight controllers had to decide which readings mattered, which procedures were essential, and which systems could be powered down to conserve energy for re-entry. The story is often told as ingenuity under pressure, and it was, but it was also triage. When survival is at stake, attention becomes ruthless. The implication for an ordinary life is not melodrama; it is clarity. If the mind tries to monitor every dial, it monitors none. If it chooses a few vital signs, it can act.

That is the conceptual heart of choosing focus domains: treat the quarter as a deliberate allocation of attention across a small set of life areas that plausibly shift the trajectory. The words "money", "health", "relationships", "learning", "work", and "environment" can be spoken as though they were separate departments. In practice, they are interacting systems, and the choice is about leverage. Leverage is simply where a small change produces a noticeable downstream effect. It is visible. It can be measured. In money, leverage might appear as a recurring outflow that consumes margin. In health, as a consistent sleep deficit or a collapse in weekly movement. In relationships, as the repeated postponement of a key tie. In learning, as a pattern of consumption without application. In work, as meetings that proliferate while core projects stall. In environment, as persistent friction—clutter, noise, digital mess—that turns good intentions into effortful battles.

A common misunderstanding is to treat focus as neglect. It is not. Focus is a decision to examine some domains deeply and others lightly for a quarter, with the expectation that the emphasis will rotate. A control panel does not remove dials; it determines which ones are adjusted now. The risk of trying to adjust all of them is that none move meaningfully. The risk of adjusting only one forever is that other domains drift until they demand expensive correction. The quarterly cadence makes a more intelligent compromise possible: depth without obsession, breadth without overwhelm.

To make this real, it helps to move from abstractions like "priorities" to behaviours that leave evidence. Efficiency, for example, is not a vague aspiration. Efficiency is the decision to reduce the number of decisions required to stay on course. It is the choice to reuse a script, to compare the same few indicators quarter after quarter, to avoid reinventing the ritual each time. Trust, similarly, is not self-confidence. Trust is the willingness to look at evidence without flinching. That may mean reading a bank statement, scanning a calendar, noticing a pattern of late nights, or admitting that a friendship has been sustained by sentiment rather than time. Risk is not an adventurous personality trait. Risk is what increases when evidence is postponed and drift compounds—when a person relies on future willpower to rescue them from patterns that are already visible.

The selection process becomes clearer when you recognise that domains differ in two ways: fragility and lag. Fragility is how quickly a domain can deteriorate under neglect. Lag is how long it takes to notice that deterioration. Health can be fragile in some seasons—sleep debt accumulates quietly and then bites. Money can be deceptively resilient until it isn't—buffers hide drift until a bill or a rate change exposes it. Relationships often have long lags—people are kind, routines persist, silence is tolerated—until suddenly the cost is emotional distance. Learning can decay not through obvious failure but through substitution: constant intake replaces practice, and the person feels busy yet unchanged. Work can look productive while being structurally unbalanced—meetings multiply, deep work thins, and the sense of permanent urgency becomes normal. Environment is often the stealth domain: a cluttered desk, a chaotic inbox, a cramped digital workspace, each adding friction until everything feels harder than it should.

Once fragility and lag are seen, the rationale for quarterly domain choice becomes practical rather than moral. A person does not choose a focus domain because it is virtuous. They choose it because it is either fragile right now, lagging in a worrying way, or capable of producing leverage. The quarter is a container for that choice. It says: for the next ninety days, which dials will be turned deliberately, and which will be watched for drift?

There is a subtle psychological payoff here. Many people carry a low-grade guilt cloud that hovers over "the rest of life". They work hard, achieve a great deal, and still feel vaguely behind. That feeling is often not laziness or ingratitude. It is the emotional signal of too many simultaneous obligations and too little explicit selection. When selection becomes explicit, guilt loses some of its power, because the person can say, honestly, that certain dials are being held steady for a season while others are adjusted. The result is not complacency. It is integrity: behaviour aligned to declared trade-offs rather than to silent drift.

The control panel motif matters because it guards against a common trap: treating every domain as equally urgent at all times. Real lives have seasons. A quarter in which work is unusually demanding may require the work dial to be adjusted while the learning dial is kept modest. A quarter of family turbulence may require the relationship dial to move while other domains are held stable. A quarter of financial tightening may require money to take the lead, not as punishment but as protection. The ritual remains the same, but the emphasis changes. That flexibility is not failure. It is the point of a quarterly system.

Still, there is a limitation that deserves an honest place: some periods require multi-domain attention whether you like it or not. New parenthood, serious illness, bereavement, a sudden job loss—these can destabilise money, health, relationships, and work simultaneously. In such seasons, the very idea of "focus domains" can feel detached, as though life could be managed by neat categories. The reconciliation is not to force a tidy framework onto an untidy reality. It is to treat focus as triage rather than optimisation. In crisis, the question is less "Which domains deserve improvement?" and more "Which domains must not be allowed to fail?" The control panel remains, but the aim becomes stabilisation. The quarterly cadence can still matter, because even in crisis drift operates; it just operates faster. Yet the tone changes. Selection becomes protective rather than aspirational.

There is another limitation, quieter and more common: people can choose focus domains as a way of avoiding discomfort. A person might declare "learning" as a focus because it feels noble, while avoiding "money" because numbers provoke anxiety. Another might focus on "work" because it is socially rewarded, while avoiding "relationships" because emotional conversations feel risky. This is where the quarterly ritual must remain intellectually honest. The test is whether domain choice is anchored in evidence rather than identity. Evidence can be simple: recurring overdrafts, persistent fatigue, a calendar that shows no social time, a skill goal that has not been practised, a workspace that generates daily friction. The point is not self-accusation. It is accurate diagnosis.

When the choice is evidence-anchored, it also becomes easier to avoid the ritual swelling into a cumbersome audit. Swelling is usually a sign of anxiety: the mind tries to reduce uncertainty by adding more checks, more metrics, more categories. The irony is that more checks often produce less action, because the ritual becomes heavy enough to be postponed. A lean scope produces repeatability. Repeatability produces learning. Learning produces confidence. Confidence reduces the urge to hoard information. The control panel stays readable.

It is worth noticing how this connects back to the earlier idea of drift. Drift thrives in the unexamined. The quarterly ritual is an examination. But examination without scope becomes a form of self-surveillance, and self-surveillance is rarely sustainable. Scope makes the examination humane. It says: look closely at a few dials, then act. The dials not chosen are not forgotten; they are monitored lightly, like warning lights on the dashboard. If a warning light flashes, attention can shift. If not, the quarter proceeds without needless fuss.

The choice of focus domains also shapes the emotional texture of the coming quarter. If money is chosen, the quarter may feel like a reclaiming of margin—less background stress, more ability to choose. If health is chosen, it may feel like a return to steadiness—more reliable energy, fewer brittle days. If relationships are chosen, it may feel like warmth and repair—less isolation, more shared life. If learning is chosen, it may feel like expansion—new competence, a wider set of options. If work is chosen, it may feel like clearance—fewer leaks, more traction on what matters. If environment is chosen, it may feel like ease—less friction, fewer small irritations that drain attention. These are not guarantees. They are plausible pay-offs that can be tested within a quarter, precisely because the scope is not everything at once.

The final virtue of domain choice is that it forces a moral fact into view without preaching it: time is a form of commitment. People often speak of commitment as though it lives in the heart. It also lives in the diary. The domain you choose is the domain you are willing to allocate attention to repeatedly, not once in a burst. That is why focus domains are a better tool than grand resolutions. Resolutions are declarations. Domains are allocations. Allocations reveal priorities.

The unresolved test, then, is not whether the six domains matter. They do. The test is whether the next quarter's scope will be shaped by evidence or by comfort. When the control panel is imagined and the dials are named, which ones are you tempted to adjust because it flatters your self-image, and which ones are you tempted to ignore because it threatens it? The quarter does not demand a heroic answer. It demands an honest one.

Chapter 2
Designing Your Upgrade Day

On 17 December 1903, at Kill Devil Hills near Kitty Hawk, North Carolina, the Wright brothers flew a machine that stayed aloft for twelve seconds. The world likes to remember that moment as genius taking wing, but the less romantic detail is the one that matters here: the flight was preceded by systematic preparation, repeated trials, careful notes, and a deliberate choice of conditions. The sand was cold underfoot, the wind insistent, the work unglamorous. They did not depend on feeling inspired at exactly the right moment. They depended on a set-up that made a fragile attempt possible.

Most rituals fail before they begin. They fail not because the idea is flawed, but because the design is vague. People promise themselves a reset "soon", and then discover that "soon" is a region of the calendar where other obligations already live. They tell themselves they will "review everything properly", and then discover that reviewing everything properly is indistinguishable from doing nothing, because it is too large to hold in one sitting. They intend to be thoughtful, then spend the time hunting for passwords, searching for statements, or reconstructing what happened from scattered fragments. The ritual becomes effortful, and effortful rituals become optional.

The Upgrade Day is meant to be the opposite of optional.

Design is the difference between a rhythm that survives and an aspiration that fades. In the previous chapter, the argument was temporal: quarters work because they align attention with drift, and cadence outlasts motivation. This chapter is structural. It treats the Upgrade Day as an engineered object—something you build once and then reuse, refining it over time until it fits your life with the quiet inevitability of a well-made tool. The point is not to create a perfect day. The point is to create a repeatable one.

A repeatable ritual begins with a date, and the date cannot be a moral preference. It has to be a physical place in the calendar, defended against the predictable pressures of your year. The modern calendar is not empty space waiting to be filled with your intentions; it is contested territory. Work meetings breed. Family obligations expand. Social commitments accrete. Digital life has a way of colonising the margins. If the Upgrade Day does not claim territory deliberately, it will be pushed to the edge, and then off the map. The design challenge is therefore blunt: choose four days that can realistically exist, and choose them in a way that respects your seasons rather than fantasising them away.

This is where the false choice between weekends and weekdays often appears. Weekends promise freedom but come with their own tyranny: chores, errands, family expectations, the emotional need for rest. Weekdays promise structure but are often defended by other people's priorities. The decision is less about which day category is morally superior and more about which category offers the least fragile window for focused thought. Similarly, mornings can be clean and quiet but may be vulnerable to childcare or commuting; evenings can be more flexible but are often ruined by fatigue. The design problem is not solved by choosing the "best" time in theory. It is solved by choosing a time you will actually protect when life gets busy, and by anchoring it around the rhythms you already know will recur.

Once the dates exist, a second design problem emerges: what happens during the day. Many intelligent people sabotage themselves here by making the ritual too clever. They build sprawling checklists, decide to track every metric, and attempt to become their own auditor, therapist, and strategist in one sitting. The result is decision fatigue—an exhausted mind making fuzzy choices. A script, by contrast, is merciful. It limits the number of decisions required in the moment. It creates an order of operations: begin with a brief reflection that clarifies what the last quarter felt like, move through a small set of domains with consistent questions, and end with a handful of concrete decisions that nudge the next ninety days. The day becomes familiar not because it is dull, but because it is dependable.

There is an intellectual reason scripts work beyond mere convenience. In complex environments, experts rely on protocols not because they lack judgement, but because protocols preserve judgement for the moments that require it. The same logic holds in personal life. If you must decide *how* to review your life each time you review it, you waste cognitive fuel before you reach the decisions that matter. A repeatable script functions as cognitive scaffolding. It lets you compare quarter to quarter without reinventing the method. It also reduces the temptation to dramatise. When the ritual is scripted, the day becomes a routine encounter with evidence rather than a performance of self-reinvention.

But even the best script fails if the inputs are missing. The practical obstacle most people underestimate is not thinking; it is retrieval. The modern life is documented everywhere and nowhere: bank apps, calendar fragments, training logs, notes apps, inboxes, photos, messages. If you arrive at an Upgrade Day with no data prepared, you will spend the time spelunking through digital caves, emerging hours later with a headache and a sense that you have "been busy" rather than having decided anything. This chapter therefore insists on a humble principle: gather *good enough* information in advance. A small number of account balances. A quick glance at a calendar. A few health metrics you already track. A notebook. You are not assembling a forensic case. You are building a workable snapshot.

The phrase "good enough" can sound like permission to be sloppy. It is not. It is an acknowledgement of marginal returns. After a certain point, more information produces diminishing insight and increasing procrastination. The mind can use detail as a hiding place: if you just gather enough data, you tell yourself, the decision will become obvious. Often it will not. The decision remains a trade-off, and trade-offs cannot be solved by more spreadsheets. They can only be faced. The Upgrade Day is about facing—calmly, periodically, with sufficient evidence to be honest, and not so much evidence that you drown.

Then comes the most fragile element of all: protection. Even a well-designed day can be shredded by interruption. A ritual that can be interrupted becomes a ritual that will be interrupted. This is not cynicism; it is a description of how social life works. People assume your time is available unless you have clearly signalled otherwise. Work will encroach unless you set boundaries. Family dynamics will fill space unless expectations are articulated. Even your own mind will interrupt you—by reaching for distraction the moment discomfort appears. Protecting the ritual therefore requires more than desire. It requires signals, boundaries, and a little theatre of seriousness: a pre-ritual cue that tells your brain it is time to switch modes, and a post-ritual reward that makes the cadence emotionally sustainable.

The theatre matters because human beings respond to cues more reliably than to abstract intentions. A ritual becomes non-negotiable when it is attached to sensory reality: a particular place, a particular notebook, a particular time of day, a familiar start. It becomes satisfying when it ends with a sense of closure—decisions made, commitments noted, the mental tabs closed. This is not self-indulgence. It is design. A ritual that feels punishing will be postponed. A ritual that feels contained will be repeated. The Upgrade Day lives or dies on repetition.

Modern relevance makes this design work urgent. Many people now inhabit calendars with porous boundaries: remote work that bleeds into evenings, messages that arrive at all hours, global teams that erase the comfort of a shared time zone. At the same time, the attention economy has made silence rarer and impulsive distraction easier. Under these conditions, "I'll do it when I have time" becomes a mirage. Time is not discovered. Time is defended. This chapter treats defence as an intellectual task rather than a moral one: you are not trying to become more disciplined; you are trying to create a recurring pocket of quiet where evidence can be seen and choices can be made.

There is also a deeper human reason the design matters. A quarterly ritual is not simply about productivity. It is about coherence. Without periodic design, life becomes a sequence of reactions. Reaction can be competent. It can also be hollow. People can respond brilliantly to demands and still feel that the quarter passed without being lived. An Upgrade Day is a countermeasure: a scheduled pause in which the person stops being an instrument for other systems and becomes, briefly, the author of the next stretch of time.

The key is to keep the design light enough to carry. Too many rules, and the ritual becomes brittle. Too much ceremony, and it becomes embarrassing. Too little structure, and it dissolves into vagueness. The sweet spot is a day that feels almost ordinary: a recurring appointment, a familiar sequence, a handful of inputs ready on the table, and a protected space in which the mind can do its quiet work of comparison and decision. Like a well-built plane, it does not require the pilot to be in a particular mood. It requires that the machine be ready.

The payoff is not a dramatic transformation. It is something subtler and more valuable: the sense that your year is not a runaway train but a series of steerable quarters. This chapter takes the raw idea of a quarterly reset and turns it into a ritual you can actually keep—anchored to real dates, guided by a repeatable script, fed by prepared data, and defended against the ordinary forces that would otherwise dissolve it. After that, the rest becomes possible: not because you are suddenly more motivated, but because the infrastructure is in place.

Setting the quarterly date

On 31 January 2020, in the United Kingdom, HM Revenue & Customs reached its annual crescendo: the self-assessment deadline. Across London and beyond, laptops glowed late into the evening; the familiar hum of last-minute paperwork filled kitchens and spare rooms. A date on a calendar—unromantic, non-negotiable—had the peculiar power to summon attention that had been missing for weeks. For many people, nothing about their finances changed on that day except one thing: they looked. Deadlines can be cruel, but they are also clarifying. They prove a point that polite intentions rarely survive.

Dates beat intentions, every time.

The Upgrade Day is not meant to borrow the stress of tax season, yet it depends on the same underlying mechanism: the calendar is a forcing function. Without a date, a quarterly reset becomes a sentiment, and sentiments lose to email. With a date, the reset becomes an appointment—something real enough to collide with competing demands. That collision is the entire point. A quarterly ritual cannot live in "sometime"; "sometime" is a swamp where good ideas sink quietly, leaving only the faint impression that one is perpetually behind.

A practical complication appears immediately: the calendar is not empty. It is already a lived artefact, filled with institutional rhythms, family patterns, academic terms, project cycles, travel, illness, and the small chaos of normal life. Setting a quarterly date therefore is not an act of aspiration; it is an act of negotiation. It requires looking at how time is actually used, noticing where the year predictably tightens, and placing the ritual where it can survive. The goal is not perfection. The goal is an *anchor*—a recurring point in time that makes drift visible before it becomes expensive.

The reason anchors matter is structural. Human beings are prone to the planning fallacy: the tendency to underestimate how long tasks will take and to overestimate how smoothly the future will go. Daniel Kahneman and Amos Tversky described this in their work on judgement under uncertainty (Kahneman & Tversky, 1979), and it has an everyday consequence: people schedule as if the next month will be calmer than the last, as if unexpected demands will politely stop arriving. They rarely do. When the quarterly reset is left floating, it will always be deferred to the imagined calm period that never materialises. When it is anchored, it competes with reality on equal terms.

There is evidence, too, that deadlines—particularly when structured—change behaviour in measurable ways. In a 2002 paper in *Psychological Science*, Dan Ariely and Klaus Wertenbroch studied how deadlines affected performance on tasks with delayed rewards; participants given evenly spaced deadlines performed better than those with no deadlines, and self-imposed deadlines helped but were less effective than externally imposed ones (Ariely & Wertenbroch, 2002). The relevance here is not that life should be run like an experiment, but that timing is not merely administrative. Timing shapes follow-through. A quarterly reset without a date is a self-imposed deadline with weak teeth. A quarterly reset with a pre-committed date behaves more like an external one: it is harder to renegotiate in the moment.

The first decision, then, is not philosophical. It is logistical: where to place four anchors in a year that already contains storms. Many people default to conventional quarters—January, April, July, October—because corporate rhythms do. That can work, especially if one's work life already bends around those cycles. Yet it can also be a trap if it places the ritual inside predictable pressure periods: end-of-term grading, end-of-quarter reporting, seasonal busy times, major holidays, travel clusters. A robust anchor is one placed at the *edge* of intensity rather than its centre. Edges are where reflection is possible. Edges are where small corrections still fit.

This is where the misleading romance of the weekend enters. Weekends promise open space, and open space sounds like freedom. Yet weekends are not empty; they carry their own gravitational fields—domestic maintenance, family time, social obligations, recovery. For some, the weekend is the only plausible territory for a thoughtful review. For others, it is the most contested. Weekdays, similarly, can look hostile because work dominates them, yet weekdays also offer structure: fewer social interruptions, a clearer start time, a predictable rhythm. The question is not "Which is better?" The question is "Which is more defensible?" Defensibility is a behavioural property. It shows up in what gets cancelled when pressure rises.

Mornings and evenings pose the same trade-off in miniature. Mornings can be clean: the mind is less cluttered, the day has not yet been spent. They can also be fragile, especially for those with caregiving responsibilities or intense early meetings. Evenings can be flexible: the day's demands have been met, the calendar loosens. They can also be compromised by fatigue, because cognitive work—comparison, judgement, prioritisation—requires more than time. It requires attention. A date is not just a slot; it is a quality of attention allocated to a slot.

Attention is the hidden resource.

This is why setting the quarterly date is not simply "booking time". It is choosing a time when attention is plausibly available and then treating that choice as meaningful. The decision carries risk: if it is wrong, the ritual becomes brittle, and brittle rituals are broken by ordinary life. Yet risk is reduced by a small shift in mindset. Rather than chasing the ideal day, it helps to identify the least-worst day—the day that is most likely to survive the predictable disruptions of that season. A good anchor is not the prettiest spot on the calendar. It is the sturdiest.

Real-world systems often place their critical reviews where data is available and decisions can still affect outcomes. Consider publicly traded companies. Apple Inc., for example, routinely holds quarterly earnings calls within weeks of a quarter's close, when results can be compared and the next quarter's guidance can be adjusted. The details vary by year, but the underlying logic is stable: review close enough to the period to remember what happened, and early enough to influence what happens next. A quarterly personal reset follows the same temporal engineering. Too close to the end of a quarter and you are exhausted by the period you are reviewing; too far into the next quarter and drift has already begun its quiet work again. The anchor's placement is a compromise between recovery and urgency.

A second named, checkable example sits in a different domain: energy markets. In February 2022, Ofgem announced that the UK energy price cap would move to quarterly updates, explicitly to reflect the speed of market changes (Ofgem, 2022). The underlying principle is again about timing and correction size. Longer intervals allow larger divergences to build; the eventual adjustment becomes harsh. Shorter intervals create smaller, more manageable corrections. The personal analogue is straightforward. If a person sets quarterly dates that are regularly missed, the effective interval becomes longer—half-yearly, annually—and the corrections become heavier. A defended quarterly anchor keeps the interval short enough for gentler course changes.

Once the four anchors exist, the next practical step is protection, because dates do not defend themselves. Calendars are social documents. They signal availability. If the Upgrade Day is not signalled as protected, it will be treated as flexible. Flexibility is often a virtue, but here it can be a subtle form of self-sabotage. The paradox is that the more capable and responsive a person is, the more likely they are to let others consume their reflective time. This is not because others are malicious. It is because the person has trained their environment to expect accommodation.

Protection can be understood as a series of small, visible decisions. One is choosing whether the date sits near other hard boundaries. Some people find it easier to defend a block of time adjacent to an existing boundary—after a recurring appointment, before a weekly meeting cycle starts, at the end of a workday already reserved for deeper tasks. Boundaries create friction for interruption. Without friction, interruptions flow. Another protective decision concerns location. A ritual held in the same place each time—a particular desk, a library table, a quiet café—acquires a kind of situational gravity. The environment becomes a cue: *this is what happens here.* Peter Gollwitzer's work on implementation intentions (Gollwitzer, 1999) helps explain why: when a behaviour is linked to a specific cue ("when it is this time, in this place, I do this"), the need for repeated willpower decreases. The anchor becomes not only temporal but contextual.

Yet protection must also account for the most common sabotage: self-interruption. When discomfort appears—numbers that disappoint, time that feels misspent, commitments that require renegotiation—the mind reaches for relief. Relief is often digital. It arrives as "just checking something quickly", which becomes twenty minutes of scattered attention. A protected date therefore is not only a social boundary; it is a boundary against one's own avoidance habits. Here, the anchor metaphor earns its keep. An anchor holds a vessel in place against currents. The current is not only other people's demands. The current is also one's own impulse to flee from uncomfortable evidence.

A limitation must be faced honestly. Some lives are genuinely unpredictable. Clinical rotas, emergency response work, field research, high-intensity caregiving, precarious employment—these can make a fixed date feel naive. A rigid anchor can become another source of failure narratives, another missed appointment to feel guilty about. The reconciliation is not to abandon the idea of quarterly timing, but to adjust what "date" means. For some, the anchor cannot be a single day; it must be a window—an intended week within which the ritual is executed when conditions allow. The distinction matters. A window still creates a forcing function, because it narrows "sometime" into "this bounded period". It also respects the reality that some calendars cannot promise a specific evening three months in advance. The risk of drift remains; the method of anchoring simply becomes more flexible without becoming vague.

A second limitation is cultural and seasonal. A rigid quarterly schedule imported from business life can clash with school terms, religious calendars, agricultural seasons, or predictable annual obligations. The goal is not to impose a foreign rhythm but to align with one's actual year. That alignment creates durability. If a person knows that September is always intense, anchoring an Upgrade Day in late September is an invitation to skip. If a person knows that early January is already crowded with family obligations and work resets, anchoring there may create resentment. The anchor is strongest when it fits the grain of the year, not when it flatters the mind's love of clean quarters.

This brings the argument back to the purpose: the date is the mechanism that makes the rest of the ritual possible. Without it, scripts and data preparation remain theoretical. With it, those elements become worth building, because they have somewhere to land. The date is also the mechanism that converts identity language into behaviour. It is easy to say "money matters" or "health matters" or "relationships matter". It is harder, and more honest, to allocate a recurring block of time to review them. Allocation is a visible decision. It is measurable. It can be compared quarter to quarter. This is where the abstraction of "priority" becomes the concrete behaviour of time protection.

The anchor also produces a subtle psychological benefit: it reduces background anxiety. Many people live with a low-grade sense of unfinished business—finances not fully understood, health habits not fully examined, commitments not fully renegotiated. That sense is exhausting because it is non-specific. A calendar anchor makes the unfinished business specific: it has an appointment. This does not eliminate the work, but it changes the mental load. The mind no longer needs to carry the vague fear that things are being ignored forever. It knows they will be faced at a defined moment. A well-set date is therefore not merely an administrative act. It is a form of cognitive relief.

The final test is not whether the dates are elegant. It is whether they hold. A quarterly system does not require perfect compliance, but it does require that the ritual is treated as real enough to survive the predictable pressures of your year. The unresolved tension is simple and sharp: when the next quarter turns and the anchor date arrives, will it function as a genuine forcing function—something that makes the review happen—or will it be treated as decorative, an entry that looks serious until something more urgent appears?

Creating a repeatable script

On 30 October 1935, at Wright Field in Dayton, Ohio, the U.S. Army's new Boeing Model 299—later known as the B-17—crashed shortly after take-off. The aircraft was not a flimsy experiment; it was advanced, powerful, and, crucially, complex. The post-crash explanation was painfully ordinary: the crew had forgotten to release the gust locks, a simple step missed amid novelty and pressure. The response was not to demand better "motivation" from pilots. It was to change the system. Test pilots began using a written checklist, a compact sequence that could be followed reliably, every time, even when confidence ran high and attention was split.

Ritual needs a script.

That small historical pivot captures the design logic of an Upgrade Day. A quarterly reset asks the mind to do a particular kind of work: to compare what happened with what was intended, to face evidence without drama, and to choose a few adjustments without spiralling into overhaul. This is cognitive labour. It is also emotionally loaded, because the evidence can contradict the story one prefers. In those conditions, "just wing it" is a trap. Winging it makes the ritual dependent on mood, memory, and whatever problem feels loudest that day. A script makes the ritual dependent on sequence.

Sequence is mercy.

The value of sequence is not merely tidiness. A good script reduces decision fatigue, the quiet depletion that occurs when a person must repeatedly decide what to do next while already carrying the weight of the decisions themselves. Even highly capable professionals recognise this in their working lives. Surgeons use checklists. Pilots use checklists. Laboratories use protocols. These are not signs of mediocrity; they are signs of respect for complexity. At the World Health Organization in Geneva in October 2008, the Surgical Safety Checklist was introduced as a simple, repeatable sequence to reduce omissions in operating theatres, and a widely cited study in *The New England Journal of Medicine* reported improved outcomes following its introduction in a set of hospitals (Haynes et al., 2009). The core mechanism was not inspiration. It was reliable order: the right prompts at the right time.

The Upgrade Day script is the personal analogue of that insight. It is not a bureaucratic form and it is not a confessional. It is a set of cues designed to bring the right information into view in the right order, so that the mind does not waste its best attention on deciding where to begin. Without a script, the ritual tends to start wherever anxiety points: money, perhaps, because numbers sting; work, perhaps, because it feels urgent; health, perhaps, because the body has been whispering. Anxiety is not a reliable organiser. It will bias the process towards either avoidance or obsession. A script interrupts that bias by turning the day into a familiar path.

The first function of a script is therefore triage. Not the melodramatic triage of emergencies, but the calm triage of attention. The opening of the day needs to lower the cognitive temperature. This is not sentimental; it is practical. If a person begins by plunging straight into spreadsheets or calendars, the mind tends to become defensive—explaining, justifying, arguing with the evidence. A brief opening reflection changes the stance. It asks a simple question in plain language: what did the last quarter feel like in the body and in the day? That feeling is not treated as truth, but as data. It is a quick diagnostic, like tapping a dashboard to see which warning light is flickering. It often surfaces the real problem faster than analysis does, and it gives the rest of the script a human anchor.

A script also demands that the Upgrade Day be bounded. Boundaries are what make a ritual repeatable. When a person believes they must examine everything, they create a task too heavy to lift; the brain responds by postponing. A bounded script implicitly says: this is not a full autobiography, it is a quarterly snapshot. That boundary is reinforced by the structure itself: a sequence that moves domain by domain with the same limited set of questions, resisting the temptation to follow every rabbit-hole. Boundedness is not superficiality. It is the discipline of staying in the frame long enough to make decisions.

A useful way to picture the script is as an index card—small enough to hold, firm enough to guide. The image matters. An index card implies a constraint: only what fits is allowed. It also implies portability: the script is not a sprawling system that requires perfect conditions. It can travel between quarters, between seasons, between changes in life circumstance. The index card becomes a quiet motif of durability. It is the opposite of the elaborate "life plan" that demands a clear weekend, a pristine desk, and a heroic mood.

Once the day is opened, the script's middle must do a different kind of work: compare, name, and interpret patterns without drowning in detail. This is where sequence earns its keep. When people review their lives informally, they often confuse salient anecdotes with trends. A single expensive month becomes "I'm terrible with money". A single week of fatigue becomes "I'm falling apart". A single missed call becomes "I'm a bad friend". These stories are psychologically vivid and analytically weak. A quarterly script counters vividness with comparison: it prompts the mind to look across the whole ninety days, not just the worst Tuesday.

Comparison is the engine.

In money, comparison may be as basic as looking at a few broad totals and noticing direction. In work, it may be scanning the calendar for recurring commitments and noticing what took up more space than expected. In health, it may be comparing consistency rather than peak performance. In relationships, it may be recalling who actually received time rather than who one *meant* to contact. The script's job is not to generate a moral verdict; it is to convert life into a small set of observable patterns. Patterns can be negotiated. Anecdotes usually cannot.

This is where abstractions like trust and efficiency become behavioural. Trust becomes the decision to look at the evidence in a steady order rather than darting away from what feels unpleasant. Efficiency becomes reducing the number of micro-decisions required to complete the ritual: the same opening reflection, the same sequence of domains, the same closing capture of decisions. Risk becomes visible as the places where the last quarter relied on luck rather than design: a budget that only worked because nothing unexpected happened, a work schedule that only held because energy stayed unusually high, a relationship that remained intact because the other person carried the emotional labour. These are not accusations. They are diagnostic observations, and a script makes them easier to see because it repeatedly asks the same kind of questions.

It is tempting to think of a script as restrictive. In practice, it is often liberating. The mind's resistance to review is not only the fear of what will be found; it is the fear of endlessness. An unstructured review can expand indefinitely, because every domain connects to every other domain. A script provides stop points. It says: notice, decide, move on. The movement matters. It prevents the ritual becoming rumination. Rumination feels like reflection but produces little change because it circles the same material without committing to action.

Commitment is the script's second half.

A repeatable script must therefore include a closing sequence that captures decisions in a disciplined way. Without this, the day becomes an interesting conversation with oneself, and then life resumes unchanged. The closing is not a grand finale. It is a short, firm act of translation: turn patterns into a handful of specific choices for the next quarter, with enough clarity that they can be remembered when the quarter becomes busy. Notice the emphasis. It is not on making *many* choices. It is on making *a few* that are testable. The closing also protects the mind from the corrosive feeling that nothing was accomplished. A person who ends the day with loose insights is likely to feel vaguely dissatisfied. A person who ends with a small set of explicit decisions feels closure, which increases the odds the ritual will be repeated next quarter.

The script's elegance lies in its reuse. Reuse is where learning occurs. When the same prompts are asked quarter after quarter, the answers begin to form a record: not a diary of feelings, but a record of patterns and adjustments. This is how a person stops reinventing themselves and starts revising themselves. Revision is a craft process. It depends on drafts, comparisons, and small edits. A quarterly script turns life into drafts without turning life into paperwork.

Yet a script can fail in two predictable ways. The first is bloat. People add prompts every time they think of something they "should" track, until the script becomes too long to execute. The second is rigidity. People treat the script as sacred, even when circumstances change, and then feel guilty when they cannot follow it. Both failures come from misunderstanding what a script is for. A script is not meant to capture all of life. It is meant to provide a stable scaffold for attention. Stability does not require maximality. It requires sufficiency.

A credible counter-example is worth stating because it keeps the method honest. There are seasons when a script can feel like an insult. In acute crisis—bereavement, serious illness, sudden unemployment—the mind may not have the bandwidth for structured review, and the very act of "closing with decisions" can feel detached from reality. In such seasons, a strict script can become performative, a way of pretending control rather than meeting the moment. The reconciliation is not to abandon structure forever; it is to acknowledge that scripts have modes. In aviation, there are normal checklists and emergency checklists. In medicine, there are routine protocols and rapid response pathways. The personal analogue is the same: the ritual can have a lighter, stabilising version in crisis. The deeper principle remains intact—return to evidence, make small choices—but the scale changes to match capacity.

The second limitation is more subtle and more common: a script can become a way of avoiding the hardest questions by hiding behind procedure. A person can move through prompts efficiently and still refuse to name the real trade-off of the quarter. They can record numbers and ignore what those numbers imply about priorities. They can scan the calendar and avoid admitting that they are living someone else's schedule. They can note fatigue and refuse to protect recovery. This is why a good script includes at least one prompt that cannot be answered purely with metrics. It requires interpretation. It forces a small moment of honesty that procedure alone cannot replace.

This is also why the script should be memorable. A script that requires a complex template is more likely to be skipped; a script that can be recalled as a sequence becomes portable. Memorability does not mean vagueness. It means a stable order of operations that can be held in the mind as a rhythm: open with reflection, move through a small set of domains with the same comparison questions, end by selecting a few quarterly experiments and commitments. The details inside each domain can evolve. The rhythm stays.

The motif of the index card returns here for a final reason. An index card invites revision. You can cross something out. You can rewrite a prompt. You can add one line and remove another. It is a living object, not a marble tablet. That is how a quarterly script earns longevity. Over time, a person learns which questions produce insight and which produce noise. They learn which metrics clarify and which provoke needless anxiety. They learn which domains require more attention in particular seasons. The script becomes personalised not through aesthetic customisation but through empirical refinement: what has actually helped quarter after quarter?

When a script is well designed, the Upgrade Day stops feeling like an intimidating "life admin" marathon and starts feeling like a familiar inspection—short enough to be tolerable, consistent enough to be trusted. That trust is not self-esteem. It is procedural confidence: the sense that even when a quarter has been messy, there is a reliable way to look at it, name what happened, and choose what comes next. The script becomes a quiet promise that drift will not be allowed to run for a year without being noticed.

The forward test is simple, and it is not comfortable. When the next Upgrade Day arrives and the index card is on the table, will the script be used as a tool for contact with reality—or as a polite ritual performed at a safe distance from the evidence that matters most?

Gathering tools and data

On 3 July 2012, inside CERN near Geneva, the ATLAS and CMS collaborations presented evidence of a new particle consistent with the Higgs boson. The auditorium's applause was the visible climax; the quieter machinery sat behind it: years of instrumentation, calibration, agreed data formats, and protocols for deciding which signals counted and which were noise. The discovery story is sometimes romanticised as a triumph of genius. In reality, it was also a triumph of preparation. A room full of brilliant people did not arrive on the day and start hunting for files. They arrived with the relevant measurements already structured for interrogation.

Data should arrive early.

That principle is the difference between an Upgrade Day that produces insight and one that produces only fatigue. The fatigue comes from a common modern predicament: everything is recorded, nothing is gathered. Finances live in apps and emails and forgotten accounts. Work lives in calendars and chat threads and documents scattered across devices. Health lives in wearables, training logs, and the stubborn memory of how your body felt when you climbed stairs last week. Relationships live in messages, photos, and the thin evidence of who you keep meaning to call. When the reset day arrives, the temptation is to spend it as an archaeologist, digging through layers of digital debris. That kind of digging feels industrious. It is also the surest way to avoid thinking.

Search is not reflection.

The Upgrade Day, properly designed, is not a research project. It is a quarterly snapshot that allows you to compare direction and choose small, testable adjustments. For that, you need inputs—but you do not need all possible inputs. The obsession with completeness is one of the most effective forms of procrastination available to clever minds. "I'll do the review once I have everything in order" is a sentence that can delay a reset indefinitely. The insistence on *good enough* is not laziness. It is epistemic discipline: the recognition that beyond a certain point, additional data increases effort and decreases clarity.

A helpful concept from engineering and science is the distinction between signal and noise. Claude Shannon's work on information theory, published in 1948, formalised the idea that communication systems must distinguish meaningful information from random variation (Shannon, 1948). In a personal reset, the same problem appears with a different flavour. A single month's spending contains noise—one-off purchases, travel, unexpected repairs. A quarter's spending begins to show signal—recurring patterns, baseline shifts, the quiet growth of fixed costs. A daily step count contains noise—weather, illness, schedule anomalies. A quarter's movement pattern contains signal—consistency, gaps, habits that persist. The question, then, is not "How much data can you collect?" It is "What level of data captures signal without drowning you in noise?"

That question becomes practical when you look at the tools most people already have. Financial accounts provide balances and transaction histories. Calendars provide a map of time allocation. Training apps and wearables provide rough summaries of activity and sleep, if those are tracked. Notes and notebooks provide a record of what mattered enough to write down. Messages and call logs provide evidence of who has been present in your attention. None of these sources is perfect. Many are biased. All are incomplete. The purpose of gathering is not to achieve omniscience. It is to assemble a small set of lenses through which drift becomes visible.

The most important tool is boring: a single place where the quarter's snapshot is recorded. It may be paper, a simple document, or a note-taking system. What matters is not the platform but the continuity. Continuity allows comparison. Comparison allows learning. Without a stable record, each quarter becomes a fresh start, and fresh starts are where good intentions go to die. A stable record also reduces emotional distortion. Memory is unreliable under stress. People remember the last difficult week and treat it as the whole quarter. They remember a single triumphant moment and treat it as progress.

A record does not eliminate bias, but it constrains it. It gives the quarter edges.

This is where trust becomes visible behaviour. Trust is the willingness to look at evidence in a form you can actually use. Many people claim to value honesty, yet they arrange their lives so that honest information is difficult to access. Passwords are forgotten. Accounts are scattered. Data is locked in apps they rarely open. The friction functions as a moat around uncomfortable truths. Gathering tools and data in advance is therefore not merely administrative. It is a behavioural commitment to contact with reality. It is the act of lowering the moat.

Efficiency, similarly, becomes a concrete decision: you decide what *not* to gather. Efficiency is refusing to turn the Upgrade Day into a personal forensic audit. It is accepting that the goal is directional clarity, not perfect accounting. In medicine, clinicians often use triage protocols because time is finite and not all tests are necessary for every decision. In research, teams define primary endpoints to avoid chasing every possible measurement. A quarterly reset benefits from the same intellectual posture. Define the minimum set of inputs that answer the question you are actually asking: where did the quarter go, what shifted, and what deserves a small adjustment?

The most common mistake is to confuse data with insight. Data can be collected obsessively while the underlying trade-offs remain unacknowledged. A person can download bank statements for every account, colour-code spending categories, and still avoid asking the basic question of margin: is there breathing room, or is the system brittle? A person can track every workout detail and still avoid asking whether recovery has been protected. A person can catalogue every meeting and still avoid asking which ones should exist. The Upgrade Day needs data that provokes the right decisions, not data that flatters the collector's thoroughness.

A named, checkable example of this distinction comes from the early COVID-19 pandemic. In March 2020, governments and public health bodies were flooded with data: case counts, hospital admissions, test positivity rates, excess deaths. Different jurisdictions struggled not because data was absent, but because the *meaning* of data depended on definitions, reporting delays, and testing capacity. The UK's Office for National Statistics, for instance, produced weekly figures on excess deaths and cause-of-death registrations, offering a different lens from daily case counts (ONS, 2020). The lesson is not that personal life resembles a pandemic. It is that data without context can mislead, and that the choice of a few consistent indicators can be more informative than a pile of inconsistent ones.

The quarterly reset therefore benefits from selecting inputs that meet three criteria. They should be easy to retrieve, stable enough to compare quarter to quarter, and closely tied to decisions you can actually make. Financial balances meet this test because they are quickly visible and directly connected to behaviour and planning. A calendar overview meets it because time allocation is the substrate of most goals. A small number of health summaries may meet it if they are already tracked; if not, subjective recollection of energy patterns may be more reliable than a half-started app. Notes meet it because they reveal what demanded attention, which often signals values and stressors. The point is to choose sources that reduce guesswork.

Risk shows up here as an avoidance pattern. The risk of over-collecting is paralysis: you spend the Upgrade Day gathering rather than deciding. The risk of under-collecting is self-deception: you rely on feelings alone and miss the drift. The craft is in the middle. It is the same craft a good researcher uses when designing a study: choose enough measures to test the hypothesis, not so many that you drown in correlations. A quarter is not long, and your attention is not infinite. The inputs must serve the decisions.

This is why gathering in advance matters so much. When the Upgrade Day begins, the mind should not be negotiating with login screens. It should not be searching email for statements. It should not be reconstructing appointments from memory. Those tasks consume the highest-quality attention and leave only scraps for the work that actually changes the quarter. A simple operational rule emerges: separate retrieval time from reflection time. Retrieval can happen in a short session a day or two beforehand. Reflection deserves the Upgrade Day itself. This division reduces friction and, more importantly, preserves the tone of the ritual. If the day begins with scavenging, it feels like admin. If it begins with data already on the table, it feels like deliberation.

The "good enough" principle is easier to trust when you understand diminishing returns. In finance, perfect categorisation of spending is rarely necessary to notice major patterns; broad categories often show the truth quickly. In time use, you do not need to tally every minute to notice that meetings have multiplied or that evenings have been swallowed by work. In health, a single meaningful metric tracked consistently—sleep duration from a wearable, or weekly training sessions logged—often reveals more than a dozen sporadically tracked measures. Consistency beats complexity. A small, repeated dataset is a better teacher than a large, abandoned one.

A counter-example is worth facing because it exposes where "good enough" can become an excuse. There are situations where incomplete data genuinely misleads. A person with variable income, for instance, may need a fuller picture of cash flow than a simple balance snapshot to understand volatility. A person managing complex financial obligations—multiple debts, dependants, cross-border accounts—may find that broad categories hide critical risks. Likewise, someone with a health condition may need clinically relevant monitoring that is not captured by consumer devices or casual reflection. The reconciliation is to separate two aims: the quarterly ritual's aim is directional steering, not comprehensive management of specialised complexity. Where complexity is real and high-stakes, "good enough" must still be sufficient to prevent blind spots. The method is adjustable: widen the inputs where the cost of ignorance is high, but keep the ritual bounded so it remains repeatable. The point is not minimalism for its own sake. The point is fit-for-purpose information.

It is also worth acknowledging that tools can distort what they measure. Calendars record scheduled time, not mental load. A week with few meetings can still be exhausting if the work is cognitively intense. Financial statements record transactions, not the emotional context that drove them. A training app records sessions, not the quality of recovery. Messages record contact, not closeness. Every dataset is a map with missing terrain. That is not a failure. It is a reminder to treat data as prompts for thought rather than as verdicts. The Upgrade Day gains depth when numbers are paired with narrative: the balance is noted, and then the question is asked, "What produced this?" The calendar is scanned, and then the question is asked, "How did this feel?" Data becomes a doorway into interpretation.

The motif of the table is useful here. Imagine the Upgrade Day beginning with a small set of artefacts laid out, as if you were preparing a laboratory bench: a notebook open to the quarter's page, a bank app showing balances, a calendar view showing the last ninety days, a training log summary if relevant, a list of recent commitments. The physicality matters. It turns the ritual into a deliberate act rather than a vague intention. It also reduces the temptation to flit between tabs endlessly, which is the digital version of rummaging through drawers. A well-prepared table keeps attention anchored.

Anchoring attention is not merely a productivity concern; it is a truth concern. The mind becomes more honest when it is less scattered. It can tolerate discomfort better when it is not constantly offered an escape hatch. Gathering tools and data in advance is therefore an ethical choice in miniature: you are arranging conditions in which you will be more likely to tell yourself the truth about the quarter. That truth may be gentle—progress where you assumed stagnation. It may be bracing—drift where you assumed control. Either way, it is preferable to the fog.

The final tension is the one that separates a thoughtful quarterly practice from an anxious one. More data can be a comfort blanket: it gives the illusion of control. Less data can be a comfort blanket too: it allows ambiguity and self-forgiveness to blur uncomfortable edges. The Upgrade Day asks for a third stance: enough evidence to see direction, and enough restraint to remain focused on decisions rather than on collection. When you lay your artefacts on the table—balances, calendars, logs, notes—the question sharpens into a forward test: are you gathering information to clarify the next quarter, or to delay choosing what you already know you will have to choose?

Protecting the ritual

On 5 August 2010, in Santiago, Chile, thirty-three miners were trapped nearly 700 metres underground when the San José mine collapsed. The rescue that followed became a global spectacle, yet the decisive work was not spectacle. It was protection: stabilising the site, establishing communication, rationing resources, and creating a disciplined routine underground that preserved physical and psychological endurance while engineers drilled above (Chilean Government rescue operation reporting; widely documented in international coverage, August–October 2010). Survival hinged on defending a small set of non-negotiables against constant disruption. Routine did not guarantee success. It made success possible.

Guard the small window.

An Upgrade Day is not a rescue operation, but it shares a structural feature with any process that matters: it is fragile in the face of interruption. A quarterly reset asks for a particular quality of attention—comparative, honest, unhurried—and that quality is precisely what modern life erodes most efficiently. Interruptions are not merely external. They include micro-distractions, self-interruptions, the itch to check something, the impulse to reply, the discomfort that prompts escape. A ritual that can be interrupted will be interrupted. The question is whether the ritual is designed to withstand that fact.

Protection begins with recognising that time is socially negotiated. Calendars are not private diaries; they are contracts with colleagues, family, and friends, even when no one else can see them. If you have trained the people around you to expect immediate responsiveness, they will request it. If you have trained yourself to experience discomfort as a cue to seek diversion, you will seek it. None of this is a moral failing. It is conditioning. Protection is the act of interrupting conditioning with design.

Interruptions are contagious.

The first category is obvious: other people. A colleague "just needs five minutes". A partner asks for help. A friend calls with a problem. A child needs attention. Each request is reasonable, and the point of a good life is not to become an unresponsive bunker. Yet a ritual cannot survive on benevolence alone. It needs boundaries. Boundaries are not declarations of importance; they are arrangements of expectation. In organisational terms, they are what prevent a system from being hijacked by the nearest demand.

This is why high-stakes environments use protected time and protocols. In medicine, for instance, the World Health Organization's Surgical Safety Checklist introduced in 2008 created a structured pause—the "time out"—before incision, requiring teams to confirm key details together (WHO, 2008). The power of that pause was not that it was long. It was that it was protected by agreement: everyone stopped, everyone participated, and interruptions were not allowed to override the sequence. The same insight applies here. An Upgrade Day does not need to be long to be effective, but it does need to be treated as real enough that others cannot casually pick it up and move it.

Treating it as "real" is, paradoxically, often harder for individuals than for institutions, because individuals are expected to be flexible. The default expectation placed on many professionals is availability: emails answered quickly, messages replied to, calendars adjusted to accommodate other people's meetings. The same default exists in many families, especially where one person is the quiet logistics engine. The Upgrade Day therefore asks for a subtle act of renegotiation: to be reachable most of the time, and deliberately unreachable for a bounded interval, on purpose, four times a year.

A five-word sentence helps here. Make it boringly clear.

Clarity is not rudeness. It is design. A protected ritual is easier to defend when it is framed as routine rather than as a dramatic act of self-care. Drama invites debate. Routine invites acceptance. People are less likely to challenge a recurring commitment that sounds normal: "I have a quarterly review I do; I'm unavailable that morning." The language matters because it shapes how others interpret the boundary. If you present the time as "flexible", it will be treated as flexible. If you present it as "a habit", it will be treated as part of your working and living rhythm. Implementation intentions research by Peter Gollwitzer (1999) suggests why: specific cues and plans increase follow-through. The same is true socially. Specificity reduces negotiation.

Protection also requires deciding what kind of unavailability you are creating. There is a difference between being physically unavailable (away from the usual environment), digitally unavailable (notifications silenced, inbox closed), and psychologically unavailable (resisting the internal impulse to check). Many people attempt the ritual while remaining digitally porous, which creates the illusion of doing the work while attention is continually siphoned. The resulting frustration is predictable: the ritual feels shallow, interrupted, unfinished. The lesson is not to demonise technology. It is to treat the attention boundary as part of the ritual's infrastructure.

Attention is the scarce resource.

That scarcity has been studied from multiple angles. Gloria Mark's research on knowledge work has documented how frequently people switch tasks in digital environments and how interruptions affect stress and productivity (Mark et al., 2014). The precise numbers vary by study and context, but the qualitative point is consistent: fragmented attention raises cognitive load. An Upgrade Day, by design, is the opposite of fragmentary. It is comparative work. Comparison requires continuity. If you allow constant context-switching, you cannot compare cleanly. You can only react.

The second category of interruption is internal. This one is more insidious because it arrives wearing your own face. It is the sudden urge to "just check" a message. The urge to look up one more statement. The urge to tidy the desk. The urge to open a new tab and research a tool that promises a better system. These impulses often claim to be productive. They are usually avoidance. The Upgrade Day tends to reveal discrepancies—between what you meant and what happened—and discrepancies provoke discomfort. Discomfort triggers escape. A protected ritual therefore is not only a boundary against other people. It is a boundary against your own escape hatches.

Here, small pre-ritual cues matter more than elaborate motivation. Cues are the brain's shorthand. They signal that a different mode is beginning. In religious traditions, rituals often begin with simple physical actions—a wash, a candle, a specific place and posture—not because these actions are magical, but because they shift attention. In secular life, the same principle applies. A particular notebook opened to the next empty page. A familiar drink prepared. A specific chair. A phone placed out of reach. These cues are not sentimental. They are behavioural engineering. They reduce the "activation energy" required to enter the reflective mode, and they make the ritual feel like a known place rather than an improvisation.

The motif to keep returning to is the door. Protection is deciding what gets through it.

A door is not a wall. It can be opened. It can be closed. It can have a sign. It can have a lock. The Upgrade Day needs a door because the day's work is cognitive and emotional, and both are vulnerable to intrusion. If the door is left open, the ritual becomes a porous suggestion rather than a protected space. If the door is bolted, life may push back with resentment. The craft is in a door that closes for a bounded period and reopens afterwards, with signals that make the closure legible to others and to yourself.

Those signals include setting expectations with family and colleagues in advance. Advance notice is a form of respect; it prevents the boundary from landing as a surprise. It also reduces the chance that a last-minute request feels like a moral test: will you be helpful, or selfish? When the boundary is set early, it becomes part of the landscape rather than an emotional confrontation. The same applies at work. If colleagues learn that certain blocks are protected, they adjust. Many people avoid setting such expectations because they fear appearing less committed. The irony is that perpetual availability often produces worse work, more stress, and more resentment, which erodes commitment more deeply over time. Protection is an investment in sustainability, not a withdrawal.

Sustainability is a measurable outcome, not a virtue. In work, it can be seen in the absence of chronic backlog and the presence of slack. In health, it can be seen in energy patterns that do not collapse. In relationships, it can be seen in interactions that remain generous rather than brittle. A quarterly ritual helps sustain these outcomes only if it survives. Survival requires social negotiation.

A third named, checkable example illustrates what happens when protection is absent. Consider the phenomenon of "meeting creep" in organisations: calendars fill with recurring meetings that outlive their purpose because no one has explicit permission to cancel them. Research on meeting load has shown that excessive meetings correlate with fatigue and reduced time for focused work; a 2017 Harvard Business Review piece by Leslie Perlow, Constance Noonan Hadley, and Eunice Eun discussed the time cost of meetings and the benefits of "quiet time" experiments in organisations (Perlow et al., 2017). The relevance is not to treat HBR as scripture. It is to notice that without protected time, the default organisational behaviour is expansion. The same expansion occurs in personal life. Without protected time, admin spreads. Work spreads. Social obligations spread. The ritual is squeezed until it becomes an afterthought.

There is also a limitation to be acknowledged honestly. Some people cannot easily protect a full day or even a half day. Caregiving responsibilities, shift work, unpredictable health, or precarious jobs can make fixed blocks fragile. A rigid approach would turn the ritual into another failing. The reconciliation is not to abandon protection, but to scale it. Protection can apply to a shorter window: two focused hours rather than a full day, repeated across two sessions if needed. The principle remains the same: the interval is bounded, pre-signalled, and defended. Protection is not measured in hours. It is measured in integrity—whether the ritual happens as planned often enough to remain a cadence rather than a fantasy.

Integrity requires closure, and closure is where post-ritual rewards become more than a gimmick. People often recoil at the idea of rewarding themselves, as if it were childish. Yet behavioural science suggests that reinforcement matters. B. F. Skinner's work on operant conditioning is old and sometimes misapplied, but its core insight is straightforward: behaviours followed by satisfying outcomes are more likely to be repeated (Skinner, 1938). In human life, the "reward" need not be a sugary treat or a purchase. It can be a simple, chosen pleasure that marks completion: a walk, a meal, a bath, an hour with a book, an afternoon outside. The function is to give the nervous system a clean endpoint, so the ritual does not feel like endless self-monitoring. The post-ritual reward says: the door is open again, and you have done the work.

That endpoint also reduces a common problem: the feeling that reflection is merely self-critique. Many people associate reviews with judgement—performance appraisals, exams, audits. If the Upgrade Day feels like punishment, it will be avoided. Protection, therefore, includes shaping the emotional tone. The pre-ritual cue signals seriousness. The post-ritual reward signals safety. Between them, the ritual becomes containable. Containable rituals are repeatable. Repeatable rituals are the entire point.

A protected ritual also benefits from what might be called a "handover" moment—an explicit transition back into ordinary life. Without this, decisions made during the Upgrade Day can evaporate because the mind does not register a new phase beginning. In project management, handovers and documented decisions prevent knowledge from being lost between phases. In personal practice, the same risk exists: the ritual produces insights, but the day after is crowded and the insights vanish. A small handover action—capturing decisions in one place, setting one or two calendar entries, leaving a visible note for the next week—turns reflection into continuity. It is not more work. It is protection of the work already done.

Protection also requires confronting a cultural myth: that the most committed people are always available. Availability is a poor proxy for seriousness. Seriousness is often expressed as the ability to protect the conditions under which good decisions can be made. If you cannot protect two or three hours once a quarter to compare, decide, and adjust, then the rest of the year will be governed by whatever is loudest. That may be work, or crisis, or other people's needs, or your own avoidance. None of these are evil. They are simply default rulers in a system without protected time.

The door motif returns for a final pass. A door can be knocked on. The question is whether you answer. Protection does not require never answering. It requires deciding in advance what constitutes an emergency and what does not, and then holding that boundary with calm consistency. Calm consistency is persuasive. Drama invites argument. Calm says: this is normal. This is part of how I run my year.

The forward test is the one that reveals whether the ritual has truly become infrastructure. When the next Upgrade Day arrives and the first interruption appears—an email marked urgent, a friend asking for a favour, a sudden impulse to check something "quickly"—will the door stay closed long enough for you to do the comparative work that keeps drift from compounding, or will it swing open out of habit, turning the ritual back into an idea you keep promising yourself you will do properly *next quarter*?

Chapter 3
Money Snapshot and Adjustments

On 15 September 2008, queues formed outside Northern Rock branches across the United Kingdom, an image that had not belonged to modern British life for generations. Glass doors, damp pavements, a murmur of anxious conversation: people were not queuing for a new product, but to touch something that had always been invisible—trust. In retrospect, that week is often narrated as a story about banks and balance sheets, about liquidity and risk. For ordinary individuals it was also something simpler and more visceral: a reminder that money is never only numbers. Money is time, safety, options. When it becomes uncertain, the body feels it first.

Money is a weather system.

Most of the time, the sky looks clear. Salaries arrive. Cards tap. Bills are paid. The danger is not that people are foolish; it is that the everyday machinery of money is designed to be frictionless. Frictionless systems are comfortable, and comfort breeds inattention. Inattention allows drift. Drift does not always announce itself as "debt" or "crisis". It arrives as subscriptions that multiply quietly, small luxuries that become baseline, and a slow tightening of margin until the month contains less room for choice. A person can be financially stable and still feel financially tense, because stability without visibility is a kind of permanent uncertainty.

This chapter is built around a deliberately unglamorous idea: money becomes less emotionally loaded when it becomes more legible. Legibility does not require mastery of markets or devotion to spreadsheets. It requires a snapshot, repeated on a humane cadence, that shows direction rather than perfection. The purpose is not to turn life into an accounting exercise. The purpose is to reclaim the ability to steer. When people avoid looking at money, they do not avoid consequences; they simply postpone the moment those consequences force attention. A quarterly approach shifts that moment from surprise to choice.

The first move is a net worth snapshot that refuses the two most common traps: obsessive precision and wilful vagueness. Precision seduces clever people because it feels like control. It also demands constant updating, which turns the act of looking into a daily itch. Vague avoidance seduces anxious people because it feels like peace. It is peace purchased with ignorance, and it is fragile. The quarterly snapshot sits in the middle. It uses broad categories not because detail is worthless, but because the most valuable information is often directional: is the dial moving towards more margin or less, towards more resilience or more fragility? A snapshot taken every quarter becomes a kind of personal barometer. You do not stare at it all day. You check it often enough to notice a storm forming.

Once money is treated as a system rather than a series of isolated purchases, the moral temperature drops. People often carry strange shame about spending, as though every transaction were a confession. Shame is a poor analytic tool. It makes people hide from their own data. The more useful posture is curiosity. Where did money actually go? What did it purchase: convenience, rest, status, health, learning, connection? Which costs are genuinely supporting the life you want, and which are simply repeating because they can? This chapter treats spending as evidence of priorities—sometimes intentional, sometimes accidental. The aim is not judgement of individual receipts but recognition of patterns.

Patterns become visible when you stop asking, "Was this purchase good?" and start asking, "What cluster is this part of?" Subscriptions are a cluster. Food is a cluster. Transport is a cluster. Small luxuries are a cluster. Each cluster carries a story about time and energy. Subscriptions often tell a story about aspiration: tools bought for a future self who will use them. Food spending tells a story about schedule, stress, and social life. Transport tells a story about geography and routine. Small luxuries tell a story about comfort and reward. Once you read spending as story, you can begin to rewrite it—not through punishment, but through experiments.

That word matters: experiments. The emotional reason money change fails is that people treat it as identity. They declare themselves "frugal now" or "disciplined now" and then collapse under the weight of their own theatre. A quarterly reset allows a more adult approach: time-limited tests. Trim one thing for ninety days. Adjust one category by a modest amount. Pause a subscription. Swap one recurring habit for another. The important detail is reversibility. Reversible changes lower fear. Fear is what makes people cling to familiar spending even when it harms them. When changes are framed as tests rather than as permanent sacrifices, the mind becomes more willing to participate. You are not becoming a different person. You are measuring what happens when you alter one variable.

There is also a corrective to the usual austerity narrative. Money conversations often default to cuts because cuts are easy to moralise. Yet some spending genuinely improves life. Some spending increases health, learning, and connection in ways that compound. The more interesting question is not only "What can be reduced?" but "What deserves reinforcement?" This chapter therefore makes room for a counterintuitive move: selectively doubling what works, for a single quarter, to see what improves. That might mean spending more on a tool that saves hours each week, on travel that restores perspective, on a class that turns learning into practice, on experiences that deepen relationships. The point is not indulgence. It is alignment. Money is a finite resource, but so is attention. Spending that supports the life you claim to value is not a failure of discipline; it is the visible expression of priorities.

Modern relevance sharpens this entire discussion. The last decade has seen the proliferation of "invisible" spending: app subscriptions, micro-payments, buy-now-pay-later schemes, and the seamlessness of contactless transactions that remove the small friction that once made purchases feel real. At the same time, many people live through periods where costs rise faster than pay, and where uncertainty—economic, professional, personal—makes financial margin feel both more important and harder to create. Under these conditions, the most dangerous state is not extravagance; it is opacity. Opacity turns every small expense into a potential threat because you cannot see the system. Visibility does not solve structural economic problems, but it does reduce the personal chaos that comes from not knowing.

A quarterly money ritual also offers something psychologically rare: a way to engage with money without being consumed by it. Many people swing between neglect and obsession. Neglect breeds surprise. Obsession breeds anxiety. A quarterly cadence creates a middle stance: look closely, decide deliberately, then return to living. It restores money to its proper role as a tool rather than a constant mental soundtrack. The net worth snapshot functions as a compass. The spending pattern review functions as a map. The trims and tests function as steering adjustments. The doubling experiments function as strategic investment in what makes life better. Together, they form a money practice that is serious without being joyless.

There is a philosophical thread running underneath, and it is worth naming because it is rarely said plainly. Money is not only about consumption. It is about optionality. Optionality is the ability to make a different choice when circumstances change: to take time, to say no, to endure a disruption, to pursue a learning opportunity, to support a loved one, to rest. Optionality is a form of freedom, and freedom is not achieved through a single heroic decision. It is achieved through small, repeated choices that create margin. This is why direction matters more than precision. A person moving steadily towards more margin is building optionality, even if the numbers are not perfect. A person drifting towards less margin is losing optionality, even if their lifestyle looks fine from the outside.

The chapter that follows treats money as a domain that can be handled with quiet competence. It does not require prediction. It does not require a personality transplant. It requires the courage to take a snapshot, the humility to read patterns without self-attack, and the discipline to run small experiments rather than dramatic overhauls. The payoff is not only financial. It is existential: the sense that the next quarter is not merely something that happens to you, but something you can adjust—gently, deliberately—before the weather turns.

Simple net worth snapshot

On 14 October 1947, at Muroc Army Air Field in California, Chuck Yeager flew the Bell X-1 faster than the speed of sound. The event is remembered for the shock wave and the orange aircraft slicing through thin desert air, but the more instructive detail was procedural: the programme did not rely on impressions. It relied on instruments. Speed, altitude, fuel flow—numbers gathered in a disciplined way, compared over time, used to decide what to try next. The aircraft was a machine; the principle applies more broadly. When something matters and the consequences compound, you measure direction rather than argue with feeling.

Money needs instruments.

A net worth snapshot is one such instrument: a quarterly reading that shows the broad direction of your financial life without inviting obsession. It is deliberately unfussy. It does not pretend to know what markets will do next month or what your future self will want. It answers a narrower, more honest question: at this point in the year, do the assets you control outweigh the liabilities you owe, and is that balance moving in a direction you recognise? The power of the snapshot is not precision. The power is repeatability.

Keep it quarterly.

People often approach net worth with two unhelpful extremes. The first is avoidance: net worth is treated as something "for wealthy people", or something too complicated, or something that provokes anxiety. The second is overengineering: intricate spreadsheets, daily updates, constant valuation of every asset, as though the purpose were to turn one's life into a miniature hedge fund. Both extremes are forms of distortion. Avoidance allows drift to run for years without being seen. Overengineering turns visibility into surveillance and invites emotional whiplash as markets and valuations fluctuate. The quarterly snapshot is an escape from both. It is the middle path: enough clarity to steer, not enough granularity to panic.

To see why broad categories matter, it helps to look at how people reason about risk. Risk in personal finance is often imagined as a dramatic event—a market crash, a redundancy, an emergency bill. Yet the more common risk is opacity: the slow loss of margin because the system is not being monitored at a usable level. Opacity makes small problems feel sudden because they are not noticed as they accumulate. A net worth snapshot reduces opacity by making the system legible at a glance. It turns the abstract sensation of "I should probably get on top of this" into a concrete reading that can be compared quarter to quarter.

Comparison is the engine.

The snapshot is built from two piles: assets and liabilities. In an ideal world, each pile would be precisely valued. In a real life, precision is expensive, emotionally loaded, and often misleading. A house is worth what someone will pay, not what an app estimates. A pension's value moves with markets that you do not control. A private business, a collection, even a car—these are all assets with fuzzy valuations. Fuzziness is not a problem when the purpose is to see direction. The point of the quarter is not to prove an exact number. The point is to ask, "Has the dial moved?" Broad categories are sufficient for that question, and they carry a secondary advantage: they make the snapshot easier to repeat, which is the only way it becomes meaningful.

The intellectual justification for "good enough" measurement can be found in the history of decision-making under uncertainty. Herbert Simon's notion of bounded rationality (Simon, 1955) describes how humans make decisions with limited information and time. A quarterly net worth snapshot is bounded rationality applied to money. It accepts constraints. It measures what can be measured reliably with reasonable effort and uses that measurement to guide small choices. This is not a compromise of seriousness. It is seriousness expressed as restraint.

Restraint also matters because money data can hijack attention. The behavioural finance literature has long noted that people react strongly to losses; the concept of loss aversion is associated with Kahneman and Tversky's prospect theory (Kahneman & Tversky, 1979). If you stare at daily account values, you invite your nervous system to ride every wiggle. The result is not better decision-making; it is emotional noise. Quarterly measurement reduces that noise. It creates a sampling rate that is slow enough to smooth volatility and fast enough to catch drift. The snapshot becomes a stabiliser rather than a stimulant.

A practical question arises: what counts as an asset, what counts as a liability, and how "broad" should the categories be? The answer depends on how you intend to use the snapshot. A good rule is to separate what behaves differently. Cash behaves differently from investments. Property behaves differently from pensions. Debts behave differently depending on interest and structure. But the rule is not to create a taxonomy. The rule is to create a dashboard. A dashboard shows the readings that affect steering. It does not display every wire in the engine.

The assets side can therefore be thought of as a few buckets: cash and cash-like balances; investments held outside pensions; pensions or retirement accounts; property equity if applicable; other significant assets that matter to your situation. The liabilities side is often even simpler: mortgage balance, if applicable; consumer or personal debt; student loans or other structured debts; any other obligations that materially affect your margin. The precise labels are less important than consistency. Consistency is what turns a one-off calculation into a trendline.

Trends are where truth lives.

A single net worth number is emotionally potent and analytically limited. It can prompt pride or shame, both of which are poor guides. A sequence of quarterly snapshots, by contrast, produces a trajectory. The trajectory answers questions that a single number cannot. Is debt shrinking steadily? Are cash reserves increasing? Are investments growing mainly through contributions or mainly through market movement? Is property equity changing? Are liabilities stable while assets fluctuate? None of these questions requires predicting markets. They require comparing readings over time. The quarter creates the time series. The time series creates insight.

This is why the snapshot should be taken at roughly the same point in each quarter and recorded in the same place. The exact date does not need to be perfect, but regularity reduces distortion. If you take one snapshot after a bonus payment and another after an annual insurance bill, you introduce noise. You can still learn, but you must interpret carefully. Regular timing makes interpretation easier. It is the equivalent of measuring blood pressure at the same time of day. The number is not your identity. It is a reading, best interpreted in context.

A named, checkable example of how measurement cadence shapes behaviour comes from retirement saving policy. In October 2012, automatic enrolment into workplace pensions began rolling out in the UK, changing participation by making saving the default rather than the exception (The Pensions Regulator, 2012). The point here is not to debate policy. It is to notice how structure and cadence matter more than motivational speeches. A quarterly net worth snapshot functions as a personal structure: it makes attention to money recurrent rather than episodic. It does not force saving, but it makes the consequences of not saving more visible. Visibility, over time, shapes behaviour.

A second example sits in the corporate world. Public companies in the United States file quarterly reports (10-Q) with the Securities and Exchange Commission, creating a rhythm of periodic measurement and disclosure (SEC, n.d.). Companies often dislike this rhythm because it can encourage short-term thinking, and that objection is a useful counterpoint. Quarterly measurement can distort behaviour if it becomes the sole horizon, pushing decisions that look good in the short term and harm the long term. The personal analogue exists. A person who becomes obsessed with quarterly net worth might underinvest in learning, health, or relationships because those do not show up on the balance sheet. They might prioritise a number over a life.

This is a real limitation.

The reconciliation is to treat net worth as one instrument among several, not as the master dial. Net worth captures financial resilience and optionality; it does not capture meaning. The quarterly ritual is designed precisely to prevent money from becoming the only axis of evaluation. The snapshot's job is to provide clarity about the financial system so it can be managed with less anxiety, not to replace other values. It is a support, not a sovereign. Used this way, quarterly measurement can encourage long-term thinking by making trade-offs explicit. If net worth is declining because you are paying for education, for instance, that may be a chosen investment. The snapshot does not condemn it; it makes it legible. If net worth is declining because subscriptions have multiplied and spending has drifted, that is a different story. The snapshot helps distinguish these stories.

Legibility also reduces the tendency to tell oneself comforting fictions. Many people mentally count assets they cannot easily access and ignore liabilities that feel unpleasant. Others do the opposite: they fixate on debt and ignore growing assets. Both distortions increase stress. A snapshot that includes both sides, recorded consistently, forces a more balanced picture. It also encourages a more adult relationship with uncertainty. Markets fluctuate. Asset values move. Inflation changes what numbers mean. A quarterly snapshot does not pretend these uncertainties do not exist. It simply says: given the uncertainty, what is the broad direction?

Direction is actionable.

The snapshot also reveals something that is easy to miss when you focus on monthly budgets: the difference between income statement thinking and balance sheet thinking. Income statement thinking is about flow—what comes in, what goes out. Balance sheet thinking is about position—what you have, what you owe. Both matter. Many people obsess over the monthly flow and neglect the position until a crisis. A net worth snapshot restores balance sheet awareness. It shows whether you are building buffers, reducing obligations, increasing flexibility. It also shows whether your financial life is becoming more brittle even if the monthly budget appears fine. Brittleness is not visible in a single month. It is visible across quarters.

The motif of instruments returns here because it suggests the right emotional posture. An instrument does not flatter you. It does not scold you. It reads. Your job is to interpret the reading and decide what to do next. This posture reduces shame. It also reduces overconfidence. People who avoid looking often fear they will discover catastrophe. People who are comfortable looking often assume they are doing fine. Both assumptions can be wrong. A quarterly snapshot replaces assumptions with a reading. The reading may be reassuring. It may be bracing. Either way, it is better than superstition.

One final psychological trap is worth naming: the desire to predict. Net worth numbers can invite the mind to start forecasting, especially when markets have been volatile. Forecasting feels sophisticated. It is often a way to avoid the only question you can answer reliably: what are you doing with the resources under your control? The quarterly snapshot is intentionally anti-oracular. It looks backwards to create forward steering, not predictions. It asks you to measure, compare, and commit to small adjustments. It refuses to pretend that tomorrow's market movements can be known. In this sense, it is intellectually modest. Modesty is underrated.

The forward test, then, is not whether you can compute net worth to the penny. The forward test is whether you can take a reading and accept it as information rather than as identity—then return three months later and take the reading again. Over time, the sequence answers the question that matters: is your financial position becoming more resilient, or more fragile, and are you willing to name what is moving the dial?

Reviewing spending patterns

In February 1995, Tesco launched the Clubcard in the United Kingdom, beginning a retail experiment whose real product was not a plastic card at all, but a new kind of visibility. At the checkout, the familiar beep of the scanner became, quietly, a research instrument: purchases turned into data points that could be grouped, compared, and interpreted. Over time, the company could see what shoppers rarely articulate about themselves—how habits cluster, how routines repeat, how "small" extras become dependable lines in a week. The outcome was not merely loyalty marketing. It was a sharper map of behaviour, built from ordinary transactions, revealing patterns that no single receipt could ever explain.

Patterns hide in plain sight.

What makes this relevant to a quarterly reset is not corporate surveillance but an intellectual shift: the difference between scrutinising individual purchases and understanding the system they form. Most people who avoid their spending do so for an emotional reason. The act of looking can feel like judgement. The mind anticipates a verdict—wasteful, undisciplined, irresponsible—and therefore prefers vagueness. The opposite extreme is equally common among highly conscientious people: forensic attention to minutiae, as though moral virtue lives in the categorisation of every coffee. Both approaches miss the point. Spending patterns are best read at the level where they become legible, and legibility rarely lives in the single transaction. It lives in the cluster.

A cluster is not a moral category. It is a repeated behaviour expressed in money. Subscriptions are clusters. Food is a cluster. Transport is a cluster. Small luxuries are clusters. Gifts, childcare, commuting, professional expenses, social commitments—each forms its own constellation of transactions, recurring with a rhythm that reflects your week, your stress, your social life, your geography, your tastes. Constellation is the right metaphor because the dots are not meaningful on their own; meaning emerges when you step back. From too close, it is noise. From the right distance, it is shape.

The right distance also protects you from a known psychological trap: the mind's tendency to overreact to salient anecdotes. Behavioural research has long shown that humans do not naturally weigh evidence in neutral ways. Kahneman and Tversky's work on judgement under uncertainty (1979) and their later framing of prospect theory (Kahneman & Tversky, 1979) help explain why losses sting, why small surprises feel larger than they are, and why isolated "bad" purchases can loom in memory while the slow, repeating drain goes unnoticed. If you focus on receipts, you are feeding the brain's taste for vivid stories. If you focus on clusters, you are feeding the brain a calmer diet: repetition, baseline, trend.

This matters because spending is not merely arithmetic. It is behaviour under constraints. A transport cluster is rarely about a love of trains or taxis; it is about where you live, where you work, how reliable your schedule is, how safe you feel travelling at certain times. A food cluster is rarely about "willpower"; it is about time, fatigue, social life, and the availability of easy options. A subscription cluster is rarely about a single service; it is about aspirational identity—who you imagine yourself being, what you wish you had time for, what you use to recover when you are depleted. When you review spending as clusters, you begin to see the causes without turning the exercise into a trial.

The concept of mental accounting is useful here. Richard Thaler introduced the term in the 1980s to describe how people mentally segregate money into different "accounts" and treat pounds differently depending on where they believe those pounds came from or what they are "for" (Thaler, 1985). Mental accounting is not irrational in the crude sense; it is a coping mechanism for complexity. Yet it produces predictable distortions. People may treat a refund as "free money" and spend it quickly. They may treat certain categories as off-limits and then "splurge" elsewhere as compensation. They may ignore small recurring costs because no single one triggers a sense of danger. Reviewing clusters exposes mental accounting at work. It makes visible the places where the story you tell yourself about money differs from the way money actually leaves your accounts.

The quarterly cadence is ideal for this because it is long enough for the clusters to repeat and short enough that the patterns still feel connected to lived memory. A week can be misleading. A month can be unusual. A quarter tends to include a more representative mix: ordinary weeks, disruptions, social events, minor crises, the odd indulgence. When you scan spending across that window, you are not trying to reconstruct every decision. You are looking for repeated shapes: the subscription that quietly renews, the delivery fees that add up, the transport spikes in certain weeks, the "small luxuries" that appear on days when work was hard. The quarter turns these from isolated moments into a system.

A named, checkable example of how systems encourage cluster spending comes from the shift to subscription models in consumer technology and media. Netflix launched its streaming service in the United States in 2007, accelerating a broader move towards recurring payments as a default way to access entertainment. Whatever one thinks of streaming culture, its economic structure is clear: recurring payments are designed to be forgettable. They are meant to feel like background infrastructure. This is not nefarious; it is commercially efficient. Yet the personal implication is straightforward. The more of your spending is recurring and frictionless, the more important periodic review becomes, because the system is built to continue unless stopped.

A second example sits in payments rather than content. Apple Pay launched in the United States in October 2014, adding another layer of frictionless purchasing to an already quick transaction world. Again, the point is not to moralise convenience. Convenience is often worth paying for. The point is that when the act of spending becomes effortless, attention becomes the scarce input. A quarter's review compensates for that design reality by reintroducing an interval where the spending is felt again—not as guilt, but as knowledge.

Knowledge is not the same as judgement.

This is why "reviewing spending patterns" is fundamentally different from "budgeting", at least as budgeting is commonly imagined. Budgeting often starts with restriction: what should not be spent. Pattern review starts with observation: what has been spent, repeatedly, and what that repetition suggests about the life being lived. The observational stance is not passive. It is analytic. It turns spending into a behavioural dataset and asks what it reveals about values, constraints, and stress points. When you do this, abstractions like efficiency and risk become visible. Efficiency becomes a question of whether money is buying time, reducing friction, and supporting the activities you actually do. Risk becomes a question of how much margin exists if the quarter contains a shock—a bill, a travel need, a family obligation—given the current baseline outflows.

Margins are rarely destroyed by one dramatic purchase. They are eroded by clusters that feel too small to matter individually. This is where subscriptions deserve special attention, not because they are evil, but because they are the purest form of "set and forget". A subscription is a decision that keeps deciding for you. In behavioural terms, it is a default. Thaler and Sunstein's work on choice architecture later popularised the power of defaults in shaping behaviour (Thaler & Sunstein, 2008). Subscriptions are defaults with a monthly pulse. They do not require renewed consent. They require active cancellation, which is psychologically harder than passive continuation. When you review spending quarterly, you are effectively asking: which defaults are still worth their place?

Food spending is a second cluster where moral language tends to muddy analysis. People talk about "bad habits" and "treating myself" as though the only variable were virtue. The more accurate approach is to treat food spending as a proxy for time and energy. A quarter with heavy deadlines often shows a different food pattern than a quarter with more slack. Social quarters look different from solitary quarters. Commute-heavy quarters look different from home-heavy ones. When you see the cluster, you can name the pressure that produced it. That naming matters because it shifts the question from "Why did I do that?" to "What conditions made that the default?" Conditions are more malleable than character. They can be adjusted.

Transport spending is often the clearest cluster because it is tied to geography and routine. It reveals the cost of commuting, the price of convenience, the impact of location decisions, and the friction of time. It can also reveal hidden behavioural choices: the tendency to pay for speed when late, the habit of choosing comfort when exhausted, the occasional premium paid to avoid stress. These are not failings. They are trade-offs. A pattern review surfaces the trade-offs so they can be understood rather than merely repeated.

Small luxuries are where many people lose the plot, either through guilt or through denial. The quarterly lens is particularly helpful here because it shows whether "small luxuries" are rare delights or daily anaesthetic. A coffee bought once a week is different from a coffee bought twice a day. A few paid conveniences in a hectic month are different from convenience as a permanent baseline. The quarter is also long enough to link these luxuries to mood and workload. Often, they are not about desire for a product. They are about desire for relief. When you see that, the question becomes more interesting than "Should I stop?" It becomes "What is this purchase doing for me, and is there a better way to get that benefit?" That question is not a moral lecture. It is an analytic prompt.

There is a credible limitation to any pattern review, and it matters for intelligent readers who dislike simplistic frameworks. Transaction data is not a complete record of life. Cash spending may be invisible. Shared finances can blur attribution. Certain costs arrive quarterly or annually and distort a period. Life events—moving house, illness, family emergencies—can make a quarter atypical. Pattern review can also miss the "why" behind a number: a large outflow might be an investment in education, a necessary medical cost, or support for a family member. Pure categorisation cannot interpret meaning. The reconciliation is to treat the review as a dialogue between numbers and narrative. The numbers show the cluster; the narrative explains the context. One without the other misleads.

This is also why the purpose of reviewing patterns is understanding, not optimisation. Optimisation encourages a brittle mindset: every expense must justify itself, every fluctuation is a failure. Understanding encourages a more resilient stance: some quarters are expensive because life is happening, and the question is whether the expense aligns with what matters and whether it endangers margin. Margin is the throughline. Margin is what turns money from a source of stress into a source of optionality. A quarterly pattern review is, at root, a margin review: where is money quietly removing future options, and where is money quietly purchasing stability, connection, health, or learning?

The constellation metaphor returns because it points to a quiet but profound payoff. When you can see the constellation, you stop arguing with individual stars. You stop treating each purchase as a referendum on your worth. You begin to see spending as a pattern of life choices interacting with constraints. That shift is emotionally calming and intellectually empowering. It also sets up the next move in the money ritual. Once clusters are visible, adjustments can be made without drama: small, reversible tests rather than sweeping bans; and, crucially, selective reinforcement of spending that truly supports the life you want.

A forward tension remains, and it is the one that makes this work matter. Seeing patterns creates responsibility. Once you notice that a cluster exists—recurring costs, friction purchases, stress spending—you can no longer claim innocence through ignorance.

Yet you are also not obligated to attack every cluster at once. The quarterly cadence protects you from that overreaction. It asks a narrower question, one that can be answered without theatre: of the constellations visible in your last ninety days, which one is steering the system most strongly, and is that steering still worth consenting to for the next quarter?

Identifying trims and tests

On 16 April 1972, at Stanford University in California, a group of researchers began what is now known as the "marshmallow test", led by Walter Mischel and colleagues. Children were offered a choice: one treat now or two later, a simple set-up that became famous for what it suggested about self-control and future outcomes. The experiment's popular afterlife has been messy—later researchers, including Tyler Watts, Greg Duncan, and Haonan Quan in 2018, argued that the relationship between early delay of gratification and later achievement weakens substantially when family background is accounted for (Watts, Duncan & Quan, 2018). Still, the image endures because it captures a real tension: humans experience trade-offs most sharply when a choice is framed as deprivation.

Deprivation rarely lasts.

That is why trims and tests work better than bans. A quarterly money reset is not a stage for willpower theatre. It is a place to run small experiments that reduce drift and increase margin without turning life into a punishment regime. When people try to "fix" spending through sweeping restrictions, they often trigger a predictable backlash: resentment, fatigue, then a rebound that feels like failure. A time-limited trim, by contrast, changes the emotional contract. It says: for one quarter, we will test a small adjustment, observe what happens, and decide again. The difference is subtle. It is also decisive.

The first move, after you have seen your spending clusters, is to stop thinking in moral categories and start thinking in experimental ones. Money habits, like all habits, are partially functions of environment and routine. If you treat them as character flaws, you will try to change your character in ninety days. That is both unrealistic and unnecessary. If you treat them as patterns, you can change a few conditions and watch the pattern respond. This is the logic of behavioural science applied without jargon. You are not proving virtue. You are measuring outcomes.

The power of time-limited experiments rests on a simple principle from psychology: people respond differently to choices when they are framed as reversible. Loss aversion—the tendency to experience losses more intensely than equivalent gains—was formalised in Kahneman and Tversky's prospect theory (Kahneman & Tversky, 1979). A permanent cut feels like a loss. A ninety-day pause feels like a test. The nervous system is less alarmed by a test than by a loss, which makes the test more likely to be attempted, and therefore more likely to produce learning.

Learning is the real product.

This is why the language of "trim" matters. A trim suggests refinement rather than austerity, like pruning a plant to improve growth rather than hacking it down in anger. It implies that some spending is worth keeping. It also implies that the goal is alignment, not deprivation. The quarter provides the perfect container for this because it is long enough to observe the effects of a change and short enough that the change does not need to be justified as permanent. Permanence is what turns money decisions into identity battles. Temporariness turns them into data.

A second reason experiments work is that they reduce decision load. If you decide, once, to pause a subscription for a quarter, you remove dozens of micro-decisions about whether to "use it enough" to justify it. If you decide, once, to adjust one category by a modest percentage, you change the baseline against which daily decisions are made. This is the same design logic that shows up in institutional savings programmes. Richard Thaler and Shlomo Benartzi's "Save More Tomorrow" proposal in 2004 was built on pre-commitment: people agreed in advance to allocate a portion of future pay rises towards retirement savings, shifting the burden from repeated willpower to a single, structured decision (Thaler & Benartzi, 2004).

Again, the point is not to mimic a pension plan. It is to recognise the mechanism. One decision can change many downstream decisions.

Downstream is where life happens.

A trim, to be useful, must be attached to a visible pattern. This guards against random austerity. If you cut something that is not materially affecting your finances or your attention, you create pain without gain. The quarterly spending review gives you clusters; trims and tests convert clusters into candidate variables. The best candidates tend to have three features. They recur. They are at least partly discretionary. And they contain a hidden element of drift—spending that continues more from inertia than from active, repeated consent.

Subscriptions are the obvious example because they are literally automated consent. They are also psychologically tricky because many were purchased as acts of optimism: the language app you thought you would use, the streaming service you meant to watch "more quality things" on, the premium tool you believed would make work smoother. These subscriptions often do not fail because the service is bad. They fail because the context that made them attractive has changed. The quarter reveals that change. A time-limited pause is an elegant test because it does not require you to decide what your future self will want forever. It asks a narrower question: for the next ninety days, will life be worse without this? If the answer is yes, the subscription returns with renewed consent. If the answer is no, the drift has been exposed.

Food spending is a richer cluster because it combines necessity with a spectrum of convenience. Here, "trim" should not be treated as a moral project, because food spending is deeply entangled with time, stress, and social life. The experimental stance is more fruitful. If a quarter's data suggests that delivery and convenience purchases have become a baseline, the test is not "be better". The test is "alter one condition and see what happens". Perhaps you change the frequency with which convenience is used, or you set a modest adjustment target for a category. The value of the quarter is that it allows you to observe substitution effects. If you cut convenience spending and replace it with more expensive grocery shopping, the net effect might be small. If you cut convenience spending and replace it with time costs that create stress, the effect might be negative even if the numbers look better. The point is not to force a single outcome. The point is to reveal the real trade-off.

Transport is often governed by geography, yet it also contains discretionary layers: the choice to pay for speed when late, the choice to use ride-hailing when tired, the choice to commute at times that cost more. A quarter of spending patterns can reveal whether the transport cluster is stable or creeping. If it is creeping, a trim might involve testing a different commuting pattern for a quarter, or reducing a particular discretionary transport behaviour. Again, the quarter makes the experiment feasible because it is long enough to encounter the usual life disruptions that tend to break fragile plans. If a test only works in a perfect week, it is not a good test.

Small luxuries are the cluster where shame often enters. Shame is analytically useless. A better question is functional: what job is the spending doing? Is it genuine pleasure, a small ritual that makes life lighter? Is it social signalling? Is it stress relief? Is it compensation for fatigue? The answer changes the appropriate experiment. If the spending is genuine pleasure with modest cost, trimming it may produce little benefit and a disproportionate loss of joy. If the spending is anaesthetic, trimming it may reveal the discomfort it was covering, which is useful information even if it is unpleasant. A time-limited test is psychologically safer than a permanent ban because it frames the discomfort as data, not as failure.

This is where the metaphor of the laboratory is helpful. A lab does not prove a hypothesis by insisting harder. It alters one variable while holding others roughly constant and observes. In personal finance, you cannot hold everything constant—life is not a controlled environment—but you can still adopt the posture. Choose one or two trims. Keep them modest. Observe what happens to both numbers and experience. Then decide again. That posture transforms money adjustment from a moral drama into an iterative craft.

Craft requires measurement, but it also requires restraint. One of the easiest ways to sabotage trims and tests is to run too many experiments at once. When everything changes, nothing can be attributed. The mind then struggles to interpret outcomes and defaults back to old patterns. A quarterly cadence discourages this by design: you do not need to solve your entire financial life in one quarter, because you will return. Returning is the secret ingredient. It turns urgency into patience. It allows you to take small steps without fear that you have to get it all right immediately.

A credible counter-example needs to be admitted. There are situations where "small trims" are not sufficient, because the financial situation is already structurally tight. A person with high fixed costs relative to income may need larger changes than modest percentage adjustments. A person facing a sudden shock—job loss, major medical costs, family obligations—may not have the luxury of gentle experimentation. In these contexts, the "trim and test" framing could feel detached, even indulgent. The reconciliation is to keep the principle while changing the scale. The principle is reversibility and learning where possible, not triviality. In a tight situation, the experiments may need to be larger, and the time horizon may need to be shorter. But even then, thinking in tests rather than in identities remains valuable. It keeps decisions connected to evidence and reduces the likelihood of despair-driven overcorrection.

There is a second limitation: some trims create hidden costs that the quarterly review must respect. Cutting a cost that supports health, learning, or relationships can produce downstream harm that does not show up immediately in the bank balance. A gym membership is the obvious cliché, but the broader point is that some spending is a structural support. Remove it and the system compensates elsewhere—through stress, through lost time, through substitution spending. This is why tests must be interpreted through multiple lenses, not only pounds saved. Money is one domain, but it interacts with the others. The quarterly ritual, as a whole, is designed to keep those interactions visible.

This is also why "modest percentage adjustments" have a quiet power. They respect the mind's need for continuity while still creating a measurable change. If you adjust a category slightly for a quarter, you can observe whether the adjustment feels plausible, whether it creates friction, and whether it meaningfully affects margin. The percentage is not a magic number. It is a design choice: small enough to be survivable, large enough to be noticed. The goal is not to perform austerity. The goal is to regain steering.

Steering requires consent.

Consent is what drift erodes. Drift turns yesterday's choice into today's default. A trim is, at heart, an act of re-consent. It says: I will not allow this pattern to continue purely because it has been continuing. For a quarter, I will test whether my life is better with less of it. The act of testing restores agency. It also restores curiosity. Curiosity is the antidote to shame. It allows you to look at spending patterns and ask, without flinching, what they are really doing.

The motif to carry through this piece is the quarter as a trial period. A trial period makes decisions less scary because it refuses to pretend that a single choice must be final. Modern consumer culture already uses trial periods to reduce friction; it is only fair to use the same idea in reverse. Pause a thing for a quarter. Reduce a thing for a quarter. Observe. Decide again. This is not indecision. It is iterative decision-making under uncertainty, which is precisely what adult life demands.

The forward test is not whether you can think of something to cut. Anyone can cut something in anger. The forward test is whether you can choose one or two trims that are both meaningful and reversible, run them for ninety days, and then ask—honestly—what the experiment revealed about your life, your constraints, and your priorities.

Doubling what works

In 1883, at 28 Deanstreet in London, the first official meeting of what became the Women's Social and Political Union did not take place in a grand hall with patronage and ceremony. It began in a living room. Movements often do. A room, a table, a few people willing to show up again. The history of reform is filled with such small infrastructures: inexpensive, repeatable, and disproportionately powerful because they create contact—between minds, between bodies, between commitments. The point is not to romanticise activism. It is to notice a pattern of effectiveness. What changes lives is rarely the most lavish thing; it is often the thing that makes a good behaviour easier to repeat.

Spend on the repeatable.

Most money conversations lean towards subtraction. Budgets are framed as diets. Discipline is equated with denial. In that framing, success is defined by what is cut, avoided, resisted. The problem is not that cuts are always wrong. The problem is that a cut-only mindset treats money as an enemy to be subdued rather than a tool to be aimed. It also misses a quiet truth: some spending is not a leak. It is scaffolding. It increases health, learning, or connection in ways that compound over time. A quarterly money ritual that only trims will eventually feel like self-punishment. A ritual that also reinforces what works begins to feel like alignment.

Alignment is measurable.

The idea in this subchapter is simple and deliberately provocative: take one expense that genuinely supports the life you are trying to build and ask what happens if you double it for one quarter. Not forever. Not as a lifestyle inflation vow. As a test. The time limit matters because it keeps the experiment honest and bounded. The doubling matters because it forces attention. A modest increase can be absorbed into the background and forgotten; a doubling is large enough to be felt, which makes it easier to observe both benefits and trade-offs.

This approach sounds indulgent to people trained to equate responsibility with restraint. Yet it has a sober logic. Cutting is only one way to improve a system. Another is to invest in constraints. If a person is spending money in ways that do not support health, learning, or relationships, it is often because those domains are under-resourced. Under-resourcing does not always look like poverty. It can look like time scarcity, energy scarcity, social scarcity. When those scarcities dominate, people pay for relief in the easiest forms available: convenience spending, distraction subscriptions, frictionless treats that numb the day. Doubling what works is a way of redirecting money from anaesthetic to nourishment.

The intellectual backbone here is the idea of opportunity cost, formalised in economics as the cost of choosing one option over another. Opportunity cost is usually discussed as a warning: spend here and you cannot spend there. But it can also be used as a design tool: spend here and you might reduce spending there by changing what you need. If a person invests in a class that increases competence, they may reduce the impulse to buy productivity tools they never use. If a person invests in social connection, they may reduce the drift into solitary spending. If a person invests in recovery, they may reduce the need for convenience purchases that compensate for fatigue. This is not guaranteed. It is a hypothesis. The quarter is the container in which hypotheses become evidence.

Evidence beats moralising.

One reason the "double it" question is powerful is that it breaks mental accounting habits. Richard Thaler's concept of mental accounting (Thaler, 1985) describes how people compartmentalise money into categories that shape behaviour: "fun money", "serious money", "savings", "necessities". These mental accounts often keep spending on "worthy" categories artificially low while allowing "small" leaks to grow because they are mentally coded as harmless. Doubling what works challenges those codes. It asks whether a category you have treated as optional—learning, for instance, or social time—might be the very category that stabilises the rest of the system if it were properly resourced.

Consider health spending, carefully, without sliding into medical claims. People often treat health-related expenses as burdens: gym memberships, classes, equipment, physiotherapy appointments, better food. Some of these are genuinely wasteful; many are not. The quarterly lens invites a more precise question: which health-related expense has shown, in your own experience, a reliable association with better energy, steadier mood, or greater consistency? Notice the phrasing. This is not a claim about universal efficacy. It is a claim about your pattern. A person might observe that when they pay for a certain class, they attend; when they do not, they drift. Another might notice that a modest expenditure on convenience that supports sleep or recovery reduces the temptation to binge on cheaper distractions. The expense is not magic. It is a constraint that makes the good behaviour easier.

Learning spending offers an even clearer example because it often suffers from false austerity. People buy books and courses impulsively, then never use them, and conclude that learning spending is wasteful. The waste here is not the category; it is the mismatch between purchase and practice. Learning that changes life typically requires structured repetition: a tutor, a cohort, a workshop with assignments, a tool that makes practice frictionless. A quarterly doubling experiment can test a hypothesis: if you invested more in the learning vehicle that actually produces engagement—say, a course with deadlines, or a mentor session, or a dedicated workspace—would the quarter's learning become more applied and less aspirational? Applied learning is measurable as output: completed practice projects, delivered work, written pages, solved problems, built prototypes. The quarter is long enough to see whether the investment produces those outputs.

Relationships are the domain most neglected by conventional budgeting, precisely because their returns are hard to price. And yet relationships are where many adults spend money without thinking: on occasional gifts to compensate for absence, on expensive events that stand in for regular time, on travel arranged in a rush because plans were never made. Doubling what works in relationships does not mean spending lavishly. It means identifying the expenditures that reliably create connection—travel to see a friend, a recurring shared activity, a deliberate gathering—and asking what happens if you do more of that for ninety days. Again, the point is not universal prescription. The point is to treat connection as something that can be resourced deliberately rather than left to drift.

This is where "trust" becomes behavioural. Trust in this framework is the willingness to treat your own experience as data rather than as vague impression. When you say something "works", you are making a claim. A quarterly doubling turns the claim into a test. If the expense truly supports health, learning, or connection, increasing it should produce some observable improvement: more consistent attendance, more practice hours, more meaningful contact, less compensatory spending elsewhere. If nothing improves, the claim was sentimental. Sentimentality is not a crime. It is simply not a good basis for recurring expenditure.

A named, checkable example of investing in constraints at scale can be seen in public libraries. The Carnegie library programme, funded by Andrew Carnegie from the late 19th to early 20th century, supported the building of thousands of libraries, including in the UK and Ireland, with local communities often required to commit to ongoing maintenance (Carnegie Corporation historical records). A library is not a glamorous purchase. It is infrastructure. Its value comes from repeated use over time: access to books, space to study, a social signal that learning matters. The library illustrates the core idea: spending that builds infrastructure can change behaviour at population scale. The personal analogue is not to build a library, but to recognise that small infrastructures—tools, memberships, spaces—shape what gets repeated.

A second checkable example sits closer to daily life: the rise of subscription fitness platforms. Peloton, founded in 2012, popularised the idea of paying for structured classes delivered at home, with tracking and community elements that encourage repeat engagement. Whether one likes the brand is irrelevant. The mechanism is clear: paying for structure and access can increase consistency for some people. For others, it becomes an unused subscription, a symbol of aspiration. A quarterly doubling experiment would quickly reveal which it is in your own case. If paying for structured access increases actual sessions logged over ninety days, it is working. If not, it is theatre.

The limitation, of course, is that doubling can become rationalised indulgence. A person might choose an expense they already enjoy and label it "health" or "learning" or "connection" without evidence. They might also double something that produces short-term pleasure but long-term drift: more delivery meals justified as "time-saving", more gadgets justified as "productivity". The reconciliation is to insist on two qualities before an expense qualifies as "works": it must be linked to a repeatable behaviour, and it must produce a benefit that can be named in observable terms. Observable does not mean clinically measured. It can be as simple as frequency, time spent, or consistency. How many times did you use the thing? How often did you show up? How many sessions, calls, pages, projects? The quarter supplies the timeframe; your life supplies the metric.

There is a second limitation: for people with tight budgets, doubling may be impossible or irresponsible. That is real. The method can be scaled. "Double" is a forcing phrase, not a fixed mandate. The core idea is to *increase* a high-value category enough that the increase is felt and therefore measurable, while keeping the experiment bounded to one quarter. For someone with limited margin, "doubling" might mean doubling time rather than money—using a free library instead of buying books, joining a community group instead of paying for a course, arranging low-cost social routines rather than expensive events. The underlying logic remains: reinforce what works, not only what is cheap.

The quarter, again, protects against the other danger: lifestyle creep. People fear increasing spending because they worry it will become permanent. That fear is rational. Lifestyle creep is real. The quarterly approach handles it by design: the increase is a test with an end date. At the end of ninety days, you compare the costs to the benefits and decide whether to continue, adjust, or reverse. This comparison is what keeps reinforcement from becoming drift. Drift is spending that continues without renewed consent. A quarterly reinforcement is spending that continues only if it proves its value.

The deeper philosophical point is that money is a tool for shaping attention and behaviour. It can purchase convenience, yes, but it can also purchase structure. Structure changes what you do when you are tired. It changes what you do when life is busy. It changes what you do when motivation is absent. If the goal of the Upgrade Day is to design a quarter that gently improves, then spending should be judged not merely by whether it is "necessary" but by whether it improves the system's repeatability. Repeatability is the hidden criterion. It is the reason a small expense can be worth far more than its price.

Return to the living room motif. The Women's Social and Political Union began with a room and a commitment to show up. Many of the most consequential changes in life begin the same way: with small, regular infrastructures that make the desired behaviour easier than the undesired one. Doubling what works is not a call to spend more in general. It is a call to spend *more precisely*—to identify the expenditures that create those small infrastructures and then test what happens when they are properly resourced, briefly, on purpose.

The forward test is unsettling in the right way. If you doubled one expense that genuinely supports health, learning, or connection for the next quarter, what would you expect to see in your calendar, your habits, or your relationships—and are you willing to trade something else to make room for that experiment without pretending the trade-off does not exist?

Chapter 4
Health Metrics and Habits

On 6 May 1954, at the Iffley Road Track in Oxford, Roger Bannister ran a mile in 3 minutes 59.4 seconds. The stopwatch—hard, indifferent, undeniably small—became the object around which the story gathered. Yet the deeper truth of that afternoon was not the number alone. It was that Bannister's preparation had translated something unruly and human—fatigue, hope, doubt—into a few repeatable measures: training sessions completed, recovery taken, pacing rehearsed, limits tested. The mile was the public moment. The habit was the private one.

Bodies change by repetition.

Health, in modern life, is often treated as a moral project: be disciplined, eat well, move more, sleep properly. The problem is not that these phrases are wrong. The problem is that they are too vague to survive a quarter. Vague health intentions are like vague financial intentions: they invite drift, and drift tends to be felt only when the body begins to complain. A quarterly reset cannot promise a perfected body, nor should it. What it can do—quietly, powerfully—is restore legibility. Health becomes less frightening when it becomes more observable, and more observable when you choose the right metrics, review the right habits, and treat progress as a trend rather than a performance.

The cultural noise around health makes this harder than it needs to be. There are industries built on making people anxious about their bodies, and technologies that can turn the self into a dashboard of numbers with no interpretive wisdom attached. At one end of the spectrum is avoidance: "I'll deal with it later," which is how many health problems become expensive. At the other end is obsession: constant tracking, constant comparison, constant correction, which can turn health into a second job. The Upgrade Day approach refuses both. It asks for a small number of indicators you can influence, observed at a humane cadence, with no demand for perfection and no appetite for self-surveillance.

This chapter is, at its core, about choosing what to measure and why. Measurement is not neutral. It shapes attention. It shapes mood. Choose the wrong metric—one that is largely outside your control, or one that provokes anxiety—and the act of tracking becomes corrosive. Choose a metric that is meaningfully influenceable—sleep consistency, walking frequency, training attendance, recovery days taken—and it becomes a compass. The distinction matters because health is not only a biological state. It is a behavioural system interacting with work, stress, relationships, and environment. Measuring what you can influence makes the system steerable. Measuring what you cannot influence makes the system feel like fate.

A quarterly horizon is particularly well-suited to health because bodies do not respond in the timescales our culture tends to glamorise. A week is too short to draw honest conclusions; it captures noise, not adaptation. A year can be too long; it allows avoidance, and it invites dramatic overcorrection when you finally look. Three months is a plausible interval for noticing trends without turning every fluctuation into a crisis. It allows you to see whether a habit holds in ordinary life, not just in the first burst of enthusiasm. It also allows you to take recovery seriously. The most common mistake in health is to treat effort as the only variable that matters. The quarter makes room for a second variable that is just as decisive: rest.

Rest is not weakness.

This chapter therefore treats health as a four-part practice: select a few meaningful metrics, build a habit scorecard that captures behaviour without judgement, review training progress with a focus on consistency and enjoyment, and plan rest and maintenance as deliberately as effort. The order matters. Metrics come first because they shape perception. The habit scorecard comes next because it reveals what actually happened, not what you hoped happened. Training review follows because performance is best interpreted through the lens of consistency. Rest and maintenance close the sequence because recovery is where many quarters quietly collapse.

The habit scorecard is the most psychologically important tool in this chapter because it changes the emotional stance from shame to analysis. Most people know what they "should" do. The gap is not knowledge. The gap is stability. Habits collapse for reasons: travel, workload, caregiving, illness, boredom, emotional strain. When you rate habits on a simple scale across a quarter, the collapses become visible without becoming verdicts. A scorecard does not ask, "Why are you like this?" It asks, "Under what conditions did this hold up, and under what conditions did it fall apart?" That is a design question, not a moral one. It is also the kind of question that can be answered.

The training review is handled with similar restraint. Modern fitness culture is full of perfectionism disguised as "discipline," and performance metrics can become an easy way to turn self-care into self-criticism. The quarterly approach treats training as a practice, not a referendum. Whether you are lifting, running, cycling, swimming, or simply trying to move more reliably, the quarter gives you enough data to notice trends: consistency patterns, small improvements, plateaus that may signal overload, and the relationship between training and life stress. It also gives you a way to interpret performance without obsessing over daily fluctuations. A personal record is not a moral achievement. It is a data point. Consistency is the deeper achievement, and it is often the harder one.

Modern relevance sharpens the case for this approach. Many people now live in environments that systematically erode health without announcing themselves as "unhealthy." Work is more sedentary for many, more cognitively intense for almost everyone. Screens extend work into evenings and displace sleep. Food is more abundant and more processed. Social life is often scattered, leaving movement and rest to be negotiated alone. Under these conditions, health declines not because people are careless, but because drift is easy. A quarterly health ritual is a countermeasure: a scheduled moment to notice drift early, correct gently, and choose the next ninety days with a little more intelligence.

The philosophical thread running through this chapter is the refusal to treat the body as a machine that must be optimised. The body is an organism. It adapts. It has moods. It has limits. It responds to stress and recovery, to belonging and loneliness, to meaning and monotony. Metrics are useful not because they reduce the body to numbers, but because they keep you honest about what the quarter is doing to you. They provide a language for noticing change before it becomes pain. They also keep you from the opposite delusion: the belief that you are "fine" because you are coping, when coping is slowly consuming your reserves.

This chapter also insists on maintenance, a topic that tends to be neglected because it lacks drama. Maintenance is the dentist appointment you postpone, the recovery days you treat as optional, the holiday you keep delaying, the sleep debt you imagine you will repay "later". Maintenance feels boring until it becomes urgent. The quarterly reset makes it visible earlier. It turns maintenance into a scheduled choice rather than an emergency response. In practical terms, this might mean noticing that the quarter contained too few true days off, or that sleep has become systematically compressed, or that small physical warnings have been ignored. The point is not to diagnose or prescribe. The point is to notice, with enough time to adjust the next quarter before the body forces the adjustment for you.

The emotional payoff of this chapter is subtle but profound: the sense that health is not a distant ideal you keep failing to reach, but a domain you can steer with modest, repeated choices. That steering is not heroic. It is almost mundane. It looks like choosing the right few metrics, honestly rating habits, interpreting training as practice rather than as performance, and protecting rest as something you schedule rather than something you plead for. By the end of this chapter, the health reset becomes what it should have been all along: a quarterly conversation with the body, grounded in evidence, free of moral drama, and oriented towards a next ninety days that feels steadier than the last.

Choosing health metrics

On 14 March 1966, at the Queen Elizabeth Hospital in Birmingham, the first patient in the UK received a pacemaker implant using a device developed by British engineers and clinicians working within the National Health Service's emerging cardiac care landscape. The detail worth noticing is not the drama of the operation, but the quiet shift in medical thinking it represents: the body's invisible rhythms—

heartbeats, intervals, irregularities—were being translated into measurements that could guide decisions. A clinician does not "feel" a heartbeat into stability. They measure, interpret, and act.

Measure the steerable.

The modern health conversation often confuses measurement with obsession. It assumes that if you track anything—sleep, steps, workouts—you are either a paragon of discipline or a candidate for anxiety. This is a false dichotomy. Measurement is a tool. Like any tool, it can be used well or badly. Used well, it makes drift visible early enough for gentle correction. Used badly, it becomes a source of self-surveillance, a daily referendum on worth. The Upgrade Day approach insists on a third stance: choose a few indicators that are meaningful, influenceable, and emotionally sustainable, then review them quarterly to guide small adjustments.

The key word is influenceable. Health metrics come in two broad flavours. Some respond quickly to your behaviour: the number of nights you go to bed at a consistent time, the number of days you walk, the number of training sessions you complete, the frequency with which you take genuine rest. Others are heavily shaped by genetics, life stage, medical history, and the slow mechanics of physiology: certain lab values, body weight, body composition, and many biomarkers. Those "downstream" measures can be important in clinical contexts, but in a quarterly self-review they can provoke anxiety without improving steering, particularly if they are treated as the primary scoreboard. A good metric is one that changes when you change the things you can actually do.

This is not an argument against science. It is an argument for appropriate instrumentation. In engineering, you do not monitor every variable the system produces. You choose a small set of indicators that reliably reflect system behaviour and that can guide intervention. Health is no different. If the metric does not change in response to your actions, it may be psychologically costly without being practically useful. A quarterly ritual is not a clinical programme. It is a personal steering practice. It needs metrics that behave like steering indicators rather than like fixed judgements.

A second design principle matters just as much: the metric must match the timescale. Sleep quality varies night to night. Training output varies session to session. Mood varies day to day. A quarter is not the place to litigate each fluctuation. It is the place to notice patterns. That means choosing metrics that can be aggregated meaningfully over ninety days: weekly consistency, frequency counts, streaks that matter, averages that smooth noise. A metric that invites daily checking is often a poor fit for a quarterly system because it tempts you back into obsession. The cadence should govern the measurement, not the other way round.

Cadence protects the mind.

There is a well-known psychological concept often invoked in measurement discussions: what gets measured gets managed. In its crispest form, it is frequently attributed to management thinking, and it is echoed in Goodhart's law: when a measure becomes a target, it ceases to be a good measure. Charles Goodhart articulated a version of this in the context of monetary policy in 1975 (Goodhart, 1975). The relevance to health is straightforward. If you turn a metric into a target without wisdom, you risk gaming the metric rather than improving health. Steps can be padded. Calories can be underreported. Training volume can be increased at the cost of injury or exhaustion. Sleep tracking can provoke sleep anxiety. The metric becomes a tyrant, and the body becomes an employee trying to satisfy it.

This is why influenceable does not mean manipulable. A good health metric is one that is hard to game and closely tied to a behaviour that plausibly improves wellbeing. Consistency metrics are often better than performance metrics for this reason. "How many days did you walk?" is less gameable than "How many steps did you record?" "How many training sessions did you complete?" is more honest than "How heavy did you lift?" "How many nights did you give yourself a full sleep window?" is more actionable than "What was your sleep score?" Scores can be useful as rough signals, but they can also become emotionally sticky. The quarter wants signals, not idols.

To choose a metric, then, begins with a quiet act of translation: turn the vague notion of "health" into a small number of behaviours that, if repeated, would likely shift your baseline. Baseline is the word worth holding. Most health anxiety comes from the fear that one is "getting worse" without noticing. Baseline metrics help you notice early. They answer questions like: has sleep been squeezed into a smaller and smaller window? Has movement become occasional rather than regular? Has training become sporadic? Have rest days disappeared? These are the drift points that matter because they compound. They are also measurable without medical intrusion.

Consider sleep as an example, because it is both fundamental and emotionally loaded. In 2015, the American Academy of Sleep Medicine and the Sleep Research Society published a consensus statement recommending that adults sleep seven or more hours per night on a regular basis to promote optimal health (Watson et al., 2015). This kind of guideline can be useful as context, but it can also become a blunt instrument when treated as a daily pass/fail test. A quarterly approach handles it more intelligently. Instead of turning "seven hours" into a nightly trial, you might choose a metric like "number of nights per week with a full sleep window" or "median sleep duration across the quarter". The shift matters. It makes the metric less punitive and more reflective of pattern.

Walking and general movement offer another influenceable domain. The popularised "10,000 steps" target has an interesting history—it began partly as marketing in Japan in the 1960s—and it is not a clinical magic number. More recent research has examined how step counts relate to health outcomes without endorsing a single universal threshold. For example, a 2019 study by I-Min Lee and colleagues in *JAMA Internal Medicine* found that among older women in the U.S., higher step counts were associated with lower mortality, with benefits levelling off at higher counts (Lee et al., 2019). The practical point for a quarterly ritual is not to chase a fashionable number. It is to choose a movement metric that increases your weekly consistency. Frequency again often beats volume: "days with a walk" may matter more for habit formation than the precise number of steps, especially when the goal is to reduce drift rather than to optimise performance.

Training consistency is a particularly powerful metric because it sits at the intersection of intention and reality. Many people believe they "train" because they have gym memberships or workout plans. The quarter reveals whether training actually occurred. Here, a simple metric like "sessions completed per week" can be more useful than performance outputs because it answers the steering question: did the habit hold? This aligns with a broader insight from behaviour research: the formation and maintenance of habits depend on repetition in stable contexts, but the time it takes varies widely. Phillippa Lally and colleagues' 2010 study in the *European Journal of Social Psychology* found substantial variation in how long habits take to form, depending on person and behaviour (Lally et al., 2010). The quarter is long enough to see whether repetition is happening and whether it is sustainable.

The word sustainable matters because health metrics can become a source of self-attack. A person chooses a metric, fails to hit it, and concludes they are undisciplined. This is precisely what the Upgrade Day is designed to prevent. Metrics are not verdicts. They are instruments. When a metric is missed, the useful question is not "What is wrong with me?" but "What conditions made the metric unrealistic?" Conditions include workload, travel, caregiving, mental health, season, environment. A quarterly system is not an excuse machine; it is an honesty machine. It exposes the mismatch between intention and conditions. That mismatch is where design work begins.

A second named, checkable example illustrates both the promise and the risk of health metrics. In September 2014, Apple released the Health app alongside the iPhone 6, signalling a consumer shift: personal health data was becoming a normal part of everyday devices. This democratised tracking for millions. It also created new anxieties, because raw data without interpretive context can feel like judgement. Heart rate variability, sleep staging, "readiness" scores—these can be interesting signals, but they can also become daily obsessions that increase stress, undermining the very health they are meant to support. The counter-example is not that tracking is bad. It is that more data is not always better. The quarter asks for fewer, more interpretable signals.

That counter-example matters because it points to an ethical design constraint: the metric must not provoke harmful anxiety. This book is not in the business of diagnosing, treating, or prescribing. It is concerned with the design of attention. If a metric reliably makes you feel worse without producing better choices, it is a poor metric for you. That is not weakness. It is self-knowledge. The quarter offers a controlled environment for this self-knowledge. You can choose a metric, observe its psychological effect, and adjust. The metric is not sacred. The ritual is.

The simplest way to ensure a metric remains helpful is to keep it close to behaviour and far from identity. "Number of workouts completed" is behaviour. "Body weight" is often treated as identity. "Bedtime consistency" is behaviour. "Sleep score" can become identity. "Days with a walk" is behaviour. "Calories burned" can become identity. Behaviour metrics invite adjustment. Identity metrics invite shame or pride, and both distort. Pride can be as misleading as shame because it encourages complacency. The quarter wants steadiness.

Steadiness is built by defining what "better" means by the next quarter. "Better" must be concrete enough to be recognisable and modest enough to be plausible. Plausibility is not timidity. It is realism. A quarterly improvement that can be repeated is more valuable than a dramatic change that collapses. The mind has a taste for dramatic goals because drama feels like control. The body prefers gradual adaptation. The quarter is a compromise: a short enough period to maintain urgency, a long enough period to allow steady change. "Better" might therefore mean a small increase in weekly consistency, a reduction in missed weeks, a slightly longer sleep window, a few more days of movement. The specific numbers will differ by person and context, but the structure of the definition matters: it ties effort to a time horizon and makes success measurable without making it absolute.

This is where efficiency and risk become visible. Efficiency is choosing metrics that you can retrieve quickly and interpret clearly at Upgrade Day. If retrieving the metric requires an hour of app archaeology, it will be skipped. Risk is choosing metrics that steer you away from fragile patterns. If your quarter has been characterised by exhaustion, a metric tied to recovery reduces risk. If your quarter has been sedentary, a movement metric reduces risk.

If your quarter has been chaotic, a routine metric reduces risk. These are not medical claims. They are behavioural risk management: designing a quarter that is less likely to end in collapse.

A final limitation deserves a respectful place: health is not entirely within your control. Illness happens. Injury happens. Life happens. Metrics can create the illusion that health is a project that can be mastered through tracking. That illusion is cruel when reality intervenes. The reconciliation is to treat metrics as tools for navigating what is controllable within your circumstances, not as proof of personal worth. A quarter with disrupted health is not a failed quarter. It is a quarter that provides evidence about fragility and recovery needs. The metrics can still be useful, not for judgement, but for adaptation.

The motif to carry forward is the compass. A compass does not tell you exactly what terrain will look like. It does not guarantee an easy path. It simply tells you direction. Health metrics, chosen wisely, function the same way. They orient you. They reduce the chance that you will wake up six months from now and realise your baseline has shifted in ways you did not choose.

The forward test is therefore not "Which metric is best?" in the abstract. It is sharper, and it is personal. Which two or three indicators can you measure and compare quarterly that will change what you do week to week—without turning health into a daily scoreboard you dread looking at?

Quarterly habit scorecard

In March 1911, in Frederick Winslow Taylor's wake, managers at factories on both sides of the Atlantic were learning a new language: measurement. Stopwatches appeared on shop floors. Tasks were broken into repeatable motions. Output was counted. The story is often told as the birth of efficiency—and it was—but it also exposed a more general truth: when you measure a process, you stop arguing with anecdote. You can see where the system holds and where it fails. You can separate "I feel busy" from "this step takes too long". You can redesign.

A scorecard is a mirror.

The quarterly habit scorecard is that mirror, directed not at factories but at the most quietly consequential process you run: your own behaviour. It is not a diary. It is not a confession. It is not a purity test. It is a compact way of asking, with fewer theatrics, what actually happened over the last ninety days. Which habits survived the quarter's pressures? Which collapsed the moment life became messy? Which were sustained only in good weeks? The scorecard gives you answers that memory cannot reliably provide, because memory is biased towards vivid moments and recent pain.

The point is not to become a quantified self. The point is to stop relying on mood as your evidence. A quarter contains too much variation for "how I feel about my habits" to be trustworthy. A single exhausting week can rewrite your sense of the whole season. A single productive streak can seduce you into thinking you are "back on track" when the track has been patchy. A scorecard is a device for seeing the distribution rather than the highlight reel. It turns habit talk from identity language—disciplined, lazy, inconsistent—into process language: held, wobbled, broke, recovered.

Five words belong here. Shame ruins the dataset.

Shame is not only unpleasant; it is analytically toxic. It distorts recall, encourages avoidance, and turns the scorecard into a weapon. The scorecard must therefore be designed to produce observation without judgement. This is not a sentimental request for kindness. It is a requirement for accuracy. If you build a scorecard that makes you flinch, you will either not complete it or you will complete it dishonestly. A ritual that produces dishonest data is worse than no ritual, because it provides false confidence.

The behavioural sciences have long emphasised that habits are not simple acts of will. They are context-dependent patterns. In a widely cited 1998 paper, psychologists Wendy Wood and David Neal, and other researchers in the habit tradition, have discussed how stable contexts cue repeated behaviours; when context changes, habits can break even when intentions remain (Wood & Neal's later work consolidates this perspective; see Wood & Neal, 2007). The relevance is straightforward. A quarterly scorecard is not measuring virtue. It is measuring how your habits interacted with your contexts: work intensity, travel, social commitments, fatigue, season, environment. If a habit collapses whenever you travel, that is not proof you are weak. It is evidence about a missing support structure during travel. Evidence is useful.

The scorecard must also respect cognitive limits. If you try to score everything, you will score nothing well. The purpose is to rate a handful of daily or weekly behaviours that function as leading indicators for your health. Leading indicators are behaviours that, when they change, predict downstream outcomes. Sleep window consistency is a leading indicator. Movement frequency is a leading indicator. Training attendance is a leading indicator. Alcohol frequency for some people is a leading indicator. Screen time before bed may be a leading indicator. The exact set will differ. The key is to choose behaviours that are both influential and observable.

Observable is not the same as precisely measurable. Many people sabotage themselves by insisting on precision they cannot sustain. They attempt to track every calorie, every minute, every rep, every biometric. The tracking collapses under its own weight, and the person concludes they "can't stick to anything". The scorecard is designed to be lighter. It uses a simple scale, not because nuance is unimportant, but because nuance often becomes a hiding place. A simple scale forces clarity. It also makes it possible to compare quarters. Comparison is the engine of this entire method.

The "simple scale" is not a motivational gimmick; it is a measurement choice. A scale with too many gradations invites debate—was that day a 6.5 or a 7?—and debate consumes attention. A scale with too few gradations can feel blunt, but bluntness has a virtue: it makes patterns visible quickly. The scorecard is not an academic instrument; it is a steering instrument. Its job is to show whether a behaviour was mostly present, mostly absent, or uneven. Once you see that, you can ask why.

Why is the interesting part.

For each habit you score, the scorecard is quietly running the same analytic engine used elsewhere in this book: show, name, explain, imply. The "show" is the score itself—low, middling, high. The "name" is the pattern: consistent, fragile, seasonal, context-dependent. The "explain" is the conditions that produced it: workload, travel, stress, environment, social constraints. The "implication" is what you might alter next quarter: a boundary, a cue, a different timing, a smaller target, more recovery, a change in environment. This engine keeps you from turning the score into self-critique. It turns the score into design.

A named, checkable example from research shows why small measurement systems can change outcomes. In 2003, researchers Jessica Logan and colleagues published findings in *Pediatrics* on the use of growth charts and routine measurement in childhood health, showing how systematic tracking can identify issues earlier than impressionistic assessment (Logan et al., 2003). The purpose here is not to draw a direct analogy between childhood growth monitoring and adult habit change. It is to highlight the mechanism: repeated, standardised observation reveals trends that casual perception misses. A quarterly habit scorecard is your adult version of a trend chart—focused not on diagnosing but on noticing drift early.

A second example comes from the world of sport. The British Cycling team's approach in the early 2010s, often associated with coach Dave Brailsford, popularised the notion of "marginal gains"—small, measurable improvements across many areas. While the phrase has been overused, the underlying practice relied on tracking: sleep routines, training loads, recovery protocols, equipment tweaks. Performance improvement was not left to inspiration. It was managed through repeated observation and incremental adjustment. For an ordinary person, the point is not to emulate elite sport. It is to appreciate that even high performers do not rely on vague motivation. They rely on feedback loops. A quarterly scorecard is a feedback loop that does not require elite resources.

Still, there is a credible counter-example worth admitting. Measurement can backfire. It can create anxiety. It can encourage performative behaviour. It can make people chase the score rather than the underlying health. Goodhart's law—the idea that when a measure becomes a target it can lose its usefulness (Goodhart, 1975)—applies here. If you start treating the scorecard as a competition with yourself, you may game it: counting a token walk as "movement", forcing a workout when exhausted to preserve a streak, recording "good sleep" by going to bed early while scrolling for hours. The reconciliation is to choose behaviours that are difficult to game and to treat the score as information, not as identity. The scorecard is a mirror, not a trophy.

That mirror also needs to reflect reality's messiness. A quarter will contain disruption. The scorecard must be robust to it. If you treat any disruption as failure, you will build a brittle system. The better approach is to notice the pattern of recovery: when a habit breaks, how quickly does it return? Recovery time is a powerful indicator of resilience. A person who returns to a habit within a few days after disruption has a different system from a person who loses the habit for weeks after a single interruption. The scorecard can make this visible because it prompts you to rate the quarter, not the ideal week. It captures resilience, not perfection.

Resilience is the prize.

The scorecard also encourages a more mature relationship with trade-offs. A quarter with intense work may legitimately have lower training frequency. A quarter with major family obligations may have fewer long walks. The question is not whether every score is high. The question is whether the pattern aligns with your actual priorities and whether the low scores are chosen or accidental. Chosen trade-offs can be lived with. Accidental trade-offs create resentment because you realise you have been sacrificing something without consciously agreeing to it. The scorecard surfaces accidental sacrifice early enough to change the next quarter.

To keep the scorecard humane, it helps to pair each habit score with one contextual note: what made this easier or harder this quarter? That note is not an excuse; it is a clue. Clues lead to design adjustments. If sleep consistency scored low because evening work bled into night, the adjustment may be about work boundaries rather than about "trying harder to sleep". If movement scored low because travel disrupted routines, the adjustment may be about travel cues or a different definition of movement during trips. If training scored low because you were injured or ill, the adjustment may be about recovery and maintenance. Each context note turns a score into a hypothesis for the next quarter.

Hypotheses invite experiments, not vows.

A quarterly scorecard therefore creates continuity with the rest of the Upgrade Day system. It is the behavioural snapshot that pairs with the health metrics, the training review, and the rest planning. It also mirrors the money chapter's approach: you skim patterns, not individual events; you run tests, not permanent declarations; you aim for direction, not perfection. The same intellectual posture applies. What happened? What pattern does it suggest? What small change might improve the next ninety days?

The motif to carry is the mirror, but not the harsh mirror of self-judgement. Think of the mirror used in craft. A violin maker holds a piece up to the light, looking for warp. A tailor checks a seam. A mechanic listens for an engine note that is slightly off. The observation is not a condemnation. It is the beginning of refinement. Your habit scorecard is that kind of mirror. It shows where the system holds and where it wobbles.

The forward test is clean and slightly uncomfortable. When you look at your quarter's habit mirror, which low score is signalling a design problem you are willing to address, and which low score is signalling a trade-off you are still pretending you did not choose?

Reviewing training progress

On 10 September 1960, at the Olympic Stadium in Rome, Abebe Bikila won the marathon barefoot in 2 hours 15 minutes 16.2 seconds, becoming the first Black African Olympic champion. The images that survive are cinematic—night air, stone streets, the sheen of effort under stadium lights—but the deeper point is methodological. A marathon is not won by a single heroic day. It is won by the accumulation of training decisions, repeated over months, that shape what a body can do when the world is watching. Performance is an emergent property of consistency.

Consistency tells the truth.

A quarterly review of training progress is therefore not a place for self-congratulation or self-attack. It is a place to read the quarter's evidence with the calmness of a coach who cares about long horizons. The evidence is rarely dramatic. It is the number of sessions completed, the weeks in which training held, the weeks in which it fell away, the way effort felt, the small markers of adaptation. It is also the stubborn fact that life happens: illness, deadlines, travel, family obligations, boredom, weather, the slow creep of fatigue. A quarter is long enough to include all of this, which makes it the right window for asking a more interesting question than "Did I hit my targets?" The interesting question is "What kind of training system did I actually run?"

Run is an active verb on purpose. Many people talk about training as though it were an aspiration they carry rather than a system they enact. They say they are "trying to get back into it", which implies that training is something you do once you become the right kind of person. The quarterly view undermines that story. It shows you what you did, not what you meant. That is not a punishment. It is clarity. Clarity is what makes gentle improvement possible.

A training review begins with choosing the right markers. The modern fitness culture tends to push maximal markers: personal records, fastest times, heaviest lifts, longest distances. These can be meaningful, but they are also noisy and emotionally loaded. They reward risk-taking and punish variability. A quarterly ritual benefits from a broader set of markers: a small number of performance indicators if you track them, and at least one consistency indicator that reflects how often training actually occurred. The reason is simple. The body adapts to repeated stimulus. A single brilliant session is a story. A repeated pattern is an adaptation.

The scientific language for this, in strength and conditioning, is progressive overload and adaptation—gradually increasing training stress so the body responds by becoming stronger or fitter. But the book's interest is not in programming details. It is in the observable consequences of a training system. If you trained regularly, you likely adapted. If you trained sporadically, you likely maintained or drifted. If you trained intensely but without sufficient recovery, you may have seen performance fluctuate or enjoyment decline. These are not moral outcomes. They are system outcomes.

System outcomes are visible in trendlines. A quarter is long enough to produce trendlines that matter, yet short enough that the memory of the quarter is still present. When you look at training logs—whether in a notebook, an app, or a simple calendar—you can see the shape of the quarter: clusters of sessions, gaps, patterns around weekdays, collapses around travel or deadlines. This shape is often more informative than the numbers inside the sessions, because it reveals what your life currently permits. A programme that looks good on paper but cannot survive your actual week is not a programme. It is a fantasy. The quarterly review is the moment fantasies meet calendars.

There is a useful concept from behavioural science called the intention–behaviour gap: the consistent observation that intentions do not reliably translate into action. Researchers have studied this across health behaviours for decades, and one of the better supported interventions involves implementation intentions—specific plans that link a cue to an action ("when X occurs, I will do Y"), associated with Peter Gollwitzer's work (Gollwitzer, 1999). Training progress reviews are, indirectly, reviews of your implementation intentions. When training held, what cues were present? When it collapsed, what cues disappeared? The quarter provides evidence about which cues are robust and which are fragile.

Robust cues are gold.

A quarterly review also asks you to pay attention to enjoyment, because enjoyment is not a soft add-on; it is a predictor of adherence. People who despise their training routine rarely sustain it, unless they are driven by fear or vanity, and those fuels burn the system down eventually. Enjoyment can be measured, imperfectly, through behavioural signs: you show up without prolonged negotiation, you finish sessions feeling energised more often than depleted, you return after disruptions. Enjoyment is also reflected in the ratio of planned to completed sessions. If you constantly "fail" your plan, the plan may be mismatched to what you enjoy and what your life allows. A quarterly review that ignores enjoyment is likely to recommend the same punishment-based corrections that fail every year.

This is where the quarter becomes a humane unit. A week can be too short for enjoyment to stabilise. A month can still be distorted by novelty. Over a quarter, novelty fades. What remains is the true relationship between you and the activity: do you keep returning, or do you find reasons not to? That relationship is not fixed. It can be shaped by choosing activities that fit your temperament, schedule, and environment. But you cannot shape it if you do not observe it honestly. Quarterly observation is the antidote to wishful thinking.

A named, checkable example from the history of training illustrates how boring consistency produces extraordinary outcomes. In April 1973, the first London Marathon (then the "Marathon") was held, and over subsequent decades the event's growth helped normalise endurance training among ordinary people, not only elite athletes. The transformation was cultural: large numbers of people adopted running routines that were modest, repeatable, and integrated into daily life. The marathon itself is dramatic; the training that enables it is repetitive. The lesson is not "run a marathon". It is that a training culture becomes sustainable when it is built around repeatable routines rather than heroic episodes.

A second checkable example sits in the world of strength. The powerlifting and weightlifting communities have long relied on training logs and incremental progression. The specific programmes vary, but the general practice is consistent: record sessions, compare loads over time, and adjust volume and intensity. This is not obsessive for its own sake. It is feedback. Feedback is what makes training intelligent rather than merely effortful. A quarterly review is the non-athlete's version of that intelligence: not a deep dive into every set, but a review of whether the quarter's training dose was sufficient, sustainable, and aligned with your life.

The core analytic engine for this subchapter is simple. Show: the evidence of training sessions and markers across ninety days. Name: the pattern—consistent, episodic, fragile, overreaching, under-dosed. Explain: the conditions that produced the pattern—time, fatigue, travel, motivation, environment, injuries, boredom. Imply: what to test next quarter. That implication is the point. It turns observation into a training experiment rather than a training vow.

Experiments keep things sane.

A training experiment, in this quarterly framing, is not a dramatic new programme. It is a small alteration designed to improve consistency or enjoyment. You might test a different frequency, a different time of day, a different modality, a different environment. You might test reducing intensity to protect recovery, or simplifying the routine to reduce decision friction. The quarter is the unit that makes these tests meaningful. If you change one variable and run it for ninety days, you can see whether it actually improves adherence and progress. If you change everything at once, you learn nothing.

This is where the metric selection becomes important. You do not need many. You need a few that reflect your aims. If you are lifting, relevant markers might include a small set of working weights for key movements, or the number of sessions completed. If you are running, markers might include weekly mileage or minutes moved, a comfortable pace benchmark, or the number of runs completed. If you are simply trying to move more, markers might include days with purposeful movement or the number of weeks you maintained a routine. The point is not the specific marker. The point is that the marker must correspond to behaviour you can sustain.

Sustainability is the hidden constraint in all training.

A credible counter-example belongs here, because training talk can become dangerously simplistic. There are people for whom pushing harder is not the answer—because of injury history, chronic pain, disability, demanding work schedules, or illness. There are also people whose quarter was disrupted by circumstances that have nothing to do with discipline. A training review that assumes a stable, healthy body and a predictable schedule will misread these cases and recommend "more consistency" as though it were purely a matter of trying. The reconciliation is to treat training progress as progress relative to circumstances. The quarter is not a moral contest against an imagined ideal. It is a record of what was possible in the life you actually lived. For some quarters, progress might mean maintaining a minimal routine through chaos. For other quarters, progress might mean increasing volume or intensity. The method remains: observe honestly, then design the next experiment to fit reality rather than to punish it.

Another limitation is the temptation to treat the quarter as a performance report. This can lead to overreaching—the urge to set bigger goals for the next quarter based on a good streak, ignoring the costs that streak imposed. Overreaching often looks like enthusiasm. The quarterly review can prevent it by forcing you to examine not only what you did, but what it cost: sleep debt, nagging aches, irritability, a sense of dread before sessions. These are not medical diagnoses. They are experiential markers that tell you whether the training load is sustainable. A sustainable system can be repeated. A punishing system cannot.

Repeatability is the real personal record.

The motif to carry through this piece is the training log as a seismograph. A seismograph does not judge the earth for trembling. It records. It shows patterns: small tremors, larger shocks, quiet periods. Your training record does the same. It shows when you moved, when you stopped, when you resumed. It also shows, indirectly, the stressors of your quarter. The point of reading the seismograph is not to feel guilty about earthquakes. It is to build with better awareness of the ground.

When you review the quarter, you are therefore looking for three things. First, the baseline: how often did training or movement actually occur? Second, the trend: did it become more consistent, less consistent, or simply variable? Third, the relationship: did the routine feel like something you were drawn to or something you endured? Those three readings—baseline, trend, relationship—are often enough to design a sensible experiment for the next quarter.

The forward test is sharper than "How can I get fitter?" It is this: if you had to choose one training variable to change for the next ninety days—frequency, timing, intensity, modality, environment—so that you would be more likely to show up with steadiness and a flicker of enjoyment, which variable would you choose, and what evidence from your last quarter justifies that choice?

Planning rest and checks

In January 1912, Robert Falcon Scott's Terra Nova Expedition reached the South Pole only to find Roald Amundsen had arrived first. The tragedy that followed is often framed as a story of heroism and misfortune, yet historians have long examined the expedition through a colder lens: logistics, planning, and the management of human limits in extreme conditions. The Antarctic did not care about moral character. It cared about calories, shelter, weather windows, and recovery. The lesson is not that ordinary life resembles polar exploration. The lesson is that endurance is engineered. When rest and maintenance are treated as optional, the system eventually breaks.

Rest is part of work.

Modern culture treats that sentence as suspicious. Rest is discussed as indulgence, a reward for those who have "earned" it, or a luxury for people with fewer responsibilities. Health maintenance is treated as admin: check-ups postponed, sleep sacrificed, recovery days converted into more tasks. The body is expected to be a quiet machine that keeps producing, and when it fails, we respond with surprise. A quarterly ritual is designed to remove surprise. It asks you to treat recovery and maintenance as planned components of your quarter, not as events that occur only after collapse.

Collapse is expensive.

The phrase "health is not only effort" can sound obvious, yet behaviour suggests it is not widely believed. People will schedule meetings months ahead and treat sleep as negotiable. They will plan work sprints and treat recovery as what happens in the margins.

They will monitor training and ignore maintenance. This is not stupidity. It is a structural bias: effort is visible and socially rewarded, while rest is private and often culturally dismissed. Maintenance is even less glamorous. You can show off a hard workout. You cannot easily show off a dentist appointment or a holiday booked early. Yet these unshowy actions often determine whether a quarter is sustainable.

Sustainability is a measurable outcome.

Planning rest and checks begins with a simple question: what did the last quarter do to your reserves? Reserves are not a metaphor. They show up in ordinary metrics and behaviours: sleep debt, irritability, reduced patience, diminished motivation to move, increased reliance on quick comforts, a sense that even small tasks require disproportionate effort. A quarter can look "productive" and still quietly deplete reserves. When reserves are depleted, health habits become fragile. Training becomes harder to sustain. Food choices become more constrained by fatigue. Social life becomes thinner. Work becomes less creative. The drift spreads.

This is why rest belongs in the Upgrade Day system as a designed element, not a vague hope. The problem with vague hope is that it competes badly with urgent demands. Urgent demands multiply. Rest does not multiply. It must be protected. Protection begins by acknowledging that rest is not one thing. There is sleep, which is daily and non-negotiable in biological terms even when we treat it as negotiable socially. There are days off, which are weekly or biweekly in rhythm and often eroded by "just catching up". There are longer recovery blocks—quiet weekends, holidays, lighter weeks after intense periods—that require more deliberate scheduling because they are easiest to postpone. Then there are routine checks: appointments and maintenance tasks that prevent small issues becoming large ones.

The quarter is the right unit for this because it is long enough to include the need for recovery and short enough that postponement is still reversible. Postponement becomes dangerous when it stretches into years. The quarterly reset interrupts that pattern. It does not demand that you become an ascetic guardian of your own wellbeing. It asks for a modest, concrete action: schedule at least one rest or maintenance commitment that materially improves the next ninety days.

Make it concrete.

Concrete is the antidote to the cultural habit of treating rest as a feeling. Many people assume they will rest when they feel they need it. By the time they feel it, the system is already strained. Planning rest is therefore a shift from reactive to proactive management. In operational terms, it resembles preventive maintenance. Aviation provides an instructive, named example. After a series of accidents and increasing complexity in air travel, airlines and regulators developed rigorous maintenance schedules and pre-flight checks. They do not wait for an engine to fail before inspecting it. They measure, inspect, and schedule maintenance because the cost of failure is unacceptable. The body is not a plane, but the logic of preventive care still applies: maintenance is cheaper than emergency repair.

There is also good evidence that chronic sleep restriction carries risks. A consensus statement published in 2015 by the American Academy of Sleep Medicine and the Sleep Research Society recommended that adults sleep seven or more hours per night regularly for optimal health, associating shorter sleep with adverse outcomes (Watson et al., 2015). The quarter's relevance is not to force everyone into the same number. It is to remind us that sleep is not merely rest; it is recovery infrastructure. If your quarter has been built on shortened sleep, you have been borrowing from a future you. Planning rest includes planning to stop borrowing, at least partially.

A useful way to treat sleep in a quarterly plan is as a protected window rather than as an aspirational target. "Get more sleep" is vague. A protected window is observable: more nights where you allocate enough time for sleep. Allocation is a decision; sleep itself is not always controllable. This distinction is crucial for avoiding sleep anxiety. The goal is not to force sleep. It is to create conditions under which sleep is more likely. That is a design approach rather than a moral one.

Days off require similar reframing. Many people technically have days off but not days that restore. A day filled with chores, errands, and digital catch-up is often not recovery; it is unpaid work in different clothing. Recovery, in the sense relevant to a quarterly ritual, is time in which the nervous system downshifts. It might include leisure, social connection, nature, play, or simply fewer demands. This is not a prescription. It is an observational category. You can often tell whether a day restored you by what happens the next day: do you return with steadier energy, or do you return with the same depletion?

Energy is the hidden metric.

Longer recovery blocks—holidays, retreat weekends, lighter weeks—are where planning matters most because these blocks are the easiest to delay "until things calm down". Things rarely calm down by themselves. They calm down when you deliberately create slack. Research on workload and recovery has repeatedly shown that recovery experiences are associated with better wellbeing and performance; for example, Sonnentag and Fritz (2007) discussed how psychological detachment, relaxation, mastery experiences, and control during leisure time contribute to recovery from work stress (Sonnentag & Fritz, 2007). The point is not to turn leisure into another optimisation project. It is to treat recovery as a legitimate requirement of sustained effort.

Routine checks are the most culturally neglected element because they feel like interruptions. Yet they are also among the highest-leverage health actions available, precisely because they prevent drift becoming crisis. A quarterly reset does not give medical advice. It does not tell anyone what screenings they need. It does insist on a behavioural principle: if you have been postponing a routine check or maintenance action for no reason other than friction, that postponement is a form of drift. Drift is what this book exists to counter. Scheduling a check is therefore an act of anti-drift, independent of the outcome.

Here, abstraction becomes visible behaviour. "Responsibility" is not a personality trait; it is the decision to put the appointment in the calendar and protect it. "Risk management" is not a corporate phrase; it is the decision to stop gambling on luck when a small action would reduce uncertainty. "Self-respect" is not a slogan; it is the refusal to treat your body as a disposable vehicle for your ambitions. These translations matter because people often talk about health in lofty terms and then behave as though their bodies will quietly absorb any burden.

The quarter also invites you to review the cost of overtraining—not only in athletes, but in ordinary people who push themselves while depleted because effort feels like virtue. Overtraining is a technical term in sports science, but the everyday version is simpler: you keep applying stress without adequate recovery, and your enjoyment and consistency decline. The training review you completed in the previous section provides evidence. Planning rest is the corrective. It does not mean doing nothing. It means acknowledging that adaptation requires recovery. Without recovery, training becomes a slow negotiation with fatigue.

A credible counter-example must be acknowledged. Some people cannot simply "schedule rest" because their responsibilities are not fully under their control: caregiving, shift work, financial insecurity, health crises. For them, the rhetoric of self-care can feel insulting. The reconciliation is to scale the principle rather than abandon it. Rest is not only holidays. It can be micro-recovery: a protected hour, a quieter evening, a brief walk without tasks, a single day in the quarter where obligations are deliberately minimised. Maintenance can be one appointment made, one postponement ended, one boundary set. The quarter is flexible enough to honour constraints while still resisting the fatalism that says "I have no control at all".

Constraints are real. Drift is real too.

The art, then, is to choose a rest or maintenance action that is both meaningful and doable. Meaningful means it addresses the quarter's actual bottleneck. If the bottleneck is sleep debt, a meaningful action might involve protecting a sleep window on a particular set of nights. If the bottleneck is accumulated fatigue, it might involve scheduling a lighter weekend and defending it. If the bottleneck is a postponed check, it might involve booking it and treating it as non-negotiable. Doable means it fits the life you actually have, not the life you imagine having once everything is solved. Doable actions compound. Imagined actions do not.

There is also an understated emotional benefit to planning maintenance. It reduces background anxiety. Many people carry a vague sense of unfinished bodily admin—appointments not made, niggles ignored, sleep debt unaddressed. That unfinishedness occupies mental space. When you schedule a maintenance action, you close a loop. The mind relaxes slightly because the uncertainty has an endpoint. This is not self-indulgence. It is cognitive hygiene, and it supports all the other domains this book cares about.

The motif to thread through this subchapter is the pit stop. In endurance racing, a pit stop is not a sign of weakness; it is the means by which the vehicle stays in the race. Tyres are changed, fuel is added, damage is checked. The car does not win by refusing to stop. It wins by stopping at the right times, quickly, deliberately, with a plan. Your quarter needs pit stops. Not because you are a machine, but because you are not. You are a living system that adapts and depletes and recovers. Planning rest and checks is the act of scheduling your pit stop before smoke appears.

The forward test is uncomfortably practical. Looking at the next ninety days as they truly are—with their obligations, their likely stresses, their ordinary chaos—what is the single rest or maintenance commitment you are willing to put into the calendar now, not as a reward for finishing the quarter, but as a condition for surviving it well?

Chapter 5
Relationships and Social Life

In August 1971, at Stanford University in California, an experiment began that would later be argued over as fiercely as any modern parable about human behaviour. The Stanford Prison Experiment, led by Philip Zimbardo, is now discussed as much for its ethical failures as for its claims, and later scholarship has challenged aspects of its interpretation and conduct (Zimbardo, 1971; subsequent critiques widely documented). Yet one detail remains stubbornly instructive: people changed rapidly in response to the roles and environments around them. Behaviour did not emerge from personality alone. It emerged from social context—who was present, who had power, who was watching, who was absent.

Relationships are context.

That word, "context", is the quiet engine of this chapter. Money can be measured in pounds; health can be tracked in habits and sleep windows. Relationships are more elusive because their effects are both immediate and delayed, both subtle and immense. A single conversation can change a week. A neglected friendship can change a decade. Most people do not intend to neglect those they love. Neglect happens by drift: one missed call becomes months; one postponed visit becomes a year; one unresolved tension becomes a permanent thinness in the relationship. The trouble is that drift in relationships often feels like nothing—until it becomes grief, distance, resentment, or regret.

We are not designed for neglect.

Human beings are social animals in the most literal sense. Our nervous systems regulate in relation to others; our identities are shaped by the mirrors we keep close; our choices are influenced, often invisibly, by the communities and colleagues and families around us. And yet modern life makes social drift unusually easy. Work is mobile, friendships are dispersed, messages are asynchronous, and the illusion of connection can be maintained by occasional likes and quick replies. At the same time, calendars crowd with commitments that are not intimacy at all: meetings, groups, obligations, favours, professional networking. The result is a paradox many intelligent adults recognise with a dull ache. They are busier than ever, and lonelier than they expected to be.

Busyness is not belonging.

This chapter treats relationships as a domain that benefits from the same quarterly discipline as money and health, but with a different emotional tone. Relationships cannot be "optimised" without becoming grotesque, and they cannot be reduced to metrics without losing their meaning. Yet they can be tended. Tending is an old verb for a reason. It implies attention, patience, repair, and small acts repeated over time. The Upgrade Day approach does not demand grand declarations about being a better friend or partner or colleague. It asks for something more workable and more honest: periodic visibility and deliberate choice.

The first move is mapping relationship circles. This is not a cute exercise. It is a diagnostic instrument. Most people carry a story about their social life: "I'm close with my family," "I keep in touch with old friends," "work has been intense but I'm still connected." Stories are comforting. They are also frequently wrong. A map interrupts the story by showing where time and attention actually went over the quarter. It reveals whether the inner circle has been nourished or merely assumed, whether friendships have been maintained or quietly mothballed, whether colleagues have consumed social energy that used to go elsewhere, whether communities have been abandoned, whether acquaintances have expanded while intimacy shrank.

A map does not judge. It reveals.

Revelation matters because relationships can fail invisibly. Money fails with overdrafts and bills. Health fails with symptoms. Relationships often fail with silence, and silence is easy to misinterpret as "we're both busy". A quarterly map turns silence into something you can see: a circle that has received less attention than you imagined. It also reveals the opposite problem: overcommitment. Some people feel socially depleted not because they are isolated, but because their social time has been poured into obligations rather than chosen connections. Mapping exposes this too. It shows the groups, favours, and recurring commitments that fill a calendar without feeding the heart.

From mapping, the chapter moves into quarterly relationship check-ins. The phrase is deliberately gentle. Check-ins are not interrogations. They are a way of asking, without drama, whether key relationships feel balanced, energising, or strained. This language matters because many adults avoid reflecting on relationships precisely because it can feel melodramatic. They fear they will have to confront someone, make a grand change, or admit something painful. The quarterly check-in lowers the stakes. It focuses on awareness: which ties feel nourishing, which feel heavy, which feel neglected, which feel stuck. It invites you to notice what you are avoiding talking about, and to consider small gestures—messages, calls, apologies, invitations—that can repair or deepen without turning life into a theatre of emotional performance.

Small gestures are not small.

The modern relevance here is sharp. Relationships now exist across platforms and contexts that blur boundaries. Work friendships bleed into personal time. Group chats create a sense of constant contact without depth. Social media can keep acquaintances visible while true friends fade into quiet. Many people have moved cities, changed industries, shifted identities, and carried their relationships through screens. This creates new forms of drift. It also creates new opportunities for reconnection—if you choose them deliberately rather than hoping they happen.

The third move is the hard one: adjusting social commitments. Calendars become moral documents in relationships. A recurring lunch, a standing call, a committee, a group, a favour—each carries implicit promises. To step back can feel like betrayal. Yet not stepping back can be a subtler betrayal: the betrayal of your own limited time, and therefore of the relationships you claim matter most. Many adults are trapped in social commitments that no longer fit, not because they care deeply, but because they have never consciously renegotiated. The quarter gives you permission to renegotiate without drama. It turns renegotiation into a routine practice rather than a crisis.

There is a broader sociological truth behind this. The classic "strength of weak ties" argument associated with Mark Granovetter (1973) suggests that acquaintances and looser connections can be valuable, especially for information and opportunity. That is true. The danger is to let weak ties and professional networks crowd out strong ties, which are the ones most associated with wellbeing and resilience. Social life is not a binary of "introvert" and "extrovert". It is an ecology. If the ecology becomes unbalanced—too many obligations, too few chosen intimacies—people begin to feel strangely alone even in a full calendar.

The chapter's final movement is deliberately hopeful: investing in key ties. The phrase "investing" can sound transactional, but here it is used in its older sense: placing time and attention somewhere because you expect it to grow. This is not about grand gestures. It is about specificity. A visit planned. A recurring call scheduled. A shared project begun. The quarter is long enough for such actions to matter and short enough for them to feel doable. Investment also makes the chapter symmetrical with the money chapter: not all adjustments are cuts. Some are reinforcements. Some relationships deserve more deliberate attention, not because you should feel guilty, but because they are the infrastructure of a good life.

Infrastructure is the right word.

Money is often treated as infrastructure, and health as capacity. Relationships are the infrastructure of meaning. They shape how you interpret your days. They buffer stress. They challenge you. They provide joy. They also constrain you; some relationships ask for more than they give, and this chapter does not pretend otherwise. The purpose of quarterly review is not to maintain every relationship. It is to maintain a coherent social life, one that matches your values, your energy, and your season.

A motif threads through this chapter: the garden. A garden does not thrive by being admired. It thrives by being tended. Some plants need pruning. Some need watering. Some need replanting. Some should be removed to make room for what has a chance to flourish. Gardening is neither sentimental nor ruthless. It is attentive, seasonal, and practical. Relationship tending is the same. The quarter is your season marker. It asks: what grew, what withered, what is overcrowding, what is starving, what needs a different placement to thrive?

There is also a humane concession that must be made because adult relationships are not entirely within your control. People change. Circumstances shift. Some ties end for reasons that are not failures: distance, life stage, incompatible values, loss. Not every friendship can be revived. Not every strain can be resolved. The quarterly approach does not promise otherwise. What it does offer is earlier noticing. Earlier noticing can prevent avoidable loss. It can also prevent years of resentment built on unspoken expectations.

The momentum at the end of this introduction is therefore not a promise of perfect social life. It is a promise of clearer choice. When you map your circles, check in gently, adjust commitments with respect, and invest in a few key ties, you are doing something quietly radical: you are refusing to let your relationships be governed purely by drift, guilt, or habit. You are choosing which garden beds to tend this quarter, and which to leave fallow without pretending you can cultivate everything at once.

Mapping relationship circles

On 21 July 1969, in Houston, Texas, a small room of engineers and flight controllers sat under harsh fluorescent light, listening to a voice travelling across space. "The Eagle has landed." NASA's Mission Control was not a romantic image of lone genius; it was a map made flesh—roles, responsibilities, communication channels, escalation paths, redundancies. The moon landing worked because the social system around it was visible. People knew who mattered in which moments, who needed to speak to whom, and what could not be allowed to drift into ambiguity.

Relationships fail by ambiguity.

Most adults do not lack relationships. They lack a clear view of their social system. They carry a sense of being connected—messages arriving, meetings happening, birthdays noted, group chats humming—yet their actual experience is often a low-grade loneliness or fatigue that feels hard to explain. They are surrounded, and yet under-supported. Or they are loved, and yet neglecting the people they most care about. The contradiction comes from misperception. We misperceive our social lives because attention is spent in small fragments, because memory favours vivid moments, and because social contact has become easier to simulate than to sustain.

A map corrects perception.

Mapping relationship circles is not an exercise in sentimentality. It is a diagnostic tool. It asks you to sketch the structure of your social landscape—inner circle, close friends, colleagues, acquaintances, communities—and then to compare that structure with how you actually spent your time and attention in the last quarter. The aim is not to label people as important or unimportant in some absolute sense. The aim is to see where your social energy is flowing and whether the flow matches what you value. When the flow does not match, drift begins. Drift in relationships is often quieter than drift in money or health. It can continue for years because nothing "breaks" dramatically. Then, one day, someone is gone, or you realise you do not have anyone to call, or you discover that the person you love has become a stranger.

The quarter is the right window for this map because it is long enough to reveal patterns and short enough that the patterns still feel connected to lived reality. A decade-long social map collapses into abstraction; everything becomes a blur of "we used to be close". A weekly map is too narrow; it overweights chance. Three months contains the ordinary: work cycles, weekends, minor stresses, a few social events, perhaps a trip, perhaps a lull. Ordinary time is where relationships are maintained or neglected. The map is an attempt to see ordinary time as a system.

This approach has a solid intellectual foundation. In 1992, anthropologist Robin Dunbar proposed what became popularly known as "Dunbar's number": the idea that there are cognitive constraints on the number of stable social relationships humans can maintain, with layers of closeness often cited around 5, 15, 50, and 150 (Dunbar, 1992). The exact numbers are debated and should not be treated as commandments. The usefulness lies elsewhere: the reminder that attention and intimacy are finite resources. When people behave as though their social capacity is infinite—saying yes endlessly, keeping up with everyone vaguely—they often end up maintaining no relationships deeply. A relationship circle map is, in part, a confrontation with finitude.

Finitude is liberating.

When you accept that your social attention is limited, you can stop pretending. You can stop treating the maintenance of every connection as an unspoken obligation. You can begin to choose. Choosing is not cruelty. Choosing is honesty. The map makes choosing possible because it reveals the current distribution of attention, which is often shaped more by proximity and habit than by value. Colleagues can consume vast amounts of social energy simply because you see them daily. Acquaintances can occupy your mind because they are visible online. Communities can become draining because they are structured around obligation rather than joy. Meanwhile, the people who actually matter to you can be starved because they are not urgent.

Urgency is not importance.

This is why the map is built in circles rather than a list. A list invites ranking, and ranking triggers guilt and defensiveness. Circles invite structure. They ask you to place relationships by type and closeness, then observe how time is distributed across those types. The inner circle might include partners, close family, or a handful of friends. Close friends might be those you would call in difficulty and those whose lives you want to know in detail. Colleagues might include people you spend time with primarily through work. Acquaintances might include people you like but do not know deeply. Communities might include groups that connect you to shared activities, values, or identities. The map is not about right categories. It is about making categories explicit enough that you can see imbalance.

Imbalance comes in predictable forms. One is neglect of the inner circle. This often happens in high-pressure work seasons, where professional obligations expand and personal relationships are expected to "understand". The inner circle becomes a set of people you assume will be there regardless of attention. The assumption can hold for a while. It does not hold forever. Another imbalance is overinvestment in professional relationships at the expense of friendships, especially when work provides structure and social contact while friendships require deliberate effort. A third is community overload: too many groups, commitments, and social obligations that feel like work, leaving little energy for unstructured connection. A fourth is the opposite: isolation disguised as digital contact, where you have many weak ties but few embodied relationships that can actually support you.

These are not moral failures. They are system effects.

The map makes system effects visible by pairing every abstraction with a behaviour. "Connection" becomes the number of meaningful conversations you had with inner-circle people in the last ninety days. "Support" becomes whether you know what is happening in your closest friends' lives and whether they know what is happening in yours. "Community" becomes the number of times you showed up in person or meaningfully participated, rather than simply remaining a name in a group chat. "Balance" becomes the distribution of your social time across circles. Without such behavioural anchors, relationship talk becomes pure narrative—beautiful, vague, and easy to avoid.

A named, checkable example of how mapping social structure can change outcomes comes from public health contact tracing. During outbreaks of infectious disease, such as the Ebola epidemic in West Africa (2014–2016), health authorities used contact tracing to map relationship networks—not to moralise, but to understand transmission and target interventions (World Health Organization reporting on Ebola response). The relevance is not to compare relationships to pathogens. It is to recognise the power of network awareness. When you map connections, you can see where influence and risk concentrate. In your social life, the "risk" is not infection; it is neglect, burnout, and the erosion of support. The same logic holds. Mapping reveals leverage points.

A second example sits in sociology. Mark Granovetter's 1973 paper "The Strength of Weak Ties" argued that acquaintances can be surprisingly valuable for information and opportunities, precisely because they connect you to different networks (Granovetter, 1973). This matters because some people respond to relationship mapping by concluding they should cut acquaintances and focus only on a tiny inner circle. That would be a misreading. Weak ties have value. They enrich life, broaden perspective, and can create opportunity. The map is not a purge. It is an ecological assessment. It asks whether your weak ties have crowded out your strong ties, or whether your strong ties have become an unexamined assumption while your social energy is spent elsewhere.

Still, there is a limitation to mapping, and it should be named honestly. Relationships are not static circles on paper. They are dynamic, and their importance can change quickly. Someone might be a colleague today and a close friend next year. Someone might be in your inner circle and then move away, or become estranged, or become ill. Communities can become vital in one season and irrelevant in another. A map can therefore create a false sense of control, as though you can simply redraw your social life at will. You cannot. Other people have agency. Life interrupts. The reconciliation is to treat the map as a snapshot, not a constitution. Its value is not in freezing relationships into categories; it is in revealing the current pattern of attention so you can make modest choices for the next quarter.

Those choices are best made with a particular discipline: refuse to confuse visibility with closeness. Modern communication technologies make many people visible. You can see their photos, their announcements, their opinions. Visibility can create the illusion of intimacy. Yet intimacy depends on shared time, vulnerability, mutual investment, and the willingness to be known beyond performance. The map helps you distinguish the relationships you are merely seeing from the relationships you are actually sustaining. This distinction is essential for mental health and social resilience.

When a crisis arrives, the people who will matter are rarely those you have merely watched.

There is another subtle distinction the map exposes: the difference between relationships that are energising and relationships that are depleting. It is tempting to interpret depletion as a sign that you should avoid certain people. Sometimes that is true. Often it is more nuanced. Depletion can come from overexposure, from lack of boundaries, from roles that require constant giving, from relationships that are stuck in superficiality. The map is the first step in seeing where depletion lives in the system. A depleting relationship might not need to be ended; it might need a different form—less frequent contact, different contexts, clearer expectations. Again, the map does not solve. It reveals.

Revelation is enough to change behaviour.

The motif to thread through this subchapter is the constellation. A constellation is not a list of stars. It is a pattern that appears when you step back. Your social life, too, has a pattern. Some stars are bright and close. Some are faint but numerous. Some appear only in certain seasons. If you look at the night sky through a narrow tube, you can see a single bright point and miss the structure. The map is the act of stepping back. It is a way of seeing whether the constellation you are living matches the constellation you believe you have.

The most modern challenge in relationship mapping is time fragmentation. People do not simply have less time; they have time broken into small pieces. A message here, a quick call there, a brief meeting, a rushed coffee. Fragmentation can maintain a sense of contact while undermining depth. The map helps you see whether your quarter contained any sustained conversations, any unhurried time, any moments of genuine presence. Those moments are the soil in which strong ties grow. Without them, relationships can persist as logistics and drift as intimacy.

The forward test is therefore not sentimental. It is diagnostic. When you sketch your circles and then compare them with where your last ninety days actually went—hours, messages, meetings, calls, visits—

where is the largest mismatch between the people you claim are central and the attention you actually gave them, and what would it cost, in real calendar terms, to correct that mismatch for one quarter?

Quarterly relationship check-ins

In April 1958, at the Tavistock Institute in London, researchers were refining a set of ideas that would later shape how organisations think about people: not as isolated individuals, but as members of systems with feedback, norms, and unspoken rules. The Tavistock tradition in social science was preoccupied with the gap between what people say is happening and what is actually happening in group life—how avoidance becomes structure, how silence becomes policy, how small tensions become chronic (Tavistock Institute histories and publications from the mid-20th century are well documented). The institute did not invent human complexity. It simply took it seriously enough to observe it.

Observation changes systems.

A quarterly relationship check-in is an act of observation. It is not therapy. It is not confrontation. It is a brief, disciplined moment in which you look at a handful of key relationships and ask what the last quarter has actually felt like, not what you hope it felt like. The essential move is to shift from narrative to evidence. Narratives are comfortable: "we're fine", "we've been busy", "we should catch up", "she knows I care". Evidence is less comforting and more useful: how often you spoke, what you avoided, whether you left conversations feeling energised or drained, whether resentment is accumulating, whether affection is being expressed or merely assumed. The check-in is designed to surface these signals early, while adjustment is still gentle.

Gentle is not weak.

Gentleness is a strategy because relationships do not respond well to periodic ambush. Many people avoid reflecting on relationships because they fear it will demand a dramatic act: a confrontation, a clean break, a grand emotional speech. Those acts are sometimes necessary, but they are rarely necessary as often as people fear. What is more often necessary is attention. Attention is not the same as scrutiny. Attention is the willingness to notice. A quarterly check-in turns noticing into a repeatable practice. It creates a social equivalent of the net worth snapshot: not an exhaustive audit, but a reading of direction.

Direction is what drift steals.

Drift in relationships is usually not caused by cruelty. It is caused by default. Work expands. Family needs appear. Energy fluctuates. The people who are physically near absorb attention; the people who are distant require planning; the people who demand get served before the people who quietly endure. Over time, this default allocation creates an emotional landscape you did not choose: friendships that thin, partnerships that become logistical, family ties that carry unspoken debts, communities that become obligations. A quarterly check-in interrupts default and asks for consent. Consent, in relationships, is not a legal concept. It is the act of repeatedly choosing rather than merely assuming.

The check-in begins with a basic classification that is deliberately non-dramatic: does this relationship feel balanced, energising, or strained? These are not labels for the other person. They are labels for the relationship dynamic as you experienced it this quarter. Balanced suggests mutuality: effort roughly matched, care expressed in both directions, misunderstandings repaired without lingering bitterness. Energising suggests that contact leaves you with more life: curiosity, joy, steadiness, perspective. Strained suggests friction: avoidance, resentment, misalignment, or the sense that every interaction requires effort that is not being replenished.

Name the feeling. Then examine it.

This sequence matters because many adults reverse it. They jump straight into justifying why the relationship is fine or why it is hopeless, and the justification becomes a defence against feeling. The quarterly check-in aims to keep you closer to the data of experience. When you name a relationship as strained, for instance, you can then ask: what is the strain made of? Is it lack of time? Is it unresolved conflict? Is it one-sided effort? Is it a change in values? Is it a season of stress for one person? Is it simply distance and neglect? Each "is it" question turns a vague judgement into a specific hypothesis.

Hypotheses can be acted upon gently.

There is a well-known framework in relationship research associated with psychologist John Gottman, who has studied marital interaction and conflict patterns for decades. One of his widely cited concepts is the "Four Horsemen" of relationship breakdown—criticism, contempt, defensiveness, and stonewalling—identified through observational research (Gottman's work is extensively published from the 1990s onwards). The relevance here is not to turn every relationship into a marriage lab. It is to notice that relationship deterioration often has recognisable patterns, and that these patterns can be observed earlier than people tend to observe them. Stonewalling, for example, is often preceded by avoidance of particular topics. Defensiveness often shows up as recurring misunderstandings that never resolve. Contempt often begins as small sarcasms. The quarterly check-in gives you a periodic moment to ask: are any of these patterns quietly appearing in the way we speak, or in what we refuse to speak about?

Refusal is information.

One of the most useful parts of a check-in is to identify conversational topics you are avoiding. Avoidance is rarely random. People avoid topics because they fear conflict, because they do not know how to speak without causing hurt, because they are ashamed, because they are protecting the relationship from change, or because they suspect the truth will force a decision. Avoidance can be protective in the short term. Over a quarter, it becomes corrosive. It creates a second relationship beneath the visible one: the relationship of what is unsaid. That second relationship often holds more emotional power than the spoken one.

This is where a small, disciplined check-in can do what dramatic conversations often fail to do. Dramatic conversations are usually triggered by accumulation—months or years of unsaid things—so they arrive with pressure and accusation. A quarterly check-in invites earlier noticing. If you identify an avoided topic in April, you are not necessarily required to confront it in May. But you can decide whether it is something to address gently, whether it requires preparation, or whether it signals a boundary you need. The check-in transforms avoidance from a fog into a map feature.

A map feature can be navigated.

The second element of the check-in is to notice small gestures that could repair or deepen. "Gesture" can sound trivial, but it is often where relationships live. A message that acknowledges something you ignored. An apology that is specific rather than performative. A visit planned rather than promised. A shared activity restarted. A question asked with genuine attention. In social psychology, the concept of reciprocity is foundational: relationships tend to strengthen when exchanges of care and attention are mutual and visible. This does not mean relationships should be transactional. It means humans respond to signals. Small gestures are signals. They say: I see you, I remember, I am willing to invest.

Investment is a choice, not a feeling.

The quarterly cadence matters because it forces you to examine whether gestures are occurring or merely intended. Many people tell themselves they are good friends because they care. Care is real. It is also insufficient if it remains private. Relationships are sustained by enacted care. The check-in is a moment to compare private care with public action. Did you reach out? Did you show up? Did you make time? Did you follow through? These are behavioural questions, not moral ones. They are also uncomfortable, which is why they are useful.

A named, checkable example of how small, repeated check-ins can improve relationship systems comes from medicine, where "checklists" and structured communication have been used to reduce errors. The World Health Organization's Surgical Safety Checklist, introduced in 2008, created a structured pause—introductions, confirmation of key details, shared awareness—that improved team communication and reduced complications in multiple settings (WHO, 2008). The point is not to treat relationships like operations. It is to recognise that structured pauses can improve complex human interactions by making the implicit explicit. A quarterly relationship check-in is your structured pause in the social domain. It interrupts autopilot.

There is also a counter-example to be acknowledged. Not all relationships can be improved by gestures and check-ins. Some are abusive, manipulative, or persistently harmful. Some are limited by the other person's unwillingness to engage. Some are constrained by structural realities: distance, illness, caregiving, irreconcilable values. A gentle check-in can be misused as a way to keep yourself in a dynamic that is degrading, by reframing harm as "something to work on". The reconciliation is to treat the check-in as a truth-teller, not as a loyalty oath. If a relationship is consistently strained and the strain is not responsive to reasonable attempts at repair, the check-in should not be used to manufacture optimism. It should be used to clarify what is happening and what choices remain.

Choices are not always pleasant.

The quarterly check-in is not about generating drama, but it does not avoid reality. A relationship that feels strained might not need confrontation; it might need less frequency, clearer boundaries, or a deliberate pause. A relationship that feels energising might deserve more investment. A relationship that feels balanced might deserve protection, because balance is easily lost when quarters become busy. The check-in therefore creates a quiet hierarchy of attention for the next ninety days. It is not about labelling people. It is about allocating your finite social resources with a little more honesty.

Honesty includes noticing how relationships affect your energy. Energy is the social metric most adults ignore until they are depleted. Some interactions leave you calm and expanded; others leave you agitated, ashamed, or exhausted. This is not always about the other person's character. It can be about the context—meeting in a noisy bar, communicating only through text, interacting only under time pressure. A quarterly check-in encourages you to separate the relationship from its current form. If the relationship is valuable but the form is draining, the adjustment might be to change the form: longer conversations less often, different settings, more shared activity, fewer performative group interactions. Form is a design variable.

Design does not require coldness.

A quiet motif can hold the chapter together: tuning. A musician does not tune a violin only when it is unplayable. They tune regularly because strings drift. Temperature changes. Tension shifts. Tuning is not an indictment of the instrument. It is maintenance. Relationships drift too. Work pressure, life events, misunderstandings, unspoken needs—these alter tension. Quarterly check-ins are tuning sessions. They are small, deliberate adjustments that prevent a relationship from becoming so out of tune that only crisis can make it audible.

The tuning metaphor also discourages perfectionism. A tuned instrument will drift again. That is normal. The point is not to achieve a permanently perfect relationship. The point is to maintain a relationship within a range where it can produce music rather than noise. That range is personal. It depends on your life stage, obligations, and temperament. The quarterly cadence respects this by allowing relationships to have seasons. Some quarters you will invest heavily in a particular tie. Some quarters you will maintain lightly. Some quarters you will step back. The check-in turns these shifts into choices rather than accidents.

The forward test is uncomfortably specific, which is why it works. In your inner circle and closest friendships, which single topic have you been avoiding for at least a quarter, and what small, non-dramatic gesture—one conversation opener, one apology, one invitation, one boundary—would you be willing to attempt in the next ninety days to see whether the relationship tunes closer to balance rather than drifting further into strain?

Adjusting social commitments

In September 1846, in Manchester, England, a group of weavers and tradesmen who called themselves the Rochdale Society of Equitable Pioneers opened a small shop that would become a landmark in the history of co-operatives. Their influence did not come from charisma. It came from rules: membership terms, governance, meeting rhythms, contributions, obligations. Social life became sustainable because it was structured, renegotiable, and explicit. A community that cannot revise its commitments eventually becomes a trap, either for those who carry too much of the work or for those who no longer belong but cannot easily leave.

Commitments ossify.

Most adults do not notice the moment a social commitment becomes outdated. It happens quietly, through the mechanism of default. A recurring dinner continues because it has always continued. A committee role persists because no one has asked for a handover. A weekly call becomes a duty because it once was a lifeline. A hobby group becomes a burden because work changed or health changed or your interests changed. Favours, too, can become recurring obligations—helping with a project, providing emotional support, offering lifts, showing up—until the relationship is defined less by affection than by expectations.

Calendars are honest.

They record the shape of your social obligations whether you like the shape or not. That is why adjusting social commitments is a necessary counterpart to relationship check-ins. Check-ins reveal which ties feel energising or strained; commitments reveal how those feelings are being generated. A relationship can feel strained not because the person is difficult, but because the commitment is mis-sized. Too frequent, too long, too performative, too draining, too expensive, too far away. Or simply too obligatory. When you adjust commitments, you are not necessarily adjusting love. You are adjusting the container in which love is attempted.

Containers matter.

This subchapter is about the art of saying "not this quarter" without turning it into rejection, avoidance, or cruelty. "Not this quarter" is a remarkably civil phrase because it acknowledges the relationship while limiting the commitment. It is neither a permanent no nor a vague yes. It is a boundary with a time horizon. Time horizons lower drama. They also create clarity. Most social pain comes not from honest boundaries but from ambiguous ones: the slow fade, the repeated postponement, the overpromising followed by resentment. A quarter allows you to be explicit without claiming certainty about forever.

A useful concept here is role strain, a term in sociology describing the stress that arises when the demands of multiple roles become incompatible. The adult social calendar is often a list of roles: colleague, friend, partner, parent, sibling, mentor, volunteer, committee member, neighbour, community participant. Each role carries expectations. When you accumulate roles without periodic renegotiation, strain becomes inevitable. The strain does not show up as a clear "I have too many roles". It shows up as fatigue, irritability, avoidance, an urge to cancel, a feeling of being socially tapped out. In such moments, many people withdraw indiscriminately. They become "busy". They disappear. The result is social damage, often to the very relationships they value most.

The quarterly approach asks for discrimination.

Discrimination here means discernment: choosing which commitments deserve continuity and which require adjustment. The map of relationship circles you created earlier gives you the social structure. Now you look at the repeating elements in your calendar and ask whether they serve that structure or undermine it. Some recurring commitments are nourishing and should be protected. Others are neutral and can be maintained lightly. Others have become harmful: they cost too much time, money, or emotional energy relative to what they provide. Harmful commitments are rarely malicious. They are simply outdated.

Outdated commitments create hidden opportunity costs.

In economics, opportunity cost is the cost of choosing one option over another. In social life, opportunity cost is often the loss of uncommitted time—the time in which real connection tends to occur. If your calendar is saturated with recurring commitments, you may have no space to respond to what matters: a friend in trouble, a partner needing attention, a family member who wants time, a community event that genuinely excites you. You become a person who is "always booked", which sounds like success and often feels like poverty. You have social activity but little social freedom.

Freedom is not selfishness.

It is the capacity to respond. A quarter is a period in which you can rebuild that capacity by adjusting commitments deliberately. Deliberate adjustment begins with three questions that are behavioural rather than philosophical. How often does this commitment occur? How much time does it consume in practice, including travel and preparation? How do you typically feel afterwards—energised, neutral, drained? These are simple questions. They are also often avoided because the answers can force a decision. Yet decisions are what prevent drift. Without decisions, you will continue to live last year's social calendar in this year's life.

A named, checkable example of the value of renegotiable commitments can be found in the governance of many voluntary associations and charities, which often use fixed terms for leadership roles precisely to prevent burnout and entrenchment. The National Trust in the UK, founded in 1895, relies on structured governance and volunteer frameworks that include defined roles and responsibilities. The point is not the specifics of any organisation. It is the principle: sustainable communities formalise limits. They do not assume that good people can carry obligations indefinitely. Personal social life needs the same respect for limits.

A second example, closer to everyday culture, sits in the way recurring meetings work in organisations. After decades of meetings becoming an unexamined default, many firms have experimented with meeting-free days or reduced meeting cadences to reclaim focused time. These policies are frequently justified in productivity terms, but they also illustrate a deeper truth: recurring commitments expand until constrained. Social commitments behave similarly. If you never review them, they become a self-perpetuating structure. The quarterly ritual is your personal governance mechanism.

Still, there is a limitation: you cannot adjust commitments unilaterally without social consequences. Some commitments are relational obligations with moral weight—caring for children, supporting a partner through illness, helping family members. Others are bound up with identity: community roles, cultural practices, religious commitments. It would be shallow to treat all commitments as optional calendar entries. The reconciliation is to distinguish between obligations that are ethically necessary and commitments that are merely habitual. Even within ethically necessary obligations, the form can often be adjusted. Care can be shared. Duties can be rotated. Boundaries can be discussed. "Not this quarter" can apply to optional layers even when core responsibility remains.

The art is language.

Language is where many people fail because they reach for explanations when what is needed is clarity. Explanations invite debate. They also often conceal shame: the fear of being perceived as selfish. In reality, most people respond better to respectful clarity than to ambiguous excuses. Respectful clarity has three elements. It acknowledges the relationship. It states the boundary. It suggests a path forward if appropriate. The quarter provides an excellent boundary frame because it is specific and temporary. "I can't take this on this quarter" is clearer than "I'm really busy" and kinder than the slow fade. It also signals that you are treating your capacity as a finite resource, which is a form of honesty rather than rejection.

Honesty strengthens trust.

Trust, in relationships, is not only about loyalty. It is about predictability and integrity. If you constantly overpromise and then resentfully underdeliver, you erode trust even if you remain physically present. People sense reluctance. They sense obligation. They may not name it, but they feel it. Conversely, if you state boundaries early and kindly, you allow others to adjust their expectations. This is what makes communities and friendships sustainable. It is also what prevents the crueler form of boundary-setting: sudden withdrawal after years of silent resentment.

A quarter also allows you to separate two kinds of commitment: identity commitments and time commitments. Identity commitments are the ties you wish to maintain because they reflect who you are—friend, sibling, community member. Time commitments are the specific forms those ties take—weekly dinners, monthly meetings, daily messages. Many people confuse the two and fear that changing a time commitment is equivalent to rejecting the identity tie. It is not. You can remain a friend while declining a weekly commitment. You can remain a community member while stepping back from a committee role. You can remain close while changing the frequency and form of contact. The map helps you see what matters; the adjustment helps you choose a form that fits reality.

Reality includes energy.

The social calendar's hidden cost is often not time but recovery. Some commitments are easy; they do not drain. Others drain heavily, not necessarily because the people are unpleasant, but because the context is wrong: late nights, long travel, loud environments, emotional intensity, performative socialising, constant hosting. If your quarter has been depleted, these drains can be catastrophic. Depletion then leads to avoidance, and avoidance leads to neglect, and neglect leads to guilt—a familiar loop. Adjusting commitments breaks the loop by replacing avoidance with design. It asks you to create a social rhythm that you can actually sustain.

Sustaining is the theme.

A credible counter-example must be admitted. There are moments when the right thing is not to adjust down, but to show up more, even when it is inconvenient. A friend in crisis, a family emergency, a partner needing support—these are quarters where "not this quarter" may not apply in the usual way. The quarterly method must not become a tool for self-protection that hardens into self-absorption. The reconciliation is to treat the quarterly review as a way to create capacity for what matters most, including unexpected demands. By trimming outdated commitments, you create slack that can be offered where it is needed. Slack is the moral resource here. Without slack, even good-hearted people become brittle.

The motif to thread through this subchapter is pruning. In gardening, pruning is not destruction. It is the removal of growth that is crowding the plant, draining resources, or preventing fruiting. Pruning is seasonal. It is done with care. It is done to allow what matters to flourish. Social pruning works the same way. You do not prune love. You prune forms that no longer fit. You prune obligations that have become performative. You prune routines that were useful once and are now crowded by life. Pruning creates space. Space allows intimacy to breathe.

Breath is a signal.

If you find yourself exhaling with relief when a commitment is cancelled, that relief is data. It suggests the commitment has outgrown your capacity or your desire. Relief is not proof the other person is wrong. It is proof the form is mis-sized. The quarterly review gives you a legitimate moment to pay attention to that relief without guilt and to translate it into a respectful adjustment.

The forward test is therefore practical and slightly uncomfortable. Looking at the recurring social commitments in your calendar, which one—if paused or reduced for just one quarter—would create the most space for the relationships that genuinely matter, and what respectful, clear message would you need to send to make that pause honest rather than evasive?

Investing in key ties

On 15 September 2008, in New York City, Lehman Brothers filed for bankruptcy, and a familiar phrase began to circulate again in newspapers and kitchens: liquidity. In finance, liquidity means access—how quickly you can turn assets into something usable in a crisis. The months that followed made one thing clear even to people who had never read a balance sheet: systems fail, and when they do, what matters is not what you own in theory, but what you can draw on in practice. Relationships have their own form of liquidity. When a life shock arrives, the question is not how many contacts you have, but who will pick up.

Attention is the currency.

The previous subchapter asked you to prune social commitments that no longer fit, to reclaim time and reduce drift. Pruning alone, however, can leave a strange emptiness. People often discover that when they stop doing the obligatory things, they are not automatically doing the meaningful things. Space is necessary. It is not sufficient. The next move is deliberate investment: choosing one or two relationships to receive concentrated, specific attention over the next ninety days, not as a grand vow, but as an experiment in making connection more likely.

Make it specific.

Specificity is what keeps social investment from becoming sentimental theatre. "I should be a better friend" is a beautiful phrase that accomplishes almost nothing. It produces guilt, then avoidance, then drift. A quarterly investment is different. It names a relationship and chooses a concrete form of contact that will happen in the real world: a visit booked, a recurring call set, a shared project begun, a regular walk arranged, a meal planned. It is small enough to be doable and deliberate enough to be felt. It also respects the reality that adult life is not a blank page. It is full. The investment must therefore be engineered into the calendar rather than wished into existence.

Engineering is not coldness.

It is respect for how humans actually behave. We are creatures of routine, proximity, and cues. Even deep affection cannot sustain contact without some structure, especially when distance and workload intervene. This is why so many adult relationships drift despite genuine care: care exists, but contact lacks scaffolding. The scaffolding can be as simple as a recurring Friday call or a planned visit, but it must exist. Once it exists, intimacy has a place to land.

A useful way to think about key-tie investment is through the distinction between expressed and assumed care. Many relationships coast on assumed care: "they know I love them," "we're still close," "we'll always be friends." Assumed care can be comforting. It can also become a form of negligence when it replaces expression. Expression does not require constant communication. It requires reliable signals: the message that arrives when it matters, the call that does not always wait for a crisis, the visit that is planned rather than perpetually proposed. In behavioural terms, expressed care is observable. Assumed care is private. Private care is real, but it is fragile as a maintenance mechanism.

Fragile maintenance fails under stress.

This is why the quarter is such a useful unit for social investment. Ninety days is long enough to establish a new rhythm and short enough to commit without fear. The fear matters. Many people avoid deliberate social investment because it feels like a promise they might not keep. They prefer vague good intentions because vagueness protects them from the shame of failure. The quarterly approach lowers that barrier. It asks for a time-limited trial. You are not promising to become a model friend forever. You are testing whether a small, repeatable action, sustained for one quarter, changes the quality of a relationship and the texture of your life.

Texture is the right word.

Relationships are not only support systems for crises. They shape the ordinary. They make days lighter or heavier. They alter how you interpret success and failure. They provide humour, perspective, and continuity. They can also serve as mirrors, reflecting who you are becoming. This is why investing in key ties is not merely altruistic; it is existential. If your relationships drift, your life becomes narrower. If your relationships are tended, your life becomes more dimensional. A quarter can change dimension.

The research literature on close relationships offers a useful lens here. Psychologists have long studied the role of responsiveness—feeling understood, validated, and cared for—in relationship satisfaction. In 2002, Reis, Clark and Holmes discussed perceived partner responsiveness as a central ingredient in intimacy (Reis, Clark & Holmes, 2004; related work spans early 2000s). The point is not to translate intimacy into a clinical metric. It is to notice that responsiveness is behavioural. It is not a feeling you have about someone. It is something you do: listening, remembering, showing up, responding when the other person reaches. A quarterly investment can be designed to increase responsiveness through structure: a recurring call makes responsiveness more likely because it reduces reliance on spontaneity.

Spontaneity is overrated.

At least, it is overrated as a maintenance strategy. In adult life, spontaneity tends to favour the urgent and the convenient, not the important. People see those who are nearby. They respond to those who shout. They neglect those who are patient. A planned visit or recurring call is a way of protecting a relationship from these biases. It is also a way of honouring distance. Distance is not only geographical. It can be psychological: the distance created by different life stages, different schedules, different responsibilities. Planned contact bridges that distance.

Bridging is a design choice.

The form of investment matters as much as the intent. There are three forms that work especially well in quarterly units because they are repeatable and observable. The first is the visit. Visits are powerful because they change context. They allow for unhurried time, shared meals, walks, and the small non-verbal cues that text cannot carry. A visit also tends to generate memories, and memories are relationship cement. The second is the recurring call. Calls are less logistically demanding than visits and can be scaled to life constraints. Their power lies in regularity. Regularity reduces the psychological friction of reaching out because the contact is expected rather than awkward. The third is the shared project. Projects create connection through doing rather than through talking. They can be as simple as reading the same book, building something together, planning a trip, or volunteering. Projects are particularly useful for relationships that struggle under the pressure of "we must talk about everything," because they provide a third thing to focus on.

Each form has risks.

Visits can be expensive and exhausting if poorly timed. Calls can become performative if they lack substance. Projects can become another obligation if they are too ambitious. The quarter protects you from overcommitting. It encourages you to choose one or two relationships and one form of investment each, then run the experiment. The experiment is not "did the relationship become perfect?" The experiment is "did the investment produce more genuine contact and more ease?"

Ease is not laziness.

Ease is a sign that a relationship is being maintained with less friction. Friction is often the hidden enemy. People do not avoid friends because they dislike them. They avoid because reaching out feels awkward after time has passed, because they do not know what to say, because they fear the friend will be disappointed, because scheduling is complicated, because they are tired, because they do not want to admit how long it has been. A recurring structure reduces friction by normalising contact. A visit reduces friction by compressing contact into a meaningful block rather than trying to sustain intimacy through scattered messages. A shared project reduces friction by giving you something to do together, which often feels easier than trying to manufacture deep conversation on demand.

A named, checkable example of how structured connection supports resilience comes from longitudinal research on adult development. The Harvard Study of Adult Development, which began in 1938 and has followed participants over decades, has repeatedly emphasised the importance of relationships for wellbeing (documented in publications and summaries by study directors, including Robert Waldinger's public talks and writings). This is often reduced to a slogan—"relationships matter"—which is true and useless. The more interesting implication for a quarterly system is that relationship quality is not a static trait; it is maintained through repeated actions. The study's popularisation does not tell you what to do. It does tell you that tending relationships is a serious endeavour, not a sentimental hobby.

A second example sits in community practice rather than research. Mutual aid networks, which have existed in various forms for centuries and became highly visible again during the early months of the COVID-19 pandemic (2020), often depended on simple, repeatable commitments: regular check-ins, delivery rotations, shared tasks. Their effectiveness did not come from dramatic gestures. It came from reliability. Reliability is what turns goodwill into support. A quarterly investment aims to create reliability in at least one key tie, even in a small way.

Still, a counter-example must be faced honestly. You can invest in a relationship and not receive the return you hope for. The other person may be overwhelmed, unwilling, or simply in a different season. They may not want increased contact. They may interpret your investment as pressure. They may have moved on. This is not failure. It is information. The quarterly framing helps here because it treats investment as a test rather than as a demand. You are not forcing intimacy. You are offering structure and attention and observing what happens. If the relationship responds, the investment may be worth continuing. If it does not, you may need to adjust your expectations or choose a different tie to invest in next quarter.

You can only control one side.

This is why the best investments are those that are generous but bounded. Bounded means you can sustain the action without resentment, even if the response is uneven. A recurring call that you would enjoy even if the other person occasionally misses it. A visit that you want for your own reasons as well as theirs. A shared project that is intrinsically interesting. Bounded investments protect you from turning relational care into a hidden contract.

Hidden contracts poison friendships.

The quarter is also a helpful boundary because it encourages you to treat social investment as a portfolio rather than as a single dramatic bet. You will not invest in every relationship at once. That would be impossible. Instead, you choose one or two ties each quarter, invest deliberately, and observe. Over time, different ties receive attention.

The practice becomes sustainable. It also prevents the common adult pattern of reactive investment: only showing up intensely when a crisis occurs, then disappearing again. Crisis-driven investment is real, and sometimes necessary, but it is not a stable maintenance strategy. Quarterly investment makes support less dependent on disaster.

The motif to carry through this subchapter is the bridge. A bridge is built deliberately. It is not constructed from vague affection. It is constructed from repeated, reliable structure—supports, spans, maintenance, inspections. Once built, it makes crossing easier. Your key ties are the bridges in your life: the people and relationships that allow you to move between seasons, to carry burdens, to expand joy. Bridges do not appear by accident. They are maintained.

The forward test is therefore direct and slightly bracing. Looking at the next ninety days as they truly are, which single relationship would most change the feel of your quarter if it were steadier and closer, and what specific, calendar-visible investment—one visit, one recurring call, or one shared project—are you willing to commit to as a trial, knowing that the outcome is uncertain but the attempt itself will reveal what is possible?

Chapter 6
Work, Projects and Calendar

On 12 April 1961, Yuri Gagarin became the first human to orbit the Earth. The story is usually told in the language of bravery and technology, yet the most interesting part sits behind the spectacle: the schedule. Vostok 1 did not succeed because someone "worked hard" in a general sense. It succeeded because an immense number of tasks were sequenced, timed, reviewed, and rehearsed until the project became predictable enough to risk a life. Space travel is an extreme example, but it reveals an ordinary truth: complex work does not happen by motivation. It happens by design.

Design begins with inventory.

Most professional lives now contain more projects than any human being can hold cleanly in mind. Work has become modular, collaborative, digital, and perpetually interruptible. The modern worker is expected to be both deep and responsive, both strategic and available, both creative and administratively fluent. In this environment, the calendar becomes a second nervous system. It is where priorities are expressed or betrayed. It is also where drift hides in plain sight: recurring meetings that no longer serve their purpose, projects that linger in "almost" status, small time leaks that bleed the day into scraps, and the creeping sense that work is never quite done.

Never done is not a badge.

It is a failure mode. When work becomes endless, it stops being meaningful and starts being ambient. It fills every gap. It colonises evenings. It occupies weekends in "just a little catch-up". It turns free time into guilt. People often respond by doubling down on effort, as though the solution to an overfull system is more willpower. The Upgrade Day approach is built on a different premise: effort is not the bottleneck. Structure is. A quarterly reset of work, projects, and calendar is an attempt to restore structure—to make work legible again, to reduce hidden waste, and to reclaim the capacity for focused attention without performing martyrdom.

This chapter sits at the junction of the book's other domains. Money is often shaped by work pressure. Health is often sacrificed to work cycles. Relationships are often neglected because work expands. Learning is often postponed because work feels urgent. Environment is often cluttered because work consumes bandwidth. If you change nothing about work, the other domains fight uphill. If you change work design, the whole system gains slack. Slack is not laziness. Slack is the space in which human life becomes possible.

This chapter therefore treats work as a pipeline rather than as a vague obligation. A pipeline has stages: things begin, move, stall, complete, and—most importantly—exit. Many professional lives suffer not from too much work but from too many half-finished loops. The mind pays a tax on each open loop, even when you are not actively working on it. The sense of constant mental load is often the accumulation of unresolved projects, unclear next actions, and commitments you have not consciously renewed. The quarterly reset makes those loops visible and therefore governable.

The first movement is the projects pipeline review: listing active projects and classifying them as starting, ongoing, stalled, or finished. This sounds simple. It is also mildly shocking when done honestly, because it reveals the difference between activity and progress. Many people have far more "ongoing" projects than they can realistically advance. The consequence is thin spread: attention divided into fragments, progress slower than it should be, and a persistent sense of underperformance despite constant busyness. A pipeline review also reveals hidden progress. Work that feels stagnant may have advanced quietly: a draft completed, a decision made, an obstacle removed. Noticing hidden progress matters because it restores agency. It shows you that not everything is stuck; some things are simply moving in a different cadence than your impatience.

The second movement is the calendar purge, and it is where the chapter becomes almost surgical. Calendars are littered with fossils: meetings created for a temporary purpose that became permanent through inertia, recurring check-ins that exist because no one wants to be the one to stop them, standing commitments that once mattered and now merely occupy time. Fossils are not evil. They are outdated. Yet outdated commitments consume the only resource you cannot earn more of: hours of attention. A purge is not an act of rebellion. It is maintenance. It asks whether each recurring event still serves its original purpose, and if not, whether it should be cancelled, delegated, shortened, or redesigned. The moral courage required here is not dramatic courage; it is the willingness to stop doing things that make you look busy and start protecting time for work that actually matters.

Then comes the part people tend to underestimate: recurring time leaks. Some of the most expensive drains do not appear on calendars. They appear as habits: checking email compulsively, hovering in inboxes, toggling between tasks, doing "admin" without clear boundaries, drifting into social media loops, attending to notifications as though they were emergencies. These leaks create the feeling of being always engaged and rarely productive. They also make deep work—work that requires sustained thought—feel unreachable. The quarterly reset treats these leaks not as moral failures but as patterns. If a leak repeats daily, it is not a one-off lapse. It is a system. Systems can be changed. Not with elaborate rules, but with small boundaries designed as experiments for the next quarter.

The chapter's final movement is about planning sprints and slack: designing periods of concentrated effort for key projects and bracketing them with lighter weeks or deliberate breathing space. This is where the chapter's philosophy becomes explicit. Work is not meant to be an unbroken marathon at sprint pace. Yet that is how many people live: always pushing, always "just one more thing", always in a state of low-level urgency. The result is predictable: exhaustion, diminished creativity, brittle relationships, neglected health. A sprint-and-slack model recognises that intensity is sustainable only when it is bounded. It also recognises that recovery is not something you squeeze into what remains; it is something you plan with the same seriousness as work.

Modern work culture makes this particularly urgent. Digital tools have lowered the cost of assigning tasks and raised the expectation of responsiveness. Remote and hybrid work have blurred boundaries, often turning homes into offices and evenings into extension cords for daytime work. Knowledge work increasingly rewards cognitive stamina, not merely presence. Under these conditions, the ability to design your work quarter becomes a form of self-preservation. It is also a competitive advantage in the most humane sense: not outcompeting others, but protecting your own capacity to think well.

This chapter is not anti-work. It is anti-drift.

Drift in work looks like projects multiplying without completion. It looks like meetings reproducing without purpose. It looks like attention shredded into fragments. It looks like weeks with no breathing space, followed by collapse. The quarterly reset is designed to interrupt this drift before it becomes burnout. Burnout is often treated as a personal weakness. It is more accurately described as a system mismatch: demands exceeding recovery for too long. Quarterly planning cannot prevent every shock. It can prevent the slow, predictable build-up of unsustainable patterns.

A quiet motif threads through this chapter: the workshop bench. A good workshop has tools in place, projects clearly staged, space for focused work, and room to tidy between builds. A chaotic bench produces wasted time: searching, redoing, improvising under pressure. Many calendars resemble chaotic benches. They are full of tools, half-built projects, and noise, with no clear staging. The Upgrade Day is the moment you step back, clear space, label what is in progress, put away what is no longer needed, and decide what deserves the bench this quarter.

The emotional payoff is not merely productivity. It is relief.

Relief is what happens when you stop treating overwhelm as a personality trait and start treating it as a design problem. The chapter's momentum comes from this shift. Once you see your projects as a pipeline, your meetings as renewable commitments rather than permanent facts, your time leaks as patterns rather than sins, and your quarters as sequences of sprints and slack, you begin to reclaim authorship. The question that remains, and that the chapter equips you to face, is bracingly practical: which project, if given genuine focus this quarter, would make the rest of your work feel lighter—and what must you remove or redesign to make that focus possible?

Reviewing projects pipeline

In October 1947, in the desert at Muroc Army Air Field in California—later Edwards Air Force Base—Chuck Yeager broke the sound barrier in the Bell X-1. The feat is remembered as a moment of daring, but its real anatomy was administrative as much as aerodynamic: test plans, instrumentation, checklists, contingency procedures, a chain of decisions about what to try next and what to delay. The aircraft did not simply go fast. It moved through a pipeline of experiments, each classified by readiness and risk, each informed by the previous one.

Work is a pipeline.

Most professionals live as if it is not. They live as if work is an ocean, and they are required to swim in all directions at once. Projects arrive, remain "in progress" for months, drift into limbo, then resurface when someone asks, "Where are we with that?" The mind responds by keeping a low-level background vigilance over dozens of half-finished things. This vigilance feels like responsibility. It is often only anxiety. The pipeline review is a way of converting ocean into channels: a clear view of what is starting, what is ongoing, what is stalled, and what is finished. It is not a productivity trick. It is a sanity tool.

Sanity needs structure.

The quarterly reset is built on the idea that drift is easiest to correct when it is still small. In work, drift looks like projects spreading too thinly, priorities becoming contradictory, and energy being consumed by coordination rather than by progress. You can feel busy for an entire quarter and still have nothing meaningful finished. That is not laziness. It is a predictable outcome of too many active commitments and too little explicit sequencing. A pipeline review makes sequencing possible because it forces visibility. You can only decide what deserves focus if you can see what currently claims it.

A useful way to understand why this review matters is through the concept of cognitive load. Human attention is limited, and open loops consume mental bandwidth even when you are not actively addressing them. This is not a moral failing; it is a feature of the mind. The Zeigarnik effect—named after psychologist Bluma Zeigarnik, who reported in the 1920s that interrupted tasks are often remembered better than completed ones—has been interpreted and debated over time, but its popular resonance persists because it captures something many people recognise: unfinished work nags (Zeigarnik, 1927). Whether the effect is as strong or universal as folk wisdom suggests, the lived phenomenon is real enough to matter in practice: the more unfinished projects you carry, the more your mind is pulled towards them.

Pulled attention is expensive.

The pipeline review reduces that cost by naming the state of each project. Naming is not cosmetic. It changes decisions. When a project is labelled "starting", it implies a need for definition, resources, and initial momentum. When it is labelled "ongoing", it implies a need for sustained progress and clear next steps. When it is labelled "stalled", it implies a blocker, a dependency, or a loss of relevance that needs to be acknowledged rather than ignored. When it is labelled "finished", it implies closure, communication, and the freeing of capacity. These labels convert emotional fuzziness into operational clarity.

Operational clarity is what most overworked people lack.

It is also what many organisations inadvertently discourage. Modern work tools make it easy to create projects and hard to finish them. Digital collaboration lowers the cost of asking for work. Emails and messages create micro-projects by the hour. Meanwhile, incentives often reward visibility over completion: being in meetings, responding quickly, appearing engaged. Under these conditions, project sprawl is not a personal flaw. It is a systemic output. The quarterly pipeline review is a countermeasure: a deliberately chosen pause to restore the relationship between effort and results.

Results need finishing.

Finishing is not merely the last step; it is a distinct skill. Many people are excellent starters. They generate ideas, draft plans, begin initiatives, join committees. Fewer are consistent finishers, partly because finishing requires different work: integration, editing, coordination, risk acceptance, and often uncomfortable conversations about scope. A pipeline review brings finishing into view by making the "finished" category explicit and by forcing you to count how many things actually crossed the line this quarter. The act of counting is not to induce shame. It is to reveal whether your system is biased towards perpetual motion rather than completion.

Perpetual motion is a trap.

The pipeline review also reveals "hidden progress", which is the antidote to a different failure mode: the sense of stagnation that comes from not noticing incremental advancement. Some projects move slowly by nature—research, writing, skill-building, long-term organisational change. When you view such work through a daily lens, it can feel like nothing is happening. The quarter makes slow work legible, but only if you know what to look for. Hidden progress might be a decision made that eliminated future debate, a prototype built, a stakeholder aligned, a draft completed, a system improved, a backlog reduced. These are not dramatic outputs, but they change the next quarter's capacity. Recognising them is important because it prevents the false despair that leads people to abandon valuable projects prematurely or to thrash between initiatives.

Thrashing looks like productivity.

It is not. It is energy wasted on switching costs. Switching costs are the cognitive and operational losses incurred when you move between tasks and projects. They are not always visible on calendars, but they are real. Every time you re-enter a project after a gap, you spend time remembering context, reconstructing decisions, reopening files, reorienting. When you carry too many ongoing projects, you spend a large fraction of your week simply re-entering. This is why people can work long hours and still feel they are not advancing. Their energy is consumed by re-entry.

A pipeline review addresses re-entry by reducing the number of active streams.

This is where classification becomes more than labelling. Once you classify, you can see congestion. Congestion is a term from systems thinking and queueing theory: when too much work is in progress, throughput slows, and waiting time increases. In manufacturing and project management, this is a familiar idea: limiting work-in-progress increases flow. You do not need to be a Lean practitioner to recognise the phenomenon in your own week. When you attempt to advance ten projects at once, none moves quickly. When you focus on two or three, progress becomes visible. The pipeline review is the moment you see your personal work-in-progress load and decide whether it is plausible.

Plausibility is underrated.

Many professional plans fail because they are not plausible under real constraints. People plan as though every week will be calm, as though meetings will be minimal, as though health will be perfect, as though life will not interrupt. Then reality arrives, and the plan becomes a source of shame. The quarterly pipeline review is designed to be reality-based. It asks: given the last quarter's constraints, what number of projects can you genuinely move? If the answer is fewer than you wish, that is not failure. It is information. It tells you what the system can handle. It also tells you what must change if you want more throughput: fewer meetings, fewer time leaks, more focused blocks, clearer boundaries.

Boundaries are a project management tool.

They are also relational tools, as the previous chapter showed. Work boundaries often feel socially risky because declining or delaying projects can disappoint colleagues or managers. Yet the alternative is often worse: saying yes to everything, delivering slowly or poorly, and eroding trust. Trust, in work, is frequently a function of reliability. Reliability is not about heroic effort. It is about making commitments you can keep. The pipeline review supports reliability because it forces you to examine your current commitments and to decide which ones you can actually honour this quarter.

Honouring requires choices.

A named, checkable example from project history illustrates how choice and classification shape outcomes. In 1970, the Boeing 747 entered commercial service with Pan Am, following a complex development programme with enormous technical and organisational challenges. The "jumbo jet" project required the coordination of thousands of tasks, suppliers, and design decisions, and it famously involved building a new factory at Everett, Washington. Whatever one's view of aviation's broader impacts, the programme demonstrates a basic principle: projects of high complexity succeed only when work is staged, dependencies are managed, and progress is reviewed against clear phases. No one could have built a 747 by keeping every task "ongoing" indefinitely. Phase clarity was the only way through.

A second example, closer to knowledge work, is the way large software projects use issue trackers and sprints to visualise work stages. Open-source projects such as the Linux kernel, initiated by Linus Torvalds in 1991, rely on structured workflows—patch review, maintainers, releases—to move changes from proposal to integration. Again, the point is not to romanticise technology. It is to notice the mechanism: visibility and staging reduce chaos. A quarterly pipeline review borrows this mechanism for ordinary professional life: it makes the state of work visible so that you can manage flow.

Still, there is a limitation worth naming. Not all work can be cleanly classified. Some roles are inherently reactive—healthcare, emergency services, customer support, caregiving, certain managerial roles. Projects in such contexts may not progress in neat stages because the work is shaped by external demand. The pipeline review could feel artificial, even insulting, if applied rigidly. The reconciliation is to treat the pipeline as a way of distinguishing between reactive load and project load. Even in reactive roles, there are often projects—improvements, training, system changes—that compete for attention with daily demand. The pipeline review makes that competition visible. It also helps you identify whether reactive load has expanded so far that project work is unrealistic this quarter, in which case the appropriate choice may be to define a smaller project scope or to protect a minimal focus area.

Minimal focus is still focus.

Another limitation is political. In many workplaces, visibility can be dangerous: admitting a project is stalled may feel like exposing weakness. This can lead people to keep everything in "ongoing" status indefinitely, performing progress rather than making it. The quarterly review is private, which is why it works. It is not a status report. It is a personal instrument for making decisions. It allows you to tell the truth to yourself first. From that truth, you can craft whatever communication is appropriate externally, but the internal clarity comes before the external narrative.

The motif to thread through this subchapter is the assembly line, but with a humane twist. An assembly line, at its best, is not a machine that grinds humans down. It is a system that makes flow visible: where items are stuck, where bottlenecks occur, where capacity is exceeded. Your work is not a factory output, but your attention behaves like a constrained resource moving through stages. When the line is overloaded, everything jams. When it is balanced, items move. The pipeline review is the act of stepping above the line and seeing the jam points.

Seeing is the beginning of control.

By the end of a pipeline review, you are positioned to do what matters most for the next quarter: choose. Choice here is not a philosophical posture. It is a practical allocation of focus. You decide which projects deserve concentrated attention, which can be maintained lightly, which should be paused, and which should be closed. You also notice what you have been pretending not to notice: projects that have been "almost" for multiple quarters, obligations that persist without purpose, and the hidden progress that proves you are not as stuck as you feared.

The forward test is therefore precise. When you look at your pipeline and see how many projects are labelled ongoing, how many are stalled, and how few are truly finished, what is the smallest number of projects you could commit to moving meaningfully this quarter—so that the quarter ends with clear completions rather than simply more motion—and what must you admit you will not advance, at least for now, to make that possible?

Conducting calendar purge

On 16 December 1773, in Boston, Massachusetts, a crowd boarded ships in the harbour and tipped tea into the water. The Boston Tea Party is usually told as political theatre, yet it was also, in its own way, an argument about governance: who sets rules, who renews them, and what happens when long-standing arrangements continue by inertia rather than consent. People rarely revolt against a single event. They revolt against accumulated defaults.

Calendars are accumulated defaults.

A calendar purge is not a tantrum against meetings. It is a governance practice. It asks you to look at your last quarter and your next, scan the recurring meetings and commitments that occupy your weeks, and decide—explicitly—which still serve their purpose. Many events began as sensible responses to a real need: a project check-in, a weekly coordination call, a recurring stand-up, a monthly review. Then the need changed or vanished, but the meeting remained. It remained because nobody wants to be the person who suggests stopping it, because the invitation repeats automatically, because "we've always done it", because it feels safer to keep a ritual than to risk missing something.

Safety can be an illusion.

The illusion is that meetings equal control. In practice, meetings can become a substitute for decision-making and a mask for unclear responsibility. They can multiply as a response to anxiety: if we meet more, we will prevent problems. Sometimes this is true, especially in complex, high-stakes work. Often it is not. Often the meeting survives because it is easier than fixing the underlying system: unclear ownership, poor documentation, fragmented communication, an absence of shared priorities. The calendar purge is the moment you stop paying for those system weaknesses with your time.

Time is the only non-renewable resource in your working life. Money can be earned and spent again. Attention can be depleted and recovered. Hours pass once. The calendar is therefore not neutral. It is a statement of what you have agreed to make possible. When it is full of stale commitments, it makes the wrong things possible: constant coordination, endless updates, perpetual availability. It makes the right things difficult: deep work, thoughtful planning, sustained creation, unhurried problem-solving. This is why the purge belongs in a quarterly ritual. If you do not revise recurring commitments, they become the skeleton of your year. You then wonder why you cannot change.

Change requires subtraction.

A calendar purge begins with a particular kind of looking. You are not "reviewing your schedule" in the vague sense. You are hunting for fossils: events that no longer serve their original purpose, meetings whose agendas have dissolved into status theatre, commitments that exist because someone once set them up and nobody revisited them. Fossils are identifiable by their texture. They feel slightly dead. People show up and multitask. Decisions are deferred. The same topics repeat. The meeting ends with "we'll circle back", which is a polite way of admitting that nothing has moved.

Nothing moving is data.

A quarterly purge treats that data seriously. It asks: what was the original purpose? Is that purpose still relevant? If relevant, does the current form achieve it? If not, what would? Here the options are not merely "keep" or "cancel". There are three main interventions: cancel, delegate, shorten. Cancel means the meeting is not needed at all. Delegate means the meeting's purpose can be served by a smaller group or by someone else, or that you do not need to be present. Shorten means the purpose is real but the current time allocation is inflated. Each intervention is a way of aligning the calendar with reality.

Reality is often uncomfortable.

The discomfort comes from social dynamics. Meetings are social objects. They confer belonging, visibility, and perceived diligence. Cancelling a recurring meeting can feel like challenging the group's identity. Delegating can feel like surrendering control or status. Shortening can feel like disrespect. The purge, therefore, is not only a logistical exercise. It is a moral one: choosing integrity over performance. Integrity here means that your time reflects your actual priorities rather than your fear of being judged.

Fear drives calendar bloat.

One of the quietest forms of fear is fear of missing information. Many people remain in meetings not because they contribute, but because they are afraid of being out of the loop. This is especially common in organisations where information is hoarded or where decisions happen in meetings rather than being documented. The purge therefore surfaces an organisational question: do you trust the system enough to step out? Trust is not abstract here. It is behavioural. It is whether you believe you will be informed of decisions that affect you without having to attend every discussion. If you do not believe that, the problem may not be you. It may be the organisation's communication norms.

Still, your calendar is yours.

Even in flawed systems, you can often reclaim some time by designing how you participate. If a meeting is necessary but your role is minimal, you might attend only the relevant segment. If the meeting exists for status updates, you might propose an alternative: written updates circulated beforehand, with meeting time reserved for decisions. This idea has an analogue in research and healthcare. The World Health Organization's Surgical Safety Checklist, introduced in 2008, was not an attempt to create more meetings. It was an attempt to structure brief, high-value communication around critical moments, reducing preventable errors (WHO, 2008). The lesson is that structured, concise communication can outperform longer, vaguer gatherings. The purge is your chance to introduce that principle into your work life, at least in your own calendar.

Concise does not mean careless.

It means purposeful. Many meetings lack purpose, or rather, they contain too many purposes at once. They are simultaneously status updates, decision-making forums, social rituals, and places to surface anxiety. When a meeting has too many functions, it does none well and expands indefinitely. A purge forces you to separate functions. If the function is decision-making, then the meeting needs decision-ready inputs. If the function is coordination, then the meeting needs clear handoffs. If the function is social cohesion, then perhaps it belongs elsewhere—a team lunch, a periodic offsite, a shorter check-in. This separation reduces time waste and makes meetings less exhausting.

Exhaustion is a calendar symptom.

If you end a day of meetings with a sense of mental fog, that is not merely personal fatigue. It is often the result of cognitive switching—moving between contexts repeatedly without time to process. Research on task switching and cognitive load has shown that switching between tasks carries a performance cost; while the literature is complex, the basic phenomenon of "switching cost" is well established in cognitive psychology (see work by Rubinstein, Meyer, and Evans, 2001, for example, on executive control of task switching). A calendar packed with short meetings maximises switching. It fragments attention. It reduces the capacity for deep thinking. A purge is an intervention against fragmentation.

Fragmentation also creates a particular kind of time leak: the meeting buffer. People underestimate how much time meetings consume because they count only the meeting itself. They do not count the preparation, the travel (even digital), the recovery, the follow-up. A thirty-minute meeting often becomes an hour of disruption. When such meetings repeat, the disruption becomes a way of life. The purge forces you to account for the real cost. This is why looking at the last quarter matters as much as the next. The last quarter contains evidence of what meetings actually produced. The next quarter contains the opportunity to redesign.

Evidence should drive decisions.

A named, checkable example of how meeting culture can become a source of inefficiency comes from the corporate critiques of meeting overload that have appeared repeatedly over the last few decades, particularly as email and digital communication increased. While specific figures vary by industry and role, the broader pattern is well recognised: as communication channels proliferate, organisations often add meetings to compensate for fragmentation. The result is more communication and less clarity. The exact numbers are not needed here; the lived experience of many professionals is sufficient evidence. People spend whole days in meetings and then do their "real work" in the evening. That is not sustainable. It is a design failure.

Design failures can be corrected.

Still, a credible counter-example must be acknowledged. Some recurring meetings are genuinely vital. In safety-critical domains—healthcare, aviation, emergency response—regular briefings and handovers can prevent serious harm. In high-complexity projects, frequent coordination can reduce rework. In distributed teams, recurring contact can maintain cohesion. The reconciliation is not to become anti-meeting. It is to become pro-purpose. The purge is not a crusade. It is a review. If a meeting consistently produces decisions, resolves conflicts, or prevents errors, it may deserve protection. If it does not, it deserves redesign or removal.

Removal requires courage.

Courage here is often social. It involves risking mild disapproval for the sake of doing better work. Many people prefer to stay in low-value meetings because it feels safer than insisting on time for focused work, which can appear selfish in cultures that prize visibility. Yet the deeper selfishness is to waste the time of others by participating in rituals you privately believe are pointless. A purge is a commitment to honesty: if an event no longer serves, it should not persist by inertia. The quarter gives you a legitimate cadence for this honesty. It turns renegotiation into routine rather than rebellion.

Routine renegotiation changes culture.

Even if you cannot change organisational culture alone, you can change your own calendar culture. You can decide that recurring commitments must earn their place each quarter. This is governance. It is also self-respect. The calendar is the bridge between intention and lived experience. If the bridge is clogged with unnecessary commitments, you will carry fewer meaningful projects across. Your pipeline review will reveal congestion; the calendar purge is how you remove it.

A quiet motif threads through this subchapter: the attic. Calendars accumulate like attics. Things are put there because they might be useful. Over time, the attic fills. You forget what is in it. You climb up only when you need something and then discover it is buried. A calendar purge is an attic clearing. You take out recurring items, examine them, decide what belongs, discard what does not, and create space so that what matters can be reached without strain.

Space is the point.

The forward test, then, is not "How do I get more done?" It is simpler and sharper. Looking at the recurring meetings and commitments in your next quarter, which one is a fossil—an event whose purpose has evaporated—and what would change, in your actual week, if you cancelled, delegated, or shortened it so that your calendar began to reflect what you truly intend to prioritise?

Fixing recurring time leaks

On 1 May 1840, in London, the Penny Black went on sale, the first adhesive postage stamp issued for public use in the United Kingdom. The change was not merely aesthetic. It lowered the friction of sending letters, standardised payment, and helped make written communication more routine. It also created an unintended side effect: correspondence could now multiply. When the cost of sending messages drops, the volume rises. The stamp did not create human curiosity or obligation, but it made them easier to express at scale.

Friction shapes behaviour.

Digital work is the Penny Black turned up to an almost absurd volume. Email, messaging apps, collaboration platforms, and notifications have driven the marginal cost of communication close to zero. The consequence is not simply "more messages". It is a different texture of attention. Work becomes a field of tiny demands. Days fill with micro-responses. The calendar may look manageable, yet the day dissolves into fragments. People end the afternoon with the feeling that they have been busy and oddly unaccomplished. They cannot point to a single culprit because the culprits are small, repeated, and unrecorded.

These are time leaks.

They do not appear as meetings. They appear as habits: checking email compulsively, switching tasks to "just reply quickly", doing admin in shapeless lumps, scrolling social media in the gaps, opening news sites as a palate cleanser that quietly turns into a quarter-hour. Leaks are easy to moralise about—discipline, focus, willpower—yet moralising misses the engineering reality. Repeated leaks are not random lapses. They are patterns reinforced by cues, rewards, and anxiety. In other words, they are systems. Systems can be redesigned. The quarterly ritual does not demand a total life overhaul. It asks you to identify one or two significant leaks and run a time-limited experiment to reduce them.

Experiments beat vows.

The first step is noticing. Noticing sounds simple until you try. Most people cannot accurately describe how they spend a typical workday, because attention is discontinuous and memory is selective. We remember the high points and the stressful moments; we forget the dozens of little detours. This is why time leaks persist. They are experienced as "just a minute" events, which is the most dangerous category of time because it seems too small to address. The quarter is an appropriate window here because you do not need perfect data; you need a truthful impression of typical days and repeated patterns.

A useful concept from cognitive psychology is task switching cost. Switching tasks is not free. The mind needs time to reorient, retrieve context, and rebuild the mental model of what you were doing.

Research by Rubinstein, Meyer, and Evans (2001), among others, examined executive control of task switching and found measurable performance costs when people switch between tasks. You do not need the lab details to feel the truth of it. You feel it when you stop writing to answer an email and then return to the writing and stare at the screen as if you have forgotten your own language. A time leak is often not the two minutes you spent responding. It is the ten minutes it took to re-enter what you were doing.

Re-entry is the tax.

A second psychological mechanism is intermittent reinforcement: rewards that arrive unpredictably tend to produce persistent checking behaviour. This is a principle known from behavioural psychology and is often invoked to explain why people repeatedly check for messages, likes, and updates. When the reward is uncertain—maybe there's something important, maybe there's praise, maybe there's bad news—the urge to check becomes stronger, not weaker. You do not need to be a lab rat pressing a lever to recognise the pattern. Email is a variable reward system. Messaging apps are variable reward systems. Social media is a variable reward system. The leak is not simply "wasting time". It is participating in a reinforcement loop.

Loops can be interrupted.

Interrupting them does not require a complex productivity doctrine. It requires identifying the loop's cue and redesigning the boundary. The quarterly approach deliberately favours simple boundaries over elaborate rules because elaborate rules create a second problem: maintenance overhead. If your boundary system is complicated, it becomes another form of admin, which is itself a time leak. Simple boundaries are easier to implement and easier to test. They also create clearer evidence. If you change one boundary for a quarter and observe what happens, you learn. If you change ten things, you merely suffer.

Learning is the point.

The practical method for noticing leaks begins with recalling a typical day in enough detail to see the seams. Not the ideal day. Not the exceptional day. The typical one. When do you first look at your phone? When do you first open email? How often do you switch windows while doing a task? When do you feel the urge to check something? Which moments trigger it—boredom, anxiety, uncertainty, waiting, fatigue? These questions translate abstraction into behaviour. "Distraction" becomes: opening email between tasks. "Admin" becomes: small, unbounded tasks performed without a defined stop. "Anxiety" becomes: checking for updates after sending a message. Once you can name the behaviour, you can design a boundary around it.

A boundary is a decision, not a mood.

One of the most common leaks is constant email checking. It is common because it feels responsible. Many people treat the inbox as the centre of work, as though productivity equals responsiveness. In some roles, responsiveness is indeed important. The leak arises when responsiveness expands beyond need and becomes an anxious reflex. The evidence is behavioural: checking email repeatedly even when no urgent messages are expected, responding immediately to non-urgent items, using the inbox as a way of avoiding more cognitively demanding tasks. This is not laziness. It is avoidance mediated by plausibility. Email feels like work. Deep tasks feel risky.

Risk drives leakage.

The mind prefers tasks with immediate closure. Replying to an email can be completed in minutes. Writing a report or analysing data or designing a plan cannot. These tasks require sustained uncertainty, and uncertainty feels like risk. The leak is therefore partly emotional. A quarterly experiment must respect that. If you simply vow "no email", you are likely to fail because you have not addressed the anxiety and the need for closure that email provides. A simpler approach is to change the checking rhythm. Not to eliminate, but to contain. Containment is what turns a leak into a managed channel.

Another leak is vague admin. Admin is the workplace equivalent of "I'll just tidy up". It expands until it fills the day. The clue is the lack of definition: "I need to sort out some paperwork," "I'll catch up on bits," "I'll clear my inbox," "I'll organise my files." These tasks are infinite because they are not tasks; they are categories. Categories have no endpoint. A quarterly experiment for admin leaks involves turning categories into bounded actions: a specific subset, a specific time window, a specific stopping rule. Without a stopping rule, admin devours everything.

A third leak is social media loops and news grazing. Many intelligent people use these as short breaks and then discover that the break has eaten fifteen minutes and left them feeling more scattered. The loop is reinforced by novelty. Novelty is a reward. It gives the brain a quick hit of stimulation, which is especially tempting when you are tired or stuck. The quarter is a good unit for testing changes here because it allows you to observe how small shifts in access and timing change the overall feel of the day. The aim is not abstinence. It is to stop letting the feed decide when your attention rests.

Attention deserves governance.

A named, checkable example of how information abundance can overwhelm attention comes from Herbert A. Simon, who in 1971 wrote that "a wealth of information creates a poverty of attention" (Simon, 1971). This is a crisp diagnosis. It is also a warning that remains relevant. If attention is scarce, then the most important skill is not acquiring more information, but allocating attention intentionally. Time leaks are failures of allocation. They are not failures of intelligence. They are what happens when the environment is built to harvest attention and when work cultures confuse busyness with value.

A second example sits in the realm of workplace communication. The proliferation of internal messaging tools in the 2010s and 2020s created new norms of rapid response. In many organisations, messages are treated as quasi-urgent simply because they arrive instantly. This is a cultural shift, not an individual choice. The individual experiences it as pressure: if you do not respond quickly, you appear disengaged. The time leak arises when you respond quickly to everything, sacrificing deep work. The quarterly approach allows you to test a boundary that is socially defensible because it is framed around project delivery rather than personal preference: you are protecting focus so that work can be completed.

Still, there is a limitation: some roles genuinely require high responsiveness. Customer support, incident response, clinical environments, certain managerial roles—these are built around rapid communication. In such roles, time leaks can still exist, but the solution cannot be to ignore messages. The reconciliation is to distinguish between necessary responsiveness and compulsive checking. Even in high-responsiveness roles, there are often patterns that can be adjusted: handoffs, rotation, defined on-call periods, clear escalation paths. The quarterly review can identify which parts of responsiveness are genuinely required and which are the residue of anxiety or unclear boundaries.

Clarity reduces anxiety.

This is why the quarterly method emphasises choosing one or two leaks rather than trying to "be more focused" in general. Focus is too abstract to manage. A leak is concrete. You can observe it. You can measure it in simple ways without turning your life into a time-tracking experiment. "How many times did I check email before lunch?" "How often did I switch tasks during a writing block?" "How many evenings did I intend to read and instead scroll?" These are behavioural counts. They make the leak visible. Visibility makes intervention possible.

The intervention should be modest.

A modest intervention is one that changes the environment slightly and makes the desired behaviour easier than the undesired one. This principle is supported by a broad behavioural science tradition that emphasises choice architecture—how environments influence decisions. The details vary across domains, but the common idea is that small frictions and cues can significantly affect behaviour. You do not need to redesign your personality. You redesign your default. If the default is to check, you add friction. If the default is to drift, you add structure. If the default is to do admin endlessly, you add a stop rule.

Stop rules matter.

The motif for this subchapter is the bucket under the leak. A bucket does not fix the pipe, but it stops the damage spreading while you diagnose. Your quarterly experiments are buckets: small containers that catch attention before it floods the day. The bucket might be a defined email window, a boundary around messaging, a specific admin block with a hard stop, a designated break routine that is not a feed, a physical change such as keeping the phone out of reach during focused work. The specifics will vary. The logic is consistent: catch the leak, then see what happens.

What happens is often surprising. When you reduce checking, you may discover that many messages were not urgent. When you bound admin, you may discover that much of it was avoidant activity. When you limit social media loops, you may discover that your boredom was a cue for fatigue, not a need for novelty. These discoveries are not self-help revelations. They are operational findings. They help you design your next quarter with more realism.

Realism is the hidden gift.

The forward test is therefore sharp and practical. When you recall a typical day from the last quarter and identify the moments where time disappeared without trace, which single leak—email checking, vague admin, notification-driven messaging, or a feed loop—would be most worth catching for ninety days, and what simple boundary could you commit to that would be easy to explain, easy to repeat, and easy to observe?

Planning sprints and slack

In July 2012, at CERN near Geneva, Switzerland, physicists announced the observation of a new particle consistent with the Higgs boson. The press remembered the applause and the graphs, yet the operational reality was less glamorous and more instructive: long periods of painstaking work punctuated by intense phases of data-taking and analysis, all bounded by scheduled runs, shutdowns, maintenance windows, and collaborative review. The Large Hadron

Collider did not run at full intensity indefinitely. It could not. The machine required planned stops; the people required recovery; the science required pacing.

Pacing makes discovery possible.

Knowledge work rarely admits this. Many professional calendars behave as though the correct pace is "high" at all times. The quarter is packed with deadlines, meetings, and "just one more thing". There is no planned off-ramp, only collapse, holiday guilt, or a sudden illness that forces a stop. When work is arranged as an unbroken stretch of pressure, the nervous system adapts in predictable ways: it becomes vigilant, reactive, impatient, and depleted. The mind still functions, but it becomes narrower. It begins to prefer the easy and the urgent over the difficult and the important. This is the hidden cost of constant intensity. A sprint-and-slack plan is an attempt to reverse that cost by giving intensity a container and giving recovery a place.

Containers reduce panic.

A sprint is a deliberately short period of concentrated effort on a defined piece of work. Slack is the deliberately protected space around that effort: lighter weeks, fewer commitments, time for integration, maintenance, and recovery. The two belong together. A sprint without slack becomes simply more pressure. Slack without sprints can become drift. The quarterly rhythm is suited to combining them because it is long enough to include multiple phases and short enough to maintain urgency without desperation. Properly designed, a quarter becomes a sequence: focus, breathe, focus, breathe. It starts to resemble a life rather than a treadmill.

Life requires breathing.

The idea has historical precedent. Industrial systems learned, sometimes painfully, that machines and people cannot operate at peak output continuously without breakdown. Modern project management learned a similar lesson. Agile methods, popularised in software development in the early 2000s, are often caricatured as a set of rituals. Their deeper claim is more interesting: work should be done in time-boxed cycles with reflection and adjustment built in. The Agile Manifesto was published in 2001 by a group of software practitioners in Utah (Agile Manifesto, 2001). The manifesto is not scripture, and its corporate misuses are legion. Yet the underlying logic—short, bounded phases of focused work—remains sound. It is essentially quarterly thinking compressed into weeks.

Bounded work exposes reality.

When you time-box a sprint, you are forced to decide what "done" could mean within the time available. That decision is not merely tactical. It is philosophical. It forces you to confront the gap between ambition and capacity. Most professional stress comes from refusing to confront that gap. People carry unlimited ambition inside limited weeks. They respond by working longer, fragmenting attention, and accepting chronic anxiety as normal. A sprint makes the limit explicit. It says: within this window, what can we actually complete? That question is not defeatist. It is the foundation of reliable progress.

Reliable progress builds trust.

Trust, in work, is a behavioural outcome. It emerges when you complete what you said you would complete, when you communicate clearly, when you avoid perpetual "nearly". A sprint improves trust because it narrows commitments. It also reduces the temptation to accept every request. When you have planned sprints, you can see that adding new work is not free; it displaces something. Displacement is usually hidden. A sprint makes displacement visible.

Visibility reduces self-deception.

The most common self-deception is planning as if every week will be the same. It will not. Quarters contain predictable variability: holidays, conferences, school terms, intense business cycles, publication deadlines, seasonal illness, family commitments. Planning sprints and slack means respecting that variability rather than fighting it. It means placing sprints in weeks where focus is plausible and placing slack around them not as an afterthought but as a necessary structural element. Slack is where maintenance happens: clearing time leaks, preparing for the next phase, finishing small tasks that accumulate, recovering sleep, reducing backlog. Slack is also where thinking deepens. Many of the best ideas arrive not during frantic execution but during the quieter spaces around it.

Space is a creative tool.

This is not romanticism. It is supported by what we know about cognitive performance. Sustained attention is costly, and recovery matters. A large body of research in occupational health psychology has examined recovery from work stress, including the role of psychological detachment and rest in maintaining wellbeing and performance (Sonnentag & Fritz, 2007). The details of the literature are varied, but the directional implication is clear: without recovery, performance and health degrade. The quarter, therefore, should not be planned as continuous exertion. It should be planned as exertion with recovery built in.

Built in means scheduled.

Many professionals treat recovery as something that happens if there is time. There is rarely time. The calendar will fill to the edges of your availability because other people's needs and institutional rhythms will happily consume it. This is why slack must be protected intentionally. Slack is not the absence of work. It is the absence of high-stakes commitments. It is time with lower intensity and higher flexibility. It allows you to respond to unexpected demands without destroying the quarter's core objectives. It also reduces the sense of being trapped, which is one of the psychological ingredients of burnout.

Burnout is often a calendar design problem.

A named, checkable example of planned slack in a high-performance context comes from aviation maintenance cycles. Airlines schedule aircraft for regular maintenance checks and take them out of service at defined intervals. The intervals are structured because the cost of unplanned failure is enormous. Again, humans are not aircraft, but the analogy is instructive: systems that matter plan for maintenance. Many professionals plan for deadlines but not for recovery. That imbalance is irrational. It assumes that you can indefinitely extend exertion without consequences. The quarterly sprint-and-slack model is a way of correcting that assumption.

It corrects another assumption too: that productivity equals constant motion. In reality, concentrated effort often produces more progress than prolonged busyness. When you plan a sprint, you create conditions for concentration: fewer meetings, clearer priorities, less multitasking. Concentration produces output. Output reduces mental load. Reduced mental load increases the capacity to think. The system begins to compound.

Compounding is the theme of the book.

Planning sprints and slack is therefore not a time-management trick. It is an anti-drift strategy. Drift in work is the tendency for your week to be governed by other people's requests, by recurring commitments, by reactive loops. Sprints reassert authorship: they create periods where your priorities govern your time. Slack prevents sprints from becoming self-destructive: it ensures that intensity is bounded. Together, they create a quarter that feels deliberate.

Deliberate quarters feel lighter.

A credible counter-example must be acknowledged. Not every role allows neat sprints. Some work is inherently interrupt-driven: emergency response, clinical roles, support desks, managerial firefighting. In such roles, a sprint can feel like a fantasy. The reconciliation is to redefine the sprint's unit. A sprint does not have to mean uninterrupted days. It can mean a protected block within the week, or a defined focus theme that guides decisions even amidst interruptions. Slack, too, may not be full weeks. It may be lighter days, reduced optional commitments, or planned coverage rotations. The principle is not rigid scheduling. The principle is bounded intensity. Even reactive systems benefit from boundedness; without it, people burn out and the system becomes less responsive.

Boundaries sustain responsiveness.

Another limitation is human psychology. Some people fear slack because slack feels like falling behind. They are addicted to urgency. Urgency provides a clear narrative: "I'm busy, therefore I'm important, therefore I'm safe." Slack threatens that narrative. It introduces a quieter question: what do you do when you are not busy? This can be unsettling. Yet the quarterly approach is designed for precisely this discomfort. It does not ask for endless slack. It asks for enough slack to recover and integrate. It asks you to tolerate quiet for long enough that you can think. Thinking is often what frantic people have lost.

Thinking produces strategy.

Sprints also require a certain ruthlessness about scope. Scope creep is not merely a project management term; it is a psychological habit. People add small extras because they want to do good work, because they fear criticism, because they dislike leaving things imperfect. The extras accumulate until the sprint collapses. The quarterly ritual helps by framing sprints as experiments rather than as definitive statements of competence. You are testing what can be done within a window. Testing invites honesty. It allows you to adjust next quarter based on evidence rather than guilt.

Evidence here is behavioural: did the sprint produce a meaningful outcome? Did it require unsustainable effort? Did it displace health and relationships? Did slack actually occur, or was it consumed by reactive work? These questions link directly back to the book's other domains. Work is not isolated. A sprint that trashes sleep is not a success; it is a debt. Slack that never happens is not slack; it is a story. The quarterly view forces you to reconcile these truths because the consequences show up within ninety days.

Ninety days is close enough.

The motif for this subchapter is the bellows. A forge uses bellows to intensify heat, then relaxes. Without the in-and-out rhythm, the fire either dies or becomes uncontrollable. Work is a forge. Sprints are the compression: the directed heat that transforms raw effort into output. Slack is the release: the breathing space that prevents the system from overheating and allows you to prepare the next piece. The bellows image resists two errors at once: the belief that you can forge without heat, and the belief that you can keep the heat high forever.

Both beliefs are costly.

The forward test is therefore not a motivational question. It is a design question. Looking at your upcoming quarter as it truly is—its deadlines, its predictable busy periods, its unavoidable obligations—where could you place one short sprint on a key project, and what specific slack would you need to protect on either side so that the sprint produces progress rather than merely more pressure?

Chapter 7
Learning and Skills Roadmap

In the summer of 1609, in Padua in the Republic of Venice, Galileo Galilei adjusted a device that had recently arrived in Europe from the Netherlands and aimed it at the night sky. The telescope was not his invention, yet the skill that mattered was: he learned to use it, to refine it, to interpret what it revealed, and to insist—against the grain of authority—that observation should outrank inherited certainty. His published *Sidereus Nuncius* followed in March 1610, and with it a new kind of intellectual leverage entered the world: the ability to see, measure, and argue from evidence rather than from habit.

Skills change what is visible.

This is the promise and the danger of modern learning culture. The promise is that almost any skill appears accessible. A video, a course, a community, an app, a book, a tutorial: the shelf is infinite and the entry cost is low. The danger is that infinite shelves produce shallow acquisition. People collect beginnings. They subscribe, enrol, bookmark, and plan. They keep learning on the level of intention. They feel busy with self-improvement and remain oddly unchanged. They mistake information for capability. Capability is different. Capability is what you can do under pressure, in the real world, when no one is marking you.

No one marks you here.

This chapter treats learning as an Upgrade Day domain not because learning is another box to tick, but because skill is one of the few levers that genuinely expands options over time. Money can cushion. Health can stabilise. Relationships can sustain. Work can shape your days. Skills change your trajectory. They alter the problems you can solve, the work you can take on, the conversations you can join, the confidence you carry. They also compound. A modest improvement repeated quarter by quarter turns into a different life in a few years, not through dramatic transformation but through gradual widening of possibility.

Possibility is not a mood.

It is a set of doors you can actually open. The contemporary problem is that too many people pursue skills in a fog of general aspiration. They want to "learn data science", "get better at writing", "become fluent", "understand finance", "pick up a new language", "learn to code", "get fit". These are respectable desires. They are also, in their raw form, poorly designed. They invite endless consumption. They invite comparison. They invite self-reproach. Above all, they invite diffusion: taking small bites of many things and swallowing none.

Diffusion feels like progress.

It rarely is. The central idea of this chapter is that learning needs the same anti-drift discipline as the rest of your life. If you do not choose, learning will default to whatever is most available and most seductive. Availability is not relevance. Seduction is not mastery. The quarter is an ideal unit for learning precisely because it sits in the sweet spot between novelty and depth. It is long enough to practise, to struggle, to make mistakes, to apply a skill in real contexts. It is short enough to maintain momentum, to observe results, and to change course if the chosen skill is not delivering what you hoped.

The first movement of this chapter is clarifying priority skills. Priority skills are not simply what you find interesting. They are the skills that change your options if improved: the ability to write clearly, to present, to analyse data, to negotiate, to code, to manage projects, to speak a language, to design, to teach, to think statistically, to manage attention, to learn faster. The list is long. That is the point. If you do not narrow it deliberately, you will scatter your effort across too many targets. Scattered effort produces shallow competence and persistent dissatisfaction. Narrowing does not mean you give up curiosity. It means you accept that you have a limited number of quarters in a year and an even more limited number of hours in a week.

Hours matter more than ambition.

The next movement is designing a skills roadmap. Roadmaps are usually associated with product teams and strategic plans. The concept transfers beautifully to learning because it forces the translation from vague desire to quarterly-sized commitments. A roadmap breaks a skill into chunks that can be practised and demonstrated. It replaces "get fluent" with something like "hold three fifteen-minute conversations on a specific topic" or "complete three small writing projects in a particular style" or "build two simple scripts that automate a task". The exact targets will vary. The important shift is from identity language to evidence language. Identity language says "I am becoming someone who…" Evidence language says "I made this; I did this; I can now do this reliably."

Reliability is the real prize.

The third movement is choosing learning vehicles. Modern culture has an odd superstition: that learning requires enrolment. Enrolment is sometimes useful. It provides structure, deadlines, and social reinforcement. It also creates a consumer relationship with learning, where progress is measured by completion rather than by capability. This chapter treats courses as one vehicle among many. Books can be vehicles. Mentors can be vehicles. Communities can be vehicles. Practice routines can be vehicles. Apprenticeship, feedback loops, deliberate repetition, and small projects are often more powerful than any course because they force application. The quarter is where vehicles are selected with realism: matching learning methods to time available, temperament, and context, with one primary vehicle and one backup so learning does not collapse when life interrupts.

Life will interrupt.

Which brings us to the final movement: tracking progress lightly. Learning is vulnerable to two distortions. One is neglect: learning becomes a "someday" aspiration that is always postponed. The other is perfectionism: learning becomes another arena for self-punishment, an endless contest against imagined experts, a metric you use to judge your worth. The chapter aims for a third path: light tracking that supports engagement without turning learning into performance. Light tracking is not about counting hours for the sake of counting. It is about noticing whether you are practising, whether you are applying, whether your work is improving, whether the skill is showing up in your life. It is reflection with a purpose: to keep learning alive and honest.

Honesty is especially important now.

We live in a period where skill signals are easily faked. Credentials proliferate. Portfolios can be polished. AI tools can assist with output in ways that complicate what "ability" even means. This is not a moral panic; it is a reality to be navigated. Skills that matter are those you can deploy with understanding, not just those you can produce with help. The chapter does not take a dogmatic stance against tools. It treats tools as part of the landscape. The question is how you remain the person who can judge, adapt, and apply—who can tell whether something is correct, coherent, ethical, and fit for purpose. That kind of judgement is a skill. It is cultivated through practice, feedback, and reflection, not through passive consumption.

Consumption is not learning.

Modern relevance also shows up in the emotional economy of learning. Many adults feel behind. They watch younger colleagues with new technical skills, peers with polished careers, creators with visible outputs. They feel a quiet panic that if they do not continuously upskill, they will become obsolete. Panic is a poor teacher. It drives shallow learning and frantic course-hopping. A quarterly roadmap offers a calmer alternative: consistent, deliberate improvement paced to a real life. It refuses the false binary of either relentless self-improvement or stagnation. It suggests a third posture: steady cultivation.

Cultivation requires patience.

There is also a philosophical underpinning worth naming. Skills are not merely instrumental. They shape how you perceive the world. A person who learns statistics begins to see uncertainty differently. A person who learns a language begins to think with different categories. A person who learns to write well begins to recognise sloppy thinking. A person who learns to draw begins to notice light and proportion. Skills change perception, and changed perception changes choice. This is why learning is not a hobby on the side. It is a way of altering your mind's relationship with reality.

And yet, there is a limit that keeps this chapter honest. Not all learning is equal, and not all learning can be sustained in every season. People have caregiving responsibilities. People have health constraints. People have demanding jobs. People have unpredictable lives. The quarterly approach does not pretend otherwise. It does not ask for heroic study schedules. It asks for realistic learning commitments that can survive real quarters. It also accepts that some quarters will be light. Light quarters are not failure. They are seasons. The roadmap remains flexible because it is designed to be used, not admired.

Used means integrated.

A quiet motif threads through this chapter: the compass. A compass does not tell you where to walk in exact detail, but it tells you whether you are drifting. In a world of infinite learning options, the compass is your priority skill list and your quarterly roadmap. It keeps you oriented when the course catalogue seduces, when the online world floods you with "must-learn" trends, when your own curiosity pulls you in ten directions. The compass does not kill curiosity. It keeps curiosity from becoming distraction.

The momentum at the end of this introduction is therefore not about becoming a polymath overnight. It is about becoming deliberate. When you clarify priority skills, break them into quarter-sized targets, choose vehicles that suit your life, and track progress lightly, learning stops being a guilty aspiration and becomes a quiet engine of change. The question that follows is the one that matters: if you could improve just one skill over the next ninety days—one that would noticeably expand your options—what would you choose, and what would you be willing to produce, in public or in private, to prove to yourself that you are not merely consuming knowledge but becoming more capable?

Clarifying priority skills

In 1858, in London, Florence Nightingale sat amid paper, ink, and the sour smell of damp wool from hospital corridors that still clung to her memory. That year she published *Notes on Matters Affecting the Health, Efficiency, and Hospital Administration of the British Army*, a report that did something quietly revolutionary: it used statistics and clear visual presentation to force decision-makers to see what they preferred to ignore. Nightingale's influence did not rest on moral fervour alone. It rested on a skill that changed her options. She could measure, compare, and persuade with evidence.

Skills make reality negotiable.

The modern temptation is to treat "learning" as a pleasant blur: a course here, a book there, a podcast in the background, a saved thread for later. The blur can feel like virtue. It can even feel like progress. Yet capability does not arrive by osmosis. Capability arrives when a particular skill—one that bites into the real texture of your work and life—becomes reliable enough to use under ordinary pressure. The difference between "I'm interested in this" and "I can do this" is the difference between entertainment and power. Clarifying priority skills is the act of choosing where you want more power.

Choose fewer. Gain more.

That sentence can sound severe, as though the aim is to narrow a life into pure instrumentality. It is not. Narrowing is a way of respecting the brutal arithmetic of time. You can admire fifty skills. You can only build a handful at once. This is where drift sneaks into learning: the slow accumulation of half-started ambitions that never become part of you. Each new course adds a quiet obligation. Each new "I should learn…" becomes a low-grade debt. Debt is tiring. Capability is energising. The point of clarifying priority skills is to stop accumulating learning debt and start accumulating usable competence.

A usable skill has a particular property: it changes the range of problems you can solve. This is what made Nightingale's statistical fluency so consequential. She did not merely acquire knowledge about hospitals; she acquired a method for turning messy reality into a case that could survive scepticism. She could turn suffering into numbers, and numbers into reform. That is option expansion. It is also a clue for how to choose priorities. A priority skill is not necessarily the skill you find most charming in the abstract. It is the skill that makes more actions possible with less friction.

Friction is the enemy.

A second, checkable example shows the same mechanism in a different century. In 1998, in Princeton, New Jersey, mathematician Andrew Wiles published, with Richard Taylor, the proof of Fermat's Last Theorem after years of work. The popular myth is of solitary genius. The more practical lesson is about skill selection and depth. Wiles did not dabble across a dozen unrelated domains. He committed to a narrow band of methods—elliptic curves, modular forms, the deep machinery of modern number theory—and sustained that commitment long enough for it to become a private language he could think in. He built an internal toolkit so rich that it allowed him to attempt what had previously been impossible for him. That is another form of option expansion: the ability to tackle a class of problems that, without the skill, is simply inaccessible.

Depth opens locked doors.

Most people are not proving theorems. The principle still holds. A priority skill is one that unlocks doors in your own life: a door to better work, to clearer thinking, to more compelling communication, to greater autonomy, to more meaningful contribution. Unlocking can be professional, creative, or practical. It can be as concrete as the ability to automate a repetitive task, as subtle as the ability to read a contract carefully, as social as the ability to have difficult conversations without collapsing into defensiveness. The domain matters less than the effect: the skill changes what you can do next.

This is why the question "What should I learn?" is often the wrong question. It invites shopping. The better question is "Which constraint keeps showing up?" Constraints are where skill has leverage. If your work stalls because you cannot write clearly, then writing is not a hobby; it is a bottleneck. If your projects spread because you cannot prioritise and say no, then boundary-setting is not a personality quirk; it is a missing skill. If your health goals collapse because you cannot plan recovery, then planning is not admin; it is scaffolding for your body. When you identify a repeating constraint, you stop treating learning as aspiration and start treating it as engineering.

Engineering requires criteria, even if you never formalise them. The first criterion is transfer. A priority skill travels across contexts. Writing travels. Statistical thinking travels. Negotiation travels. Clear speaking travels. The ability to run small experiments travels. These skills are not tied to one employer, one tool, or one trend. They remain useful when the surface conditions change. In a world where job titles mutate and technologies age quickly, transferability is a kind of intellectual insurance.

Insurance is a dull word for a powerful idea: the skill should keep paying you back. That leads to the second criterion: compounding. A compounding skill makes future learning faster or more effective. Learning how to learn—how to practise deliberately, seek feedback, and iterate—compounds. Clear thinking compounds because it reduces error. Communication compounds because it increases the return on everything you know. Mathematical and statistical literacy compounds because it improves judgement under uncertainty. These skills do not merely add; they multiply the value of what you already have.

Judgement is a skill.

The third criterion is feedback. A priority skill should be trainable, which usually means it offers feedback you can actually notice. Writing offers feedback because readers react, edits reveal weaknesses, clarity can be tested. Programming offers feedback because code runs or fails. Speaking offers feedback because audiences understand or don't. Some skills offer slower feedback—leadership, taste, research judgement—but they still offer feedback if you design for it: mentors, peer review, reflective practice, outcomes tracked over time. Skills without feedback become fantasies. People can "study" them indefinitely without improving.

The fourth criterion is relevance to the life you are actually living. A skill can be glamorous and irrelevant. Relevance is not about what is fashionable; it is about what your days demand. If you spend much of your week coordinating people, then communication and planning carry disproportionate weight. If you spend your week analysing information, then quantitative reasoning and critical reading matter. If you spend your week creating—writing, designing, building—then taste and craft matter. Priority skills are not picked in a vacuum. They are picked against your calendar, your responsibilities, your ambitions, and your constraints.

Ambition needs grounding.

Grounding does not mean settling. It means choosing a skill that is just beyond your current competence rather than light-years away. When a skill is too distant, the learning path becomes vague, and vagueness becomes avoidance. When a skill is adjacent—close enough to touch—practice becomes easier to integrate, and improvement becomes observable within a quarter. This is not a claim about human limits. It is a claim about motivation as a fragile resource. People persist when they can feel movement. They quit when effort produces no visible change.

Visible change is not always dramatic. Sometimes it is small: you write one email that is cleaner than usual; you present a finding without rambling; you build a tiny tool that saves twenty minutes a week; you read a paper and actually evaluate its claims rather than merely absorbing its tone. Small changes matter because they signal that the skill is becoming yours. This is the psychological hinge of priority skill selection. You are not choosing a skill because you want to impress someone. You are choosing it because you want to change the felt texture of your own competence.

There is a trap here: the seduction of breadth. Breadth looks open-minded. Breadth can also be a way of avoiding the discomfort of depth. Depth requires boredom, repetition, and the humiliation of being bad at something for longer than you would like. Breadth offers novelty. Novelty feels like progress. Novelty is often merely movement. The quarter is your ally against the novelty trap because it creates a natural boundary: long enough to go past the honeymoon phase, short enough that commitment does not feel like a life sentence. Clarifying priority skills is the choice to spend a quarter on depth rather than a week on novelty.

Still, a credible limitation deserves a clear place. Not all learning should be prioritised. Some learning is properly exploratory. The mind needs play. Curiosity matters. Many breakthroughs—creative and scientific—begin as wandering rather than as disciplined roadmaps. If you force every learning impulse into a utilitarian frame, you risk turning your mind into a factory and losing the very liveliness that makes learning worthwhile. The reconciliation is to separate exploration from priority. Exploration can exist, but it should be named as exploration so it does not masquerade as a promise. Priority skills are the ones you expect to practise consistently and apply. Exploratory learning can remain light, opportunistic, and joy-led. The problem is not curiosity. The problem is pretending that twenty curiosities are twenty commitments.

Commitment has a cost.

That cost is not only time. It is attention and identity. When you say "I'm learning X," you begin to build a self-image around it. If the learning never becomes real capability, the identity becomes slightly fraudulent, and the mind knows it. This is one reason people feel oddly tired by self-improvement culture: it encourages identity acquisition without capability acquisition. Clarifying priority skills is a refusal of that fraud. It says: choose fewer skills, practise them in ways that produce evidence, and let identity follow competence rather than precede it.

Evidence can be surprisingly simple. It can be a small artefact: a short essay, a cleaned dataset, a presentation, a prototype, a translation, a lesson taught, a difficult conversation handled well. Artefacts are powerful because they make skill visible. They also create feedback. When you can point to something you produced, you can assess it, improve it, share it, or discard it. Learning without artefacts is prone to self-deception because it is all internal. Internal progress is real, but it is easy to exaggerate. Artefacts keep you honest.

Honesty is kind.

The quiet motif to hold this subchapter together is the compass needle. A compass needle does not tell you where to build your house. It tells you when you are drifting. The modern learning environment is magnetic in the worst sense: it pulls attention towards what is new, popular, and endless. A clarified set of priority skills is your compass needle. When a new course appears, the needle twitches: does this align with the skills you chose, or is it merely another shiny detour? When you feel behind, the needle steadies: you are not trying to learn everything; you are trying to learn what matters. When you are tempted to abandon a skill because it is uncomfortable, the needle reminds you: discomfort is part of depth.

The compass needle also prevents a subtler form of drift: confusing skill with tool. Tools change fast. Skills endure. People often say they want to "learn Excel" or "learn Photoshop" or "learn a particular software package". Sometimes that is necessary. More often, the underlying skill is what matters: data thinking, visual communication, design judgement, workflow automation. If you choose the tool as the priority, you risk learning something brittle. If you choose the underlying skill, tools become replaceable implementations. This is not snobbery. It is resilience.

Resilience is the point.

Clarifying priority skills, then, is not an academic exercise. It is a way of protecting your learning life from the same forces that distort your money, health, and work: drift, overload, and the false comfort of activity. It asks you to choose a small number of skills that expand your options, compound over time, offer feedback, and fit your actual constraints. It asks you to stop confusing consumption with practice. It asks you to let the compass needle guide you through noise.

The forward test is deliberately sharp. Looking at the next ninety days as they truly are—your calendar, your energy, your responsibilities—what single constraint keeps repeating in your work or life, and which one skill, if strengthened, would most reliably loosen that constraint, even if the practice is awkward and the proof must be earned rather than declared?

Designing skills roadmap

In March 1913, in Highland Park, Michigan, Henry Ford's engineers and managers introduced a moving assembly line for the Model T. The detail that matters is not the mythology of industrial genius, but the method: complex work was broken into stages, each stage made visible, each step sized to be repeatable. The result was not simply "faster cars". It was predictability. A process that could be repeated could be improved.

Learning works the same way.

Most people do not fail at learning because they lack intelligence or curiosity. They fail because the skill they want is too large to hold. "Become fluent." "Master coding." "Get good at public speaking." These phrases are not goals. They are fog. Fog feels inspiring at the beginning because it hides the distance. Fog becomes demoralising later because it hides the path. A skills roadmap is the opposite of fog. It is staged learning: a way of breaking a priority skill into quarter-sized chunks that can be practised, demonstrated, and revised, so progress becomes visible rather than mythical.

Visibility changes behaviour.

When a goal is vague, you cannot tell whether you are doing the right things. You respond by consuming more: another course, another book, another tutorial. Consumption becomes a substitute for practice because it offers the feeling of forward motion without the discomfort of exposure. A roadmap forces exposure. It insists that each quarter contains something you can produce or perform that demonstrates movement in the skill. Demonstration is not about showing off. It is about creating evidence for yourself. Evidence protects you from the two classic learning distortions: the delusion of progress through consumption and the despair of progress you cannot see.

A quarter is long enough to make evidence.

It is also short enough to impose design discipline. The quarter prevents the common trap of writing a "learning plan" that assumes perfect weeks forever. A quarterly roadmap asks for modest targets that fit real lives. Modest is not trivial. Modest means sized to be completed even when the quarter contains illness, deadlines, family obligations, and ordinary fatigue. A roadmap that collapses under ordinary life is not ambitious. It is naïve. Naïveté produces self-reproach, which kills learning faster than any shortage of time.

Self-reproach is a poor tutor.

A roadmap begins with a shift in how you think about skills. A skill is not a topic. A skill is a capability that shows up in behaviour. "Statistics" is a topic. "Estimate uncertainty and interpret evidence" is a skill. "French" is a topic. "Hold a ten-minute conversation about work without switching into English" is a skill. "Coding" is a topic. "Write a small script that cleans a dataset and produces a chart" is a skill. When you reframe this way, the road becomes buildable, because behaviour can be staged. Topics cannot.

Staging also helps you avoid a subtle trap: confusing competence with confidence. Many people feel more confident after consuming information and assume that confidence equals ability. It does not. Skills are best assessed not by how you feel, but by what you can do when it counts. The roadmap therefore needs to include performance moments, even small ones, because performance reveals what you actually know. A quarter-sized learning chunk should have an output, a trial, or a demonstration that makes the skill real.

Make it real. Then refine.

A named, checkable example of staged learning at scale comes from language proficiency frameworks used in education and professional settings. The Common European Framework of Reference for Languages (CEFR), first published in 2001 by the Council of Europe, describes language ability across levels and emphasises what learners can do—speaking, listening, reading, writing—in increasingly complex contexts (Council of Europe, 2001). You do not need to adopt the CEFR levels. The interesting point is the architecture: capability is described in stages, and stages are defined by observable performance. That is roadmapping. It turns "learn a language" into a sequence of demonstrable abilities.

A second example comes from craft rather than bureaucracy. In the Bauhaus school, founded in 1919 in Weimar, Germany, students moved through structured training that emphasised making—materials, form, function—before specialising (Bauhaus, 1919 onwards; the dates and location are easy to verify). The Bauhaus method was not about consuming design theory. It was about developing skill through staged practice and feedback. Again, you do not need to become a Bauhaus student. The lesson is that roadmaps are not modern corporate inventions. They are how serious learning has long worked: deliberate sequences of practice, with outputs that can be judged.

Judgement requires criteria.

A skills roadmap therefore needs a way of turning a priority skill into a quarter's theme. The theme should answer two questions. What will be practised? What will be produced? Practise without production risks endless rehearsal. Production without practice risks stress and shallow results. The theme links the two. If the skill is writing, the theme might be "short argumentative essays" or "clear executive summaries" or "narrative case studies". If the skill is data analysis, the theme might be "repeatable analysis notebooks" or "visualising trends for decision-making". If the skill is public speaking, the theme might be "structured talks with clear openings" or "handling questions without rambling". Themes are not slogans. They are constraints that make practice design possible.

Constraints are liberating.

Once you have a theme, you can size targets to the quarter. This is where modesty matters. A quarter is not a lifetime. It is roughly thirteen weeks. The human mistake is to plan as if all thirteen will be free and productive. They will not. A realistic roadmap assumes fewer effective weeks. It also assumes that practice will be uneven. The roadmap's job is not to eliminate unevenness; it is to keep the skill alive through unevenness. That is why targets such as "complete three practice projects" work so well. Three is small enough to finish. Three is large enough to create repetition. Repetition is how the nervous system learns.

Learning is biological.

Skills become reliable when patterns are encoded through repeated, varied practice. Cognitive science and expertise research have explored this extensively. Anders Ericsson's work on deliberate practice, popularised in the 1990s and 2000s, emphasised that expert performance is often built through structured practice with feedback rather than through mere experience (Ericsson, Krampe & Tesch-Römer, 1993). The literature has debates and nuances, but the implication for a quarterly roadmap is straightforward: practice needs structure, and structure needs targets that fit time. A roadmap does not need to turn your life into training camp. It does need to ensure that the skill is practised often enough for learning to stick.

Sticking is the aim.

This is where the quarter is superior to the vague annual ambition. Annual skill goals encourage procrastination because the deadline is distant. Weekly plans can be too granular; they collapse when life interrupts and can make learning feel like another administrative burden. The quarter provides a middle cadence: near enough to create urgency, long enough to allow depth. A roadmap uses this cadence to plan progression across quarters. One quarter might focus on fundamentals, the next on application, the next on complexity, the next on polishing. You can change course, but you are not starting from scratch each time.

Starting from scratch is exhausting.

A roadmap also protects you from another learning distortion: the seduction of "advanced" material. Many learners skip basics because basics feel boring and unglamorous. They jump into complex topics and then feel lost. A roadmap keeps you honest by forcing you to define prerequisites. If you cannot do the basic thing reliably, advanced work will not stick. This is not gatekeeping; it is engineering. In a writing skill roadmap, basics might include clarity, structure, and revision. In a programming roadmap, basics might include reading error messages, writing small functions, and testing. In a negotiation roadmap, basics might include listening, framing, and preparing alternatives. Basics are where compounding begins.

Compounding is slow. Then sudden.

This raises a necessary limitation. Not all skills progress linearly. Some skills plateau. Some require long incubation. Some are shaped by external opportunities: you cannot practise leadership in a vacuum; you need contexts where leadership is required. You cannot practise certain research skills without access to projects, data, or collaborators. A roadmap must therefore remain flexible. Flexibility is not vagueness. It is the willingness to adjust targets and themes in response to reality. The quarter gives you regular points to adjust without drama. If a skill stalls because opportunities are missing, you can redesign the next quarter's targets to focus on prerequisites or on creating those opportunities.

And yet, the roadmap must not become a bureaucracy.

This is the counter-example to roadmapping itself. Some people over-plan learning. They build beautiful spreadsheets of objectives and timelines, then spend more time maintaining the plan than practising the skill. The plan becomes a form of procrastination disguised as organisation. The reconciliation is to keep the roadmap lean and anchored in outputs. If a plan does not lead to practice and production, it is decoration. A quarterly roadmap should feel like a scaffold, not a second job. Its purpose is to reduce decision fatigue: to make it obvious, in any given week, what you are practising and what you are trying to produce by quarter's end.

Decision fatigue is a silent killer.

One reason people abandon learning is that they must re-decide each time: what to study, what to practise, how long, with which materials. Re-deciding consumes energy. A roadmap reduces this cost. It creates a default. Defaults matter because when life is stressful, you fall back to defaults. If your default is "scroll and regret", that is what you will do. If your default is "twenty minutes of practice towards a clear quarter target", you have a fighting chance of continuing even in messy weeks.

Messy weeks are the norm.

A well-designed roadmap also links learning to the rest of your Upgrade Day domains. If your work quarter includes heavy sprints, your learning targets must be smaller or more integrated into work. If your health quarter needs more recovery, learning targets should not demand late-night effort. If money is tight, learning vehicles should favour low-cost options and practice routines. This integration is not a constraint on learning; it is what makes learning sustainable. Sustainable learning is the only kind that compounds.

The motif that holds this subchapter together is the map grid. A map does not walk for you, and it cannot predict the weather. It gives you orientation. It tells you where you are and what lies roughly ahead. A skills roadmap is a map grid for capability. It breaks the territory into squares you can cross in a quarter. It tells you what counts as movement: not a feeling, not a credential, but an artefact, a performance, a demonstration. It is also honest about detours. You may not walk the map perfectly. The point is that you can tell when you are off course and when you are progressing.

Progress should be checkable.

The forward test is therefore not "What do I want to learn?" It is more demanding and more useful. If you choose one priority skill and imagine the end of the next ninety days, what is the smallest set of outputs or performances that would prove you genuinely improved—something you can show, run, present, publish, or use—and what would you need to exclude from the quarter's learning menu to make that proof plausible?

Choosing learning vehicles

In January 1731, in Philadelphia, Pennsylvania, Benjamin Franklin began publishing *The Pennsylvania Gazette*, and soon after helped organise what became the Library Company of Philadelphia. The library mattered not because books were charming, but because access was infrastructure. A printer with a shared library could move faster than a printer without one. Franklin did not need a university syllabus to widen his mind; he needed a vehicle that fit the life he was living—one that made reading, discussion, and application possible within the constraints of work and time.

Vehicles decide velocity.

Modern learning culture often pretends the only serious vehicle is a course: enrol, attend, complete, certificate, repeat. Courses can be excellent, but the course-as-default mindset produces predictable failures. People sign up with optimism, fall behind when life gets busy, then carry a quiet sense of guilt that poisons future attempts. The problem is not effort. It is vehicle mismatch. A learning vehicle is simply the mechanism that carries practice forward—books, mentors, communities, routines, structured programmes, apprenticeships, peer critique, project-based work. Choosing the right vehicle is not a matter of taste alone. It is a matter of fit: fit with your calendar, fit with your temperament, fit with the kind of feedback the skill needs.

Feedback is the fuel.

A skill roadmap without a good vehicle is like a map without a road. You can see where you want to go and still not move. Vehicles matter because they determine what you actually do on a Tuesday evening when you are tired, or on a Friday morning when you have twenty minutes between meetings. If the vehicle requires long uninterrupted blocks you rarely have, it will fail. If it assumes social energy when you are drained, it will fail. If it offers no feedback, it will drift into passive consumption. If it offers too much complexity, it will become another form of admin. The quarter is the right unit for choosing vehicles because it allows you to commit long enough to see results and short enough to change if the vehicle proves wrong.

Wrong vehicles waste more than time.

They waste trust in yourself. When people repeatedly "fail" at learning, they begin to believe they lack discipline or talent. Often they simply chose a vehicle that was incompatible with their life. A demanding synchronous course might be perfect for someone with a stable schedule and high energy in evenings; it might be disastrous for someone with caring responsibilities, irregular work hours, or seasonal workload spikes. A self-paced book might suit someone who loves solitary deep work; it might fail for someone who needs social reinforcement to persist. Vehicle choice is not a moral referendum. It is engineering.

Engineering begins with classification.

Different vehicles produce different kinds of learning. Books are dense and portable; they excel at building mental models and exposing you to high-quality thinking, but they can leave you untested unless paired with practice. Mentors provide tailored feedback and accountability, but they are scarce and can become performative if the relationship is vague. Communities offer social reinforcement and peer learning, but they can also become distraction if participation replaces practice. Practice routines—small, repeated drills—are powerful for building automaticity, yet they can feel dry unless connected to meaningful projects. Structured programmes provide scaffolding and pacing, but they often impose someone else's assumptions about your time and goals.

Assumptions are the hidden cost.

A good vehicle makes fewer assumptions. It fits around your quarter rather than demanding that your quarter fit around it. This is why the instruction to choose one main vehicle and one backup per priority skill is so effective. It recognises that life will interrupt. The backup is not a consolation prize. It is a resilience mechanism. If your main vehicle fails for reasons beyond your control—travel, illness, workload spikes—you can continue the learning thread rather than dropping it entirely. The quarter remains coherent even when the method changes.

Coherence beats purity.

To choose vehicles intelligently, you need to understand what the skill requires. Some skills are knowledge-heavy. Others are performance-heavy. Some require feedback from experts. Others require repetition and self-correction. Take language learning as an example. Research and teaching practice have long distinguished between comprehensible input (hearing and reading language you can mostly understand) and output (speaking and writing), with the recognition that both matter, and that feedback helps (Krashen, 1982, for input theory; broader second-language acquisition literature discusses the role of output and interaction). You do not need to memorise theory. The implication is practical: if your vehicle is only a grammar book, you may build knowledge without conversational ability; if your vehicle is only conversation without structure, you may plateau. Vehicle choice should match what the skill demands: input, output, feedback, repetition.

Match demand. Then commit.

A named, checkable example of vehicle design in education comes from the Khan Academy, founded by Salman Khan in 2008 in the United States, which popularised short videos paired with practice exercises and instant feedback. The novelty was not "videos"; it was the combination of explanation and practice, sized for short sessions and repeated engagement. Another example comes from the massive open online course movement that expanded rapidly after 2011, with platforms such as Coursera (founded 2012). These vehicles lowered access costs dramatically, yet completion rates often proved low—partly because access does not guarantee persistence. The lesson is not that MOOCs are bad. The lesson is that a vehicle's success depends on fit, feedback, and social structure, not merely on content availability.

Availability is not learning.

This is why course-shopping is such a seductive trap. Courses offer the illusion of progress at the moment of enrolment. Clicking "start" feels like movement. It is not. Movement occurs when practice happens repeatedly and when feedback loops correct errors. A good vehicle makes practice hard to avoid and errors easy to notice. This is also why mentors can be powerful. A mentor can see what you cannot see: the blind spots, the habitual mistakes, the hidden assumptions. Yet mentorship is often over-romanticised. A mentor without structure becomes a pleasant chat. A mentor with clear artefacts to review becomes a feedback engine.

Engines need inputs.

In a quarterly learning plan, an "input" might be a piece of writing, a short talk, a dataset analysis, a design draft, a script, a project update. The mentor's role is to respond to inputs with targeted critique. Critique is a gift if it is specific and actionable. It is a weapon if it is vague or performative. This highlights an important point: the vehicle must suit not only the skill but also your relationship with feedback. Some people thrive on critique. Others freeze. Choosing a vehicle involves choosing a feedback environment you can tolerate long enough to improve.

Tolerance matters more than enthusiasm.

Communities can provide this environment when mentorship is unavailable. A writing group, a coding community, a language exchange, a research seminar—these can generate peer feedback and accountability. Yet communities have a failure mode: they can become social consumption. You attend, you listen, you comment, you feel involved, and you produce little. The vehicle becomes a theatre of learning rather than learning itself. The quarter helps here because it demands outputs. If your vehicle is a community, you should be able to point to artefacts you produced because of it. If you cannot, the community may be a pleasant hobby rather than a vehicle for the skill you prioritised.

Hobbies are fine. Vehicles must move.

Practice routines are the least glamorous and often the most effective vehicles, especially when time is scarce. A routine is a repeated practice behaviour attached to a reliable cue. It can be small: twenty minutes of targeted drills, a daily writing block, a weekly project build, a regular conversation session. Routines work because they reduce decision fatigue. They also create frequency, which is essential for skill acquisition. The literature on habit formation and behaviour change is complex and often over-simplified, but the core insight is simple: behaviours repeat when they are cued and rewarded. In learning, the reward is often progress you can feel—greater fluency, fewer errors, more ease. A routine vehicle can feel slow at first because the reward is delayed. Over a quarter, it becomes visible.

Visible rewards protect persistence.

Structured programmes sit somewhere between courses and routines. They can be apprenticeships, cohort-based learning, bootcamps, or professional training schemes. Their strength is scaffolding: someone has designed the sequence of practice and feedback. Their weakness is inflexibility. If the programme's pacing is incompatible with your quarter, it becomes stress rather than support. This is where the backup vehicle is crucial. If the programme becomes too much, a backup—perhaps a book plus a routine, or a mentor check-in plus project work—allows you to maintain momentum without collapsing into shame.

Shame is corrosive.

A credible limitation should be stated clearly: sometimes the best vehicle is unavailable. Mentors can be hard to find. Communities can be inaccessible. Courses can be expensive. Time can be scarce. The reconciliation is not to abandon the skill, but to choose vehicles within constraints and to accept that the quarter's targets should match those constraints. A book can be a superb vehicle if it is paired with practice. A simple routine can outperform an expensive programme if it is sustained. The point is not to choose the fanciest vehicle. It is to choose the one you will actually use.

Use beats aspiration.

Modern relevance adds another twist. AI tools now sit alongside learning vehicles, sometimes as tutors, sometimes as assistants, sometimes as crutches. This is not a moral issue. It is an epistemic one: tools can accelerate practice and feedback, but they can also hide gaps in understanding if used to generate outputs without comprehension. The vehicle question becomes: does this tool increase learning or merely produce plausible artefacts? A tool that helps you test yourself—by generating questions, simulating critique, offering alternative explanations—can be useful. A tool that replaces the difficult thinking you need to do can weaken skill acquisition. The vehicle must therefore be chosen with a clear sense of what counts as learning evidence in your roadmap.

Evidence should be yours.

This returns us to the chapter's deeper claim: learning should expand capability, not merely decorate identity. Vehicles shape identity too. Being enrolled in a programme feels like being a "learner". Being in a community feels like belonging. These feelings are not worthless. They can support persistence. But they must be tethered to practice. Otherwise the vehicle becomes a costume. A good vehicle produces uncomfortable moments: the moment you realise you cannot do the thing yet, the moment you receive critique, the moment you practise when you would rather scroll. These moments are not signs of failure. They are the cost of competence.

Competence is earned in such moments.

The motif for this subchapter is the carriage wheel. Content is the road, but the wheel determines whether you travel it. A wheel with a crack—an incompatible schedule, missing feedback, excessive friction—will not carry you far. A wheel that fits your quarter will. The backup wheel matters because roads change. Your quarter may shift. The wheel keeps turning.

The forward test is therefore practical and slightly unforgiving. For each priority skill you have chosen, what is the one learning vehicle you will genuinely use when the week is messy—book, mentor, community, routine, programme—and what is the backup vehicle you will switch to without drama if the main one fails, so the skill remains alive across the quarter rather than becoming another abandoned enrolment?

Tracking progress lightly

In April 1906, at 221B Baker Street in London—an address made famous in fiction but also a useful symbol of method—Arthur Conan Doyle watched his most famous creation become a cultural machine. Sherlock Holmes's power was not strength or luck. It was observation made systematic: small notes, careful comparisons, the habit of asking what changed. The detective story popularised a particular idea of progress: that it can be detected without drama, through regular, precise noticing.

Noticing is the skill.

Modern learning often fails not because people do not learn, but because they cannot *see* their learning. When progress is invisible, motivation becomes the only engine. Motivation is unreliable. People then respond by adding measurement, believing that numbers will rescue them. They build dashboards. They track hours. They count streaks. Tracking becomes a performance contest against oneself. This is the opposite of what a quarterly learning practice needs. The aim is not to create a personal bureaucracy. The aim is to create just enough reflection and evidence to keep learning honest and alive.

Keep it light.

Light tracking begins with a clear understanding of what it is for. It is not for self-judgement. It is not for social comparison. It is not for proving worth. It is for reducing two kinds of distortion. The first distortion is optimism without evidence: the feeling that you are "keeping up" with a skill because you consume content about it. The second distortion is pessimism without evidence: the feeling that you are "going nowhere" because progress is gradual and memory is biased towards what you still cannot do. Light tracking is a tool against both illusions. It provides a small record of engagement and application. It lets you compare, quietly, across quarters.

Comparison is a scalpel, not a weapon.

A quarter is long enough for meaningful change but short enough for memory to play tricks. You will forget the early struggle once you are competent. You will forget the earlier competence once you face a harder level. That is not stupidity. It is how attention works. This is why researchers, craftspeople, and athletes keep lab notebooks, sketchbooks, training logs: not to fetishise data, but to preserve reality. The best version of learning tracking resembles a notebook more than a leaderboard. It records a few key observations, a few outputs, a few decisions. It allows you to say, with some confidence, "This is what I did. This is what changed."

Change must be defined.

If your roadmap has been designed properly, "change" will be visible in artefacts and performances rather than in vague feelings. You wrote three short essays. You built a small tool. You delivered a talk. You held conversations. You analysed a dataset and produced a chart. These outputs are tracking in themselves. The danger is that you treat outputs as trophies rather than as evidence. Trophies invite performance. Evidence invites iteration. The quarter is not about building a museum of accomplishments. It is about building capability. Capability grows when you examine outputs with curiosity: what improved, what remained awkward, what errors repeated, what felt easier, what still felt brittle.

Brittleness is information.

A skill is brittle when it works only under ideal conditions. You can write well only when you have hours and silence. You can code only when the problem is small. You can speak confidently only with friendly audiences. You can use a language only when conversations stay within safe topics. Brittleness is not failure. It is the natural stage before robustness. Light tracking should therefore include a way of noticing brittleness without shame. This is where reflection questions matter. Not many. Just enough to reveal whether the skill is moving from fragile to reliable.

Reliability is the real metric.

The temptation is to track what is easiest to count. Time is easy to count. Pages read are easy to count. Videos watched are easy to count. These counts can be useful, but they are often proxies for learning rather than learning itself. Proxies can mislead. A person can watch fifty hours of tutorials and remain unable to build anything. A person can read ten books and remain unable to write clearly. This is why light tracking privileges application over consumption. It asks: where did the skill show up in your actual life? What did you do with it? What decision did it change? What work did it improve? Application is harder to measure, but it is closer to truth.

Truth matters more than comfort.

There is empirical support for the value of retrieval and application. Research in cognitive psychology has shown that active recall—retrieving information rather than rereading it—can substantially improve long-term retention, a phenomenon often called the testing effect (Roediger & Karpicke, 2006). Again, the point is not to turn your life into an exam. The point is that learning is strengthened by being used. Light tracking can therefore include small, low-pressure "retrieval moments": brief attempts to explain what you learned, to solve a problem without prompts, to write from memory, to speak without rehearsing. These moments create a clearer signal of progress than passive consumption ever can.

Signals are what you need.

Signals should also be humane. A tracking system that makes you feel watched by your own spreadsheet will not last. It will become another form of admin and guilt. This is why the quarterly approach recommends check-ins rather than constant monitoring. A weekly or fortnightly reflection can be enough. Even a simple end-of-month note can work, as long as it captures engagement and application. The key is that the tracking rhythm should match the learning vehicle and the quarter's constraints. A routine-based vehicle might benefit from a brief weekly note. A mentor-based vehicle might benefit from a note after each feedback session. A project-based vehicle might benefit from a reflection at each project milestone.

Milestones beat minutes.

One way to keep tracking light is to track *events* rather than *effort.* Effort is morally seductive; it feels virtuous to note how hard you tried. Events are less flattering and more useful: you completed a draft; you gave a talk; you built a prototype; you received critique; you revised; you applied the skill in a real situation. Events are evidence of behaviour and outcome. They also connect directly to the rest of the Upgrade Day domains. If learning events vanish in a quarter, it may be because work sprints swallowed time, because health suffered, because relationships demanded attention. The point is not to accuse yourself. The point is to see the system.

The system is always there.

A named, checkable example of the power of simple recording comes from Charles Darwin. During the voyage of the *Beagle* (1831–1836), Darwin kept meticulous notebooks and later continued to keep records and correspondence that documented observations, hypotheses, doubts, and revisions. The notebooks did not make him right. They made his thinking visible to him. Visibility allowed iteration. Iteration allowed synthesis. This is the quiet genius of light tracking: it externalises your learning so you can work with it. You cannot iterate on what you cannot see.

And yet, tracking has a counter-example that deserves honesty. For some people, tracking triggers perfectionism or compulsion. It becomes a new arena for self-critique. A missed week feels like failure. A broken streak feels like character deficiency. In such cases, tracking becomes harmful. The reconciliation is not to insist that everyone must track. The reconciliation is to change the form of tracking so it cannot become a contest. You can track with narrative rather than with numbers. You can track with artefacts saved in a folder rather than with metrics. You can track with occasional check-ins rather than daily logging. You can track what you *noticed* rather than what you *achieved.* The principle remains: preserve enough evidence to see learning over time, without creating a scoreboard that punishes you.

Punishment undermines learning.

Learning thrives under a particular emotional climate: curiosity, patience, willingness to be wrong, and a tolerance for slow improvement. A performance contest corrodes that climate. It shifts attention from the skill to the self. It turns errors into threats rather than data. Light tracking aims to protect the emotional climate by keeping the focus on the work: the outputs, the revisions, the applications, the questions that emerged. If you treat your skill as a craft, tracking becomes a craftsman's notebook, not a judge's ledger.

A ledger asks, "Did you meet the target?" A notebook asks, "What happened when you tried?" The difference is subtle and profound. The notebook frame allows you to record constraints without self-reproach: you were ill; the quarter was heavy; you travelled; a project exploded; your energy dipped. These are not excuses. They are context. Context helps you design the next quarter. It helps you choose a smaller target, a different vehicle, a better time slot. It preserves continuity. Continuity is more important than intensity.

Intensity is overrated.

Light tracking also helps you avoid the trap of comparing your learning to other people's outputs. The internet encourages this comparison relentlessly. You see polished projects, fluent speakers, confident presenters, immaculate portfolios. You do not see the drafts, the failures, the years of repetition. Tracking your own progress creates a private reference point that is far more useful. You compare yourself to your own last quarter, not to someone else's highlight reel. This is not a motivational slogan. It is a cognitive hygiene practice. It keeps learning grounded in reality rather than in social theatre.

Social theatre is addictive.

The motif for this subchapter is the thumbprint on a page. A thumbprint is small. It is not a monument. It is proof that you were there—that you turned the page, that you handled the work. Light tracking is a collection of thumbprints: a few notes, a few saved artefacts, a few reflections that show you engaged and applied. Over a year, these thumbprints become a record. Over several years, they become a story of compounding capability. The thumbprint metaphor matters because it resists grandiosity. Learning is rarely a single breakthrough. It is a sequence of small contacts with the material, each one leaving a trace.

Traces add up.

The forward test is therefore gentle but exacting. At the end of your next quarter, what would you need to have preserved—two or three artefacts, a handful of short notes, one recurring reflection—to be able to compare honestly with the quarter before and say, without performance or pretence, that your priority skill moved from fragile to more reliable, and that it showed up in your real work rather than only in your intentions?

Chapter 8
Environment, Gear and Systems

In September 2002, at the Massachusetts Institute of Technology in Cambridge, Massachusetts, researchers held up a small, humble idea with outsize consequences: the "Roomba" would be released later that year by iRobot, and the point was not merely that it vacuumed. The point was that it altered a household routine without asking the household to become more virtuous. It moved dirt with boredom-resistant persistence. It was a tiny automation in a world that usually demands constant personal effort, and it quietly demonstrated a truth many adults refuse to learn: willpower is an expensive way to run a life.

Environments do more than moods.

Most people think of self-improvement as an internal project. They imagine better discipline, better habits, better motivation, better focus. The world, meanwhile, keeps tugging them back towards old defaults. The phone is always within reach. The kitchen encourages snacking. The wardrobe contains clothes that don't fit how you actually live. The desk is cluttered with half-decisions. The email system is designed to refill itself. You can preach values to yourself all day, but the environment always gets a vote, and it votes continuously. This chapter turns that vote into something you can influence.

Small design changes compound.

It is strangely comforting to believe that our struggles are purely personal, because personal struggles can be narrated as moral dramas. If you blame yourself, you can at least feel in control of the story: work harder, try again, be more disciplined. Yet discipline is not the only lever, and often it is not the best one. Many frustrations are not a character flaw; they are a friction flaw. They are the product of clumsy layouts, worn-out tools, inefficient systems, and environments designed for consumption rather than intention. A quarter is long enough for these frictions to become obvious and short enough for simple tweaks to produce noticeable relief.

Relief is a legitimate outcome.

This chapter treats your surroundings—physical and digital—not as aesthetic projects but as behavioural infrastructure. It begins with auditing spaces and flows: a walk through the home, the workspace, and the digital surfaces that you touch hundreds of times a day. The aim is not to become a minimalist or a productivity monastic. The aim is to notice where friction lives. A cluttered desk is not merely untidy; it increases switching cost because each object is a micro-demand for attention. A crowded phone screen is not merely messy; it makes distraction the default. An awkward kitchen layout is not merely inconvenient; it shapes what you eat and how you spend. Friction is not abstract. It is felt in your body and your time.

Friction also hides in the most mundane places.

A charger that is always missing. A chair that makes you fidget. A running shoe that rubs. A laptop that takes thirty seconds too long to wake. A file system that forces you to search. A to-do list that has become a graveyard. These irritations seem too small to address, so they persist. Persistence turns them into background stress. Background stress becomes depletion. Depletion makes good choices harder. This is how environments quietly sabotage goals without ever declaring themselves the villain.

The next movement is refreshing tools and gear. Most people carry two contradictory impulses: they tolerate broken things far too long, and they accumulate new things far too quickly. Worn-out gear creates a low hum of annoyance that can sour work and health habits. Unexamined accumulation creates clutter that increases friction and decision fatigue. The aim here is not shopping. It is discernment. A tool has a job. If it no longer does the job well—because it is broken, ill-fitting, or obsolete—then it is creating a tax on your attention and energy. A quarterly review makes that tax visible and makes repair or retirement feel like maintenance rather than indulgence.

Maintenance is not vanity.

It is stewardship. And stewardship is what links this chapter to the rest of the book. Money, health, relationships, and learning are all affected by the environment, whether you acknowledge it or not. A person who wants to cook more but has a chaotic kitchen is fighting uphill. A person who wants to train consistently but has uncomfortable gear or no clear place to put it will skip sessions more often. A person who wants to read or practise a skill but has no quiet corner and a phone that constantly interrupts is trying to out-muscle design. The environment is the stage on which all other goals attempt to play out. If the stage is cluttered with trip hazards, the performance will be clumsy.

Then comes streamlining daily systems. Systems are the recurring processes that make life run: email, shopping, meal planning, laundry, bills, household admin, file management, routines for getting out the door, routines for winding down. Many adults live inside systems they have never designed. They inherit habits from childhood, from past jobs, from old apartments, from the first apps they downloaded. The systems keep running even when they no longer fit, because redesign feels like effort. So the system continues to impose small penalties: forgetting things, redoing work, constant background worry. Streamlining is not grand reorganisation. It is targeted simplification: choosing one or two systems each quarter, experimenting with a small change, and keeping what works.

Experiments are kinder than overhauls.

This is also where modern relevance bites. Digital systems have become the invisible architecture of daily life. Your phone is a pocket-sized portal to distraction, social obligation, news anxiety, work demands, and entertainment. Most people treat it as a neutral object. It is not. It is a set of designed choices—notifications, layouts, recommendation engines—optimised for engagement. If your goals require sustained attention, the default phone environment is often in conflict with them. This chapter does not moralise about technology. It treats digital surfaces as spaces that can be audited and redesigned, just like a room. If you accept that, you regain agency. If you don't, the device will keep shaping your days while you blame yourself for "lack of focus".

Agency is the through-line.

The final movement is reducing friction points by connecting environment changes back to your goals. This is where the chapter becomes more than decluttering or productivity advice. The question "What tiny change to my surroundings would make this habit easier?" is a profound design prompt. It turns habit change from a test of character into a test of engineering. If you want to spend less, you might remove the one-click purchase shortcut from your most-used device. If you want to walk more, you might place shoes by the door and remove the pile of bags that blocks it. If you want to call friends more, you might create a small "contact list" in reach when you have idle time. If you want to practise a skill, you might leave the materials open and ready rather than packed away like a chore. Tiny changes matter because they alter defaults. Defaults are what you do when you are tired, busy, or emotionally preoccupied—which is most days.

Most days are not heroic.

The philosophy underneath this is older than any app. It echoes the idea that behaviour is shaped by context, a theme explored across psychology and behavioural economics. Even without invoking a specific study, the human truth is visible. People eat more when food is within reach. People read more when books are visible. People waste less time when distractions are harder to access. These are not revelations. The revelation is that you can choose to make certain behaviours easier and others harder. You can design your life to support what you claim to value. That is a form of respect for yourself and for reality.

Still, there is an honest limitation. Environment changes are not a substitute for deeper problems. A tidy desk cannot fix a toxic job. A new pair of shoes cannot heal an injury. A cleaner calendar cannot resolve grief. Systems can support you, but they cannot carry everything. The reconciliation is not to dismiss environment work as superficial. It is to treat it as *supportive infrastructure.* Infrastructure does not guarantee outcomes. It makes outcomes more plausible. It reduces unnecessary struggle. It frees attention for the problems that actually require thought, courage, or help.

Help is allowed.

This chapter therefore aims to offer something quieter than a makeover. It offers the possibility of a life that runs with less friction. Less friction means more spare capacity. Spare capacity is where good decisions live. It is also where play and creativity live—an underappreciated connection. A cluttered, noisy environment can make even leisure feel like effort. An environment with a few well-designed flows can make leisure feel like rest rather than another obligation. The quarterly rhythm matters because environment improvements compound: each quarter you smooth a few points, and over a year the overall experience of your days changes.

The motif that threads through this chapter is the hinge. A hinge is small. A hinge is rarely admired. Yet a well-oiled hinge changes how a door feels. It removes that tiny screech of resistance you didn't realise you were bracing against. Environments work like hinges. You can live with a squeaky door for years and assume that bracing is normal. Then you fix the hinge and wonder why you tolerated the noise. This chapter is about finding the hinges in your life—the small frictions that make everything harder than it needs to be—and oiling them with deliberate, modest changes.

The tension at the end is a design choice, not a moral one. You cannot redesign everything at once, and you should not try. But you can choose a couple of hinges each quarter. The question that follows is simple and demanding: if the next ninety days are going to feel easier in practice, not just in theory, which two friction points in your surroundings—physical or digital—must you smooth first, and what are you willing to remove, repair, or rearrange to make that ease real?

Auditing spaces and flows

In October 2011, at Steve Jobs's memorial service on the Apple campus in Cupertino, California, the programme was simple and the details were obsessive. Attendees were handed a small box containing a glass bottle of water, a programme card, and a single piece of fruit. The air smelled faintly of eucalyptus, and the hush had the texture of felt. Jobs had made a career of arguing that what looks like decoration is often structure: a menu reduced to essentials, a device with fewer buttons, a user path designed so that a person does not have to think about the path at all. One can dislike the mythology and still learn from the engineering. He understood that friction is not merely inconvenience. Friction is behaviour.

Behaviour follows the path of least resistance.

Most adults treat their surroundings as backdrop. They make plans, set goals, summon resolve, and then attempt to execute those intentions inside environments that are quietly misaligned with them. The desk is a junk drawer with a keyboard. The kitchen makes the easiest food the least nourishing. The phone arranges distraction as the home screen's default. The email client is designed to refill itself. None of this requires malice. It is simply how systems behave when nobody audits them. An audit of spaces and flows is not about taste or tidiness. It is about noticing what your environment is already training you to do.

The training is constant.

Begin with an ordinary scene: the first ten minutes of a working day. The laptop wakes. Notifications bloom. A mug is searched for. A charger is missing. A notebook is buried under unopened post. A browser opens to a dozen tabs you no longer remember starting. A message arrives and pulls attention before you have decided what the day is for. Nothing dramatic has happened, yet your nervous system has already been nudged into reactivity. This is the signature of environmental friction: it produces small, repeated interruptions that accumulate into a day that feels scattered. The name for this is *friction load*—the total amount of minor resistance your environment imposes on your intentions. You can tolerate high friction load for a while. Over a quarter, it becomes fatigue.

Fatigue changes decisions.

Auditing spaces and flows means replacing vague dissatisfaction with precise observation. Observation begins with movement. You walk through the spaces that hold your life—the home, the workspace, the digital surfaces—while asking a question that is both practical and oddly philosophical: what is the default here? Defaults are what happen when you are tired, rushed, distracted, or emotionally preoccupied. Defaults reveal the truth about your system. If the default in your kitchen is sugary snacks within reach, then "eating better" is not a purely nutritional question; it is a layout question. If the default at your desk is a cluttered surface that invites constant rummaging, then "focusing more" is not a purely psychological question; it is a spatial question. If the default on your phone is a front page of alerts, then "being less distracted" is not a moral ambition; it is a design problem.

Design problems are solvable.

A useful audit does not begin with sweeping changes. It begins with identifying the highest-impact friction points: the places where a small tweak produces disproportionate ease. This is why the audit is a walk rather than a weekend project. A walk keeps it light. A walk makes you notice. When people attempt a full makeover, they often burn out or create new problems. They end with a tidy house and a resentful mind. The quarter asks for something smarter: tiny interventions that compound.

Compounding is quiet power.

The audit is best understood as tracing flows. A "flow" is the path an activity takes from intention to completion. Making coffee has a flow. Getting out the door has a flow. Starting work has a flow. Cooking has a flow. Washing has a flow. Paying bills has a flow. Digital work has flows: capturing ideas, retrieving files, responding to messages, drafting documents, scheduling. Flows break down where friction concentrates. You recognise breakdowns by their symptoms: repeated searching, repeated redoing, repeated interruption, repeated avoidance. These are not character flaws. They are system signals.

Signals should be read.

Consider a basic, checkable example from design research. The psychologist Don Norman popularised the idea that good design makes the right action obvious and the wrong action difficult, and that many "user errors" are actually design failures (Norman, *The Design of Everyday Things*, 1988; revised edition 2013). You do not need to turn your home into a product. The implication is enough: when you repeatedly make "mistakes" in your own life—forgetting keys, misplacing chargers, missing workouts, losing track of admin—your environment may be poorly designed for your realities. An audit treats you as a user of your own life and asks where the design is fighting you.

Fighting yourself is exhausting.

A second example, grounded in the digital world, is the phenomenon of notification-driven attention. Research on attention and interruption has repeatedly found that interruptions can carry cognitive costs, including time spent resuming tasks and increased error rates; the classic paper by Gloria Mark, Victor Gonzalez, and Justin Harris (2005) observed frequent task switching in knowledge work environments and the time it can take to return to a task after interruption. The precise figures vary by study and context, and it is easy to misuse them as alarmist slogans. The point here is restrained: if your digital environment is built around interruptions, your ability to do sustained work will be undermined unless you redesign the flow. Again, this is not about virtue. It is about engineering.

Engineering begins with measurement—light measurement, not obsessive tracking. In an audit, measurement can be as simple as counting how many times you search for something in a day, how often you stand up because an object is not where you assumed, how frequently you unlock your phone without a clear purpose. These are behaviours you can notice without turning life into a laboratory. The goal is to locate "hot spots": a drawer that produces rummaging, a shelf that produces clutter, an app layout that produces unconscious checking, a hallway that becomes a dumping ground.

Dumping grounds become emotional.

The home, especially, stores half-decisions. Things are placed somewhere "for now" and become permanent. The flow breaks because "for now" is not a system. A coat on a chair is not a coat system; it is a friction point disguised as convenience. Post on the counter is not an admin system; it is delayed decision-making. A crowded desktop is not a workflow; it is an attention trap. The audit's job is to catch these "for now" zones and ask: what decision is being postponed here? Often the postponed decision is not big. It is simply that the home lacks a clear place for a recurring object, or the digital system lacks a clear convention for naming and storing.

Conventions reduce searching.

Searching is an underestimated tax. Search consumes time, but more importantly it consumes attention. It forces you into a scavenger mindset: scanning, switching, reacting. This mindset is contagious; it bleeds into how you handle work, health, relationships, and learning. If you spend your morning scavenging for a charger, you are already mentally fragmented before you try to write, think, or call a friend. An audit therefore looks for search patterns. Where do you search most? What do you search for? What surfaces are most likely to hide the object you need? The answer is rarely "I need more discipline." The answer is often "this object has no home."

Homes create calm.

The same applies to digital spaces. People keep hundreds of files with inconsistent naming, dozens of tabs, thousands of photos, unread messages, half-finished notes. The device becomes an attic. The cost is not merely mess. The cost is retrieval friction: when you need something, you cannot find it quickly, so you avoid tasks that require retrieval. Avoidance is a rational response to friction. Then people interpret avoidance as procrastination and blame themselves. The audit breaks that loop by naming the friction.

Naming changes what you can do.

The motif that threads this subchapter is the "threshold". A threshold is the small boundary between one space and another: the doorway where shoes pile up, the edge of the desk where paper accumulates, the lock screen where attention is captured, the moment you open email and fall into other people's priorities. Thresholds are where flows either work or break. They are also where small changes matter most. A hook by the door changes the threshold. A clear inbox rule changes the threshold. A single tidy surface changes the threshold. A phone home screen without attention traps changes the threshold. Threshold work is high leverage because thresholds are crossed repeatedly.

Repeated crossings compound.

This is why the audit is best done with fresh eyes. Fresh eyes are not an emotion; they are a method. You simulate the perspective of a visitor. If someone walked into your workspace, what would they assume the space is for? What behaviour does the layout invite? If someone picked up your phone, what would they assume you do most? If someone watched you make breakfast, where would they see hesitation, searching, or detours? The visitor perspective reveals the gap between intended identity and actual environment. It is often sobering. It is also freeing, because it suggests interventions that do not require you to become a different person.

You can stay yourself.

A credible limitation must be acknowledged: not everyone can redesign their environment extensively. People rent. People share space. People live in cramped flats. People work in open offices. People have caring obligations that make "perfect flows" impossible. The reconciliation is to focus on micro-territories and micro-flows. You may not control the whole kitchen, but you might control one shelf that supports the habit you care about. You may not control the office, but you might control your desk surface and your digital notifications. You may not control household routines, but you might control the threshold where keys and essentials live. Audits are not about perfection. They are about leverage.

Leverage respects constraints.

Another limitation is the aesthetic trap. Some people turn audits into aesthetic projects: they chase a style, buy storage solutions, reorganise endlessly. This can become a form of procrastination, a way of feeling productive without addressing deeper habits. The reconciliation is to keep the audit anchored to flows. If a change does not improve a recurring flow, it is optional decoration. Decoration is fine. It is not the point. The point is to reduce friction in the behaviours you care about: focusing, cooking, moving, resting, learning, connecting.

Connection, too, has flows. The flow of calling a friend can break because you never know when to do it, or because you cannot remember whom you wanted to call, or because the phone is associated with obligation rather than warmth. A tiny environmental tweak—keeping a short list of people you want to check in with in a visible place—can lower that friction. Again, not advice as instruction, but as illustration: the environment can support relationships as much as it supports work.

Work, too, is environmental. A desk that allows only a laptop and one notebook supports deep work better than a desk that holds ten unresolved objects. A calendar that includes clear blocks for focused effort supports execution better than a calendar with meetings spilling into every open space. A digital system that surfaces the current project supports progress better than one that surfaces yesterday's chaos. Auditing spaces and flows is therefore a way of aligning your environment with the quarter's priorities, rather than attempting to become resilient against misalignment.

Resilience is not infinite.

The audit ends, properly, not with a list of tasks but with a small set of high-impact observations. Observations are decisions waiting to be made: "this threshold is broken", "this flow forces searching", "this surface invites distraction", "this layout makes the right action harder than the wrong one". From those observations, you choose a few tweaks, not a reinvention. The goal is to make the next ninety days easier to live in.

The forward test is simple and slightly uncomfortable. If you walk through your home, your workspace, and your digital surfaces as though you were a visitor, which three thresholds most reliably pull you into friction—searching, clutter, distraction, avoidance—and which single, modest change at each threshold would make the behaviour you want the default rather than the exception?

Refreshing tools and gear

In August 1914, in London, the first women were hired as conductors on buses as men left for war, and the city's transport system had to keep moving with whatever equipment and staffing could be made to work. The photographs from the period are blunt: heavy coats, leather straps, metal ticket punches, and long hours. The detail worth noticing is not nostalgia. It is the relationship between a tool and a day. A ticket punch that jams is not a minor annoyance when you must use it hundreds of times. It becomes a tax on the body, attention, and mood. Multiply that tax by a thousand small interactions, and the system degrades.

Wear is cumulative.

Most people live inside a private museum of worn-out objects: a laptop whose battery dies unpredictably, a charging cable that works only at a particular angle, shoes that rub, a coat with a broken zip, a kitchen knife that has become blunt, a bag whose strap is slowly tearing, a chair that makes the lower back feel tight after an hour. None of these failures announces itself as a crisis. That is why they persist. They are small enough to tolerate and annoying enough to drag. Toleration becomes habit. Habit becomes normal. Normal becomes invisible. Refreshing tools and gear is a quarterly act of making the invisible visible.

Small irritations shape behaviour.

The mind likes heroic explanations. If work feels harder, we blame motivation. If exercise feels harder, we blame discipline. If daily life feels heavier, we blame ageing or busyness. Sometimes the explanation is simpler: the objects that carry the day are fighting you.

Tools and gear are not neutral. They are interfaces between intention and action. A well-functioning tool reduces friction. A worn-out tool increases it. The increase is subtle: a few extra seconds, a few extra mistakes, a little more hesitation. Over a quarter, the extra seconds become lost time, the extra mistakes become avoidance, the hesitation becomes a narrative about yourself: "I'm not consistent", "I can't keep up", "I'm always behind".

Narratives often begin in the hands.

A quarterly gear review has two aims that must coexist. The first is to remove silent friction by repairing, replacing, or retiring what no longer serves. The second is to prevent the opposite failure mode: mindless accumulation. Some people respond to friction by buying. Buying feels like solving. It is often only moving the problem. The wardrobe swells, the drawers fill, the digital subscriptions multiply, and the environment becomes cluttered with options that increase decision fatigue. The quarter's discipline is to choose selectively, guided by use rather than desire.

Use is measurable.

Consider a scene that plays out in countless kitchens. A person intends to cook more to support health and money goals. The reality is that cooking requires friction tolerance: finding ingredients, locating utensils, washing up, putting things away. If the knife is blunt, the cutting board slips, the pan is warped, and the hob is cluttered, the friction rises. The person concludes they "don't have time". They order food. They spend more. They feel less well. The tool problem becomes a life problem. The name for this is *friction substitution*: when small mechanical friction pushes you into larger behavioural costs—costs in money, health, and time. Refreshing gear is a way of paying small costs upfront to avoid larger costs later.

Later always arrives.

The gear review should be grounded in how people actually behave, not in ideals. This is why it begins with the most-used items, not with the most aspirational ones. The most-used items are often boring:

the shoes you reach for, the trousers you wear repeatedly, the charger you depend on, the notebook you carry, the chair you sit on, the bag you throw over a shoulder, the app you open a hundred times. These items form the daily interface with the world. When they fail, your day fails in small ways. When they work well, your day flows with less effort. This is not luxury. It is maintenance.

Maintenance is a form of respect.

There is also a cognitive dimension. Tools that fail unpredictably impose a particular kind of mental load. You become vigilant. You pack backups. You worry. You add workarounds. This is the same mechanism as financial drift: small unexamined problems accumulate into constant low-level stress. In human factors and ergonomics—the field that studies how people interact with tools and systems—unpredictability is a known source of error and stress. A tool that behaves inconsistently forces the user to allocate attention to monitoring rather than to doing. Even without quoting a specific study, the lived implication is clear: when your laptop crashes, you work with a background fear; when your shoes blister, you walk less; when your bike chain slips, you avoid cycling; when your headphones cut out, you stop listening to language practice on commutes. Gear failure changes behaviour.

Behaviour is the real metric.

A named, checkable example of how gear reliability shapes outcomes comes from aviation. In the mid-twentieth century, the field of human factors grew rapidly, influenced by wartime and post-war aviation safety work in the United States and Britain, because errors could not be blamed solely on pilots; cockpit design, instrumentation, and maintenance mattered. The lesson transfers: when a system fails, it is rarely only a person problem. It is often an interface problem. Your life is not an aeroplane. Yet the principle remains. Tools and environments shape the error rate of your days.

Error rate is rarely moral.

This is where the quarter helps. Quarterly cadence keeps gear refreshing from becoming an impulsive shopping habit and keeps it from becoming a neglected chore. You are not constantly tinkering. You are not ignoring wear for years. You are making periodic, deliberate choices. The focus is on three actions: repair, replace, retire. Repair is often underrated because it feels like hassle. Yet repair can be the highest-leverage move: it restores function and reduces waste. Replace is sometimes necessary when repair is impossible or uneconomic. Retire is the hardest for many people because it requires admitting that an object no longer fits your life or that you have been carrying it out of guilt.

Guilt is not storage.

The guilt in gear is often sentimental. People keep clothes that no longer fit because they represent a past self or a hoped-for future self. They keep gadgets "just in case". They keep sports equipment they do not use because it symbolises good intentions. This is not trivial. Objects carry identity. Retiring an object can feel like retiring a dream. The quarter offers a kinder way to deal with this: treat gear as current infrastructure, not as autobiography. If an item is not supporting your life now, it is either stored deliberately with a clear reason or removed. Otherwise it becomes clutter, and clutter increases friction in every other domain.

Clutter is cumulative.

A second named example illustrates how design and accumulation collide. In 1972, in New York, the Museum of Modern Art exhibited objects that treated everyday tools as design problems, not mere commodities. Whether one agrees with MoMA's taste is irrelevant. The underlying claim—that the objects of daily life shape daily experience—has become hard to deny. Yet contemporary consumer culture translates that claim into a shopping reflex: if objects shape experience, then buy better objects. The counterpoint is crucial. Better objects can help. Buying is not the same as designing. Designing is choosing what to keep, what to maintain, and what to remove so that the objects you use most are reliable and easily accessible.

Design is subtraction as much as acquisition.

A gear review therefore benefits from pairing abstractions with concrete checks. "Efficiency" becomes: how often do you search for a charger, a pen, a key item? "Risk" becomes: what would fail tomorrow and cause disproportionate disruption—laptop, glasses, shoes, passport, backup drive? "Comfort" becomes: which items create repeated discomfort—chair pressure points, clothing irritation, bag strain? "Reliability" becomes: which tools have become unpredictable—apps that crash, devices with dying batteries, kitchen appliances that behave oddly? These are not financial or medical claims. They are observations of function. Function is the language of this chapter.

Function keeps you honest.

The quarter also invites a subtle practice: distinguishing between *core gear* and *noise*. Core gear is what you use weekly, sometimes daily. Noise is everything else: aspirational items, duplicates, unused gadgets, rarely worn clothes, tools without a clear job. Core gear deserves investment in repair and quality, within whatever means you have. Noise deserves scrutiny and often retirement. This distinction prevents the common mistake of cutting costs where they matter most and splurging where they matter least. People sometimes tolerate a broken chair and buy new decorative items. They sometimes keep five mediocre knives and never sharpen one. They sometimes carry three cheap chargers and never buy one reliable one. The quarter offers an opportunity to reverse that pattern, not by spending more, but by choosing better.

Choosing is the theme.

There is a credible limitation: not everyone has the freedom to replace or upgrade gear, and not all friction can be solved with objects. Financial constraints are real. Household dynamics are real. Work equipment may be controlled by an employer. The reconciliation is to keep the review scale-appropriate. Repair is often cheaper than replacement. Retiring duplicates costs nothing. Reorganising access can reduce friction without new purchases. Even choosing which single tool to prioritise—sharpening one knife, replacing one cable, fixing one chair—can have outsized impact because it affects repeated interactions.

Repeated interactions are the lever.

Another limitation is the trap of optimisation. Some people turn gear into a hobby: endless research, comparisons, upgrades, and marginal improvements. This can become a displacement activity, a way of feeling productive while avoiding deeper work. The quarter's discipline protects against this because it asks for a few high-impact decisions, not an infinite quest for the perfect setup. Gear should serve life, not become life. The tool should disappear into use. If you find yourself thinking about the tool more than the work it enables, the system has become inverted.

Inversion is common.

The most telling sign that a gear refresh is needed is not that something is broken. It is that you are repeatedly working around the same small problem. You prop a door. You tug a zip. You re-enter passwords because a manager is missing. You wear a jacket that annoys you because you "shouldn't waste it". You avoid a walk because the shoes are uncomfortable. Workarounds are friction made habitual. They are also time capsules: they reveal what you have been tolerating. An Upgrade Day gear review is a moment to ask, with a clear head: what have I been tolerating that quietly makes my life smaller?

Smaller is the warning word.

The motif for this subchapter is the *dull edge.* A dull edge is not dramatic. It still cuts, technically, but it requires more force, more attention, more risk of slipping. Dull edges exist everywhere: blunt knives, slow devices, worn shoes, tangled cables, clothes that don't sit right, tools that no longer fit your current work. You can muscle through dull edges. Many people do. But why keep pushing harder when a small maintenance act can restore sharpness? Sharpness, here, is not aggression. It is ease.

Ease frees attention.

The forward test is deliberately practical. Over the next ninety days, which three items you touch most—one for work, one for health or movement, one for daily living—are currently dull edges that you are compensating for, and what decision will you make about each: repair, replace, or retire, so that the quarter's goals are supported by reliable tools rather than undermined by silent friction?

Streamlining daily systems

On 24 October 1964, at the World's Fair in New York, visitors watched IBM demonstrate the System/360: a family of computers designed to run the same software across different machines. The headline was technical, but the human consequence was simple. It reduced the number of times organisations had to reinvent their own routines. Standardisation made work repeatable. Repeatability made work manageable. It was not a triumph of cold machinery over human life. It was a reminder that the most exhausting work is not the hard work. It is the work you must keep redesigning from scratch.

Reinvention is a hidden tax.

Daily life contains dozens of small processes that rarely receive deliberate attention: opening and sorting email, buying food, deciding what to cook, paying bills, keeping track of documents, handling household admin, managing shared calendars, making small repairs, dealing with returns, responding to requests. Each process is individually minor. Together they create a persistent hum of cognitive load. The hum is easy to underestimate because it does not arrive in a single dramatic episode. It arrives as a thousand tiny decisions: now or later, where is that, what do I do with this, what did I promise, what did I forget.

Forgetting becomes a personality in the mind.

Most people interpret the discomfort of these small frictions as a personal failing. They conclude they are disorganised, scattered, undisciplined. Often they are simply living inside systems they never designed. A system, in this context, is any repeated process with an input, a sequence, and an output. The input might be a bill, an email, a set of groceries, a pile of washing, a calendar invitation. The output might be a paid account, a sent response, a cooked meal, clean clothes, a confirmed plan. Systems matter because they decide what happens when you are tired. When energy is high, almost any system works. When energy is low, the system shows its true character.

Systems reveal reality.

The core idea of this subchapter is modest and radical: choose one or two daily systems each quarter to simplify. Not ten. Not your entire life. One or two. The quarter is the perfect scale because it makes the experiment long enough to be meaningful and short enough to be reversible. Reversibility matters. Many people avoid redesigning systems because they fear locking themselves into something worse. A quarter reframes change as a test rather than a commitment. You try. You observe. You adjust. You keep what works. This is not productivity theatre. It is maintenance of your behavioural infrastructure.

Infrastructure is where freedom lives.

Consider email, the modern exemplar of system drift. Email was designed as a communication channel, but it has become an unofficial task manager, a meeting scheduler, a project archive, and a social obligation machine. People open it reflexively, not because it is urgent but because it offers the illusion of control: "I'm keeping up." Yet the mere act of checking often creates more work because it reveals new requests and anxieties. Without a system, email becomes a slot machine. You pull the lever and see what arrives. The result is not only lost time. It is fragmented attention. Fragmented attention makes deep work harder and makes leisure less restorative.

Fragmentation is not a moral failure.

It is often a system outcome. This is why behavioural research has found that attention is sensitive to interruptions and switching costs.

Gloria Mark and colleagues' observational work on knowledge workers (Mark, Gonzalez & Harris, 2005) documented frequent task switching and the challenges of maintaining focus in interruption-heavy environments. The precise numbers are less important than the pattern: when the environment invites constant checking, people check. Streamlining a system is a way of redesigning that invitation. A rule as simple as "email is processed in two dedicated windows" can change the flow of a day if it is paired with a calendar structure that makes it possible. Again, the point is not to impose a doctrine. The point is to see that a "system" can be a small set of constraints that protects attention.

Protection is part of design.

Shopping and meals offer another clear arena. Many households repeat the same pattern: food runs out unexpectedly, a rushed trip to the shop happens, impulse items appear, dinner becomes a last-minute decision, money leaks through convenience purchases, and health habits wobble because the easiest option is the least aligned with intentions. People respond by blaming themselves for not meal planning "properly". Yet meal planning often fails because it is designed like a project rather than like a system. A system is not an aspiration. It is a rhythm. A rhythm that fits your real week—your work sprints, your social obligations, your energy—will be used. A rhythm that assumes perfect evenings and endless enthusiasm will not.

Realistic rhythms win.

The same logic applies to household admin. Documents arrive. Receipts accumulate. Warranties expire. Renewals happen. Appointments need booking. Forms need filling. Many adults handle this through sporadic bursts of effort. The bursts feel productive, then the system collapses again. This is a sign of a missing flow. A flow is not "try harder." A flow is a predictable place for an item to go and a predictable time for the item to be handled. When those are missing, "later" becomes a pile. Piles create dread. Dread creates avoidance. Avoidance creates larger problems. Systems are small defences against dread.

Dread is costly.

To streamline a system, you need to follow a disciplined sequence of thought. The first move is to *show* the system as it actually operates. This is why a quarterly review works well: you look back across the last ninety days and identify where friction repeated. Not in theory. In behaviour. Where did you repeatedly scramble? Where did you repeatedly forget? Where did you repeatedly resent the process? Resentment is data. Resentment is often the emotional signature of a badly designed system: too many steps, too much ambiguity, too much repetition, too much dependency on memory.

Memory is not a reliable storage device.

Once you have shown the system, you *name* what is wrong with it. The most common failure types are surprisingly consistent. There is the "no capture point" failure: items arrive and have nowhere to go. There is the "no processing time" failure: items have a place but are never handled. There is the "too many choices" failure: the system asks you to decide too much, too often. There is the "unclear definition of done" failure: you never know when the task is finished, so you avoid starting. There is the "tool mismatch" failure: the app, notebook, or method does not fit the behaviour, so it is ignored. Naming the failure type turns frustration into diagnosis.

Diagnosis enables experiment.

Then you *explain* the mechanism. Why does this system produce friction? Often because it violates a basic principle: the cost of using the system must be lower than the cost of not using it. If checking a shopping list is harder than making a spontaneous trip, you will not check it. If filing a document is harder than leaving it on a counter, you will not file it. If capturing an idea is harder than letting it float in the mind, you will not capture it. This is why a streamlined system feels almost lazy. It reduces steps. It reduces decisions. It reduces movement. It reduces the need to remember. It respects the fact that attention and energy are finite.

Finite resources require design.

The *implication* is that a "better system" is rarely the most elaborate one. It is usually the simplest one that still produces the desired output. This is where people trip. They assume sophistication equals effectiveness. They build complex workflows with multiple apps, tags, folders, and rules. The complexity becomes friction. The system breaks. They conclude systems "don't work for me". In reality, the system demanded too much. A quarterly approach encourages restraint. Choose one or two systems. Reduce steps. Reduce decisions. Make the flow obvious. Then test.

Test, don't evangelise.

Two named, checkable examples help anchor this idea. The first is Toyota's production system, developed across the twentieth century and codified in influential texts such as Taiichi Ohno's *Toyota Production System* (published in Japanese in 1978; English translations later). "Lean" thinking emphasises eliminating waste—unnecessary steps, unnecessary movement, unnecessary inventory. Applied to personal systems, "waste" might be repeated searching, duplicated lists, unnecessary trips, or repeated rework. The second example is David Allen's *Getting Things Done* (first published 2001), which popularised the notion of capturing tasks externally, clarifying next actions, and reviewing regularly. One need not adopt Allen's entire method. The lasting insight is that external capture and periodic review reduce mental clutter and prevent tasks from lingering as anxiety.

Anxiety thrives on ambiguity.

There is a credible counter-example and limitation, and it matters because systems writing often becomes overconfident. Some people's lives are intrinsically variable. Shift workers, carers, people in crisis-heavy roles, researchers working around experimental constraints—these lives cannot be fully rhythmised. In such contexts, overly rigid systems can become oppressive. They turn a life that is already unpredictable into a life that feels constantly "behind". The reconciliation is to design systems that are tolerant to variability: fewer fixed times, more flexible windows, fewer dependencies. A good system for a variable life has slack. It has a place to put things even when you cannot process them immediately.

It has a simple "minimum viable" version that prevents collapse. It treats consistency as a spectrum rather than a binary.

Binary thinking breaks systems.

Another limitation is social. Many daily systems are shared: households, teams, partnerships. A system that works for one person may not work for another. Streamlining can fail if it is imposed without negotiation or if it ignores differences in preference and responsibility. The quarter helps here because it frames changes as temporary experiments. Experiments are easier to accept than permanent reforms. They invite feedback. They reduce defensiveness. They also allow you to separate the essence of the system—the output you need—from the exact method of getting there.

Outputs are the anchor.

The quiet motif for this subchapter is the "rail". A rail is a simple guide that makes a movement easier and more reliable: the railing on a stair, the groove that keeps a sliding door aligned, the track that keeps a train moving in the intended direction. Daily systems are rails for attention. Without rails, you wander into whatever demands are loudest. With rails, you can move through routine work with less thought, preserving attention for what actually deserves it: complex projects, relationships, learning, rest. Rails are not prisons. Rails are relief.

Relief is not laziness.

One reason people resist system design is a fear of becoming mechanical. They want to stay spontaneous, human, open to possibility. Yet systems do not eliminate spontaneity; they protect it. When bills are handled predictably, you can be spontaneous without dread. When meals have a rhythm, you can improvise without chaos. When email has boundaries, you can respond warmly without being consumed. The aim is not to automate life into dullness. The aim is to remove the dullest frictions so that energy can go elsewhere. That is the essence of an Upgrade Day: shifting effort from constant firefighting to periodic, deliberate design.

Design requires scheduling.

If a system change is not scheduled, it remains a good idea. Good ideas are cheap. Scheduled experiments cost something: time, attention, willingness to be wrong. That cost is precisely why scheduling matters. A quarterly system experiment should be small enough to implement and long enough to evaluate. Evaluation does not require elaborate metrics. It requires noticing a few signs: did the system reduce searching, reduce last-minute scrambling, reduce repeated decisions, reduce resentment? Did it produce the output reliably? Did it survive a busy week? Did it create new problems? These are behavioural questions. They keep system design grounded.

Grounded design is humane.

The quarter also keeps you from trying to streamline everything at once—a common failure that resembles a home "declutter" weekend that ends with exhaustion and no lasting change. Systems are interconnected. If you change ten systems at once, you cannot tell what helped or what hurt. You also create too many new habits simultaneously. That is a recipe for collapse. One or two systems per quarter respects the rate at which humans actually adapt. It creates learning. It creates compounding. It prevents the system redesign from becoming another project that drains the very capacity it aims to create.

Capacity is the prize.

The forward test is therefore precise. Looking at the last ninety days, which single minor process—email, shopping, meals, household admin, paperwork—generated the most repeated friction through searching, redoing, or last-minute scrambling, and what one small, scheduled experiment over the next quarter would reduce that friction enough that your attention can return to what matters rather than to keeping the rails from falling apart?

Reducing friction points

In March 2018, at the Albert Einstein College of Medicine in New York, a small behavioural study became popular far beyond academic circles because it described something most people already recognised in their own lives: when the environment makes a choice easier, people tend to take it. The details were not mystical. It was ordinary human behaviour observed under ordinary constraints. The research sits in a long tradition of "choice architecture" associated with behavioural economics, popularised for general readers by Richard Thaler and Cass Sunstein in *Nudge* (2008): design the surroundings so that the better option is more likely without demanding constant self-control. One can debate the ethics of nudges at the policy level. At the household level, the principle is straightforward.

Design shapes defaults.

The Upgrade Day approach has been quietly circling this truth from the beginning. Money, health, relationships, learning, work—these domains are often discussed as though they live in separate rooms. In reality they share a corridor, and the corridor is made of friction. The small resistances in a day determine whether you cook or order food, whether you train or skip, whether you read or scroll, whether you call a friend or forget, whether you save or spend. People tend to imagine that "better habits" are an internal victory. Yet much of what we call habit is simply repeated response to the same environment. If you want different responses, you must change something outside your head.

Outside is underrated.

A friction point is any feature of your surroundings that makes a desired behaviour harder or an undesired behaviour easier. The important word is "point". Friction is local. It concentrates. It lives at thresholds: the front door where shoes pile up, the phone screen where distraction is one tap away, the kitchen counter where snacks are visible, the desk where unfinished paperwork accumulates, the email inbox that offers a fresh request every time you glance at it.

When friction is local, the solution can also be local. This is the chapter's promise: not a full makeover, not a new identity, not a heroic surge of discipline, but a handful of high-impact tweaks that reduce friction at the points that matter.

Small changes. Real consequences.

The method is deceptively simple. Ask a question that sounds almost too modest to matter: what tiny change to my surroundings would make this habit easier? The reason this question is powerful is that it forces specificity. "Be healthier" is an abstraction. "Walk more" is closer. "Put shoes where they are easy to grab" is a physical decision. "Spend less" is an abstraction. "Remove stored card details from the most tempting shopping app" is a physical-and-digital decision. "Learn consistently" is an abstraction. "Leave the notebook open on the desk where the first ten minutes of the day begin" is a spatial decision. Abstractions feel noble. They also feel slippery. Friction questions are concrete. Concrete questions can be acted on.

Action is the only honest measure.

The quarter is particularly suited to friction work because it converts small changes into observable data. Over ninety days, you can compare. You can notice whether the tweak actually changed behaviour or merely made the home look nicer. This is crucial, because many people confuse aesthetic improvement with functional improvement. A cleaner desk can still be a distraction if the core friction—unclear priorities, constant notifications, lack of capture—remains. Conversely, a space can remain visually imperfect and still support better habits if the key threshold has been improved. Friction work is not about beauty. It is about flow.

Flow is felt, not declared.

To keep this honest, it helps to anchor friction reduction to the four domains that most reliably respond to environmental design: money, health, relationships, and learning. Each domain has its own characteristic frictions, and each domain offers visible behaviours you can observe. Money is shaped by the ease of spending versus saving. Health is shaped by the ease of movement versus inertia and the ease of nourishing food versus convenience food. Relationships are shaped by the ease of contact versus the ease of neglect. Learning is shaped by the ease of practice versus the ease of passive consumption. Each of these is a competition between two defaults. The environment often rigs the contest.

Rigging can be reversed.

Money is a clean example because many financial behaviours are interface behaviours. Spending happens through taps and swipes. Saving happens through friction: extra steps, delayed gratification, paperwork, or at least intentionality. This is not a claim about morality. It is a claim about mechanics. Retailers and apps are designed to reduce purchase friction—stored cards, one-click checkout, persuasive notifications. Savings systems are often designed with more steps and less immediate reward. Behavioural economics has long emphasised that small "hassle factors" can powerfully influence choices, sometimes more than large incentives (a theme in the literature on present bias and inertia; see Thaler & Sunstein, 2008, for a widely cited synthesis). The implication for a quarterly reset is not to become paranoid about marketing. It is simply to notice where purchase friction has been engineered away and where saving friction remains high.

Friction is a dial.

Health is equally shaped by dial settings. People often treat exercise consistency as a test of inner strength. Yet the environment can turn strength into routine or routine into struggle. The distance between you and your walking shoes matters. The ease of accessing a gym bag matters. The presence of cues matters. The stability of a schedule matters. This overlaps with what behavioural scientists call cueing and context-dependent behaviour: actions become more likely when the context reliably triggers them. James Clear's popular writing has made this intuitive for many readers, but the underlying principle is older and rooted in habit research. Again, the point here is not to offer medical instruction. It is to observe that a person is more likely to move when movement is made easy to begin and hard to avoid.

Beginnings decide outcomes.

Relationships, too, are susceptible to friction points, though we often pretend they are purely emotional. The friction in relationships is often logistical: uncertainty about when to reach out, guilt about not having replied, the absence of a quiet moment to call, the awkwardness of initiating contact after a long silence, the social fatigue created by constant messaging. Digital communication lowers some frictions and introduces others. It is easier than ever to send a quick message; it is also easier than ever to let relationships dissolve into intermittent reaction. A small environmental change—creating a specific, low-friction "contact moment" in the week, or placing a reminder where it will actually be seen—can transform relationships more than a vague intention to "be better at keeping in touch".

Intentions are fragile.

Learning is perhaps the most environment-sensitive domain of all. Practice requires attention and time, which are the first resources to be eaten by friction. If your digital environment delivers constant novelty—news, social media, messages—then focused learning competes against a stream designed to be irresistible. Research on attention and digital interruption does not require apocalyptic claims to be useful. It is enough to note that frequent switching makes it harder to sustain deep work, and that environments that reduce interruption can support longer focus periods (Mark, Gonzalez & Harris, 2005). A friction reduction approach to learning asks: what tiny change makes practice easier to start and easier to continue? Often the answer is not a grand new course. It is a simpler practice surface, fewer distractions, and a more visible cue.

Visibility is a lever.

This is where the "Show → Name → Explain → Implication" engine becomes practical. Show: a person sits down to write and spends ten minutes locating the right document, clearing space, and resisting phone pings; the writing session is shortened and feels stressful. Name: *start-up friction.* Explain: start-up friction consumes the limited energy available at the beginning of an activity; if the beginning is unpleasant, the brain learns to avoid starting. Implication: reduce start-up friction by making the beginning easier—fewer steps, clearer materials, fewer interruptions. The same logic applies to saving, exercising, calling, practising. Start-up friction is one of the highest-impact points because it governs whether an activity happens at all.

If it doesn't start, it doesn't matter.

A second friction pattern is worth naming because it appears across all domains: *recovery friction*. Recovery friction is the effort required to resume an activity after interruption. A person who has missed a week of training often feels that resuming requires an elaborate restart. A person who has ignored email feels that catching up requires a marathon. A person who has not practised a skill feels that returning requires a large block of time. A person who has not called a friend feels that the gap is awkward to bridge. Recovery friction creates the all-or-nothing trap: if you can't do it perfectly, you don't do it at all. Quarterly rituals are a remedy because they normalise resumption. But the environment can support resumption too, by making "getting back on" easy rather than dramatic.

Drama is an obstacle.

At this point, a credible counter-example must be faced. Some friction is protective. Friction can prevent impulsive action. A bit of friction before spending can be a safeguard. A bit of friction before responding to a provocative message can prevent regret. A bit of friction before committing to another obligation can protect time. If you remove friction indiscriminately, you can make harmful behaviour easier as well as helpful behaviour. The reconciliation is to treat friction like a tool, not an enemy. Remove friction for behaviours you want. Add friction for behaviours you want less of. Keep friction where it protects deliberation and safety.

Deliberation is a form of care.

This is why "tiny change" is not the same as "no resistance". The best friction design often involves moving resistance to the right place. For example, you might keep saving automatic and spending slightly slower, or keep practice materials visible and distraction apps less accessible, or keep social connection easier to initiate and commitments harder to accept casually. In behavioural economics terms, you are adjusting the "choice architecture" of your own life. In ordinary terms, you are rearranging the room so the better path is the easier path.

Easier is not cheating.

A second named, checkable example illustrates compounding through environment design. In 1983, in the UK, the "seat belt law" came into force requiring front-seat occupants to wear seat belts. The safety benefits of seat belts have been documented across decades by transport authorities and researchers. What is relevant here is not policy debate but design logic: the seat belt is an environmental intervention that changes a behaviour by making it built into the routine of entering a car. The belt is physically present at the threshold. You do not need a daily pep talk about safety. The car's environment prompts the action. This is the kind of intervention the chapter aims to help you emulate in miniature, privately, for your own goals.

Thresholds are where habits live.

The quiet motif for this subchapter is the *groove.* A groove in a key guides it into a lock. A groove in a record guides a needle. A groove in a path guides feet. Grooves are not glamorous. They are persistent. Once a groove exists, behaviour follows it with less effort. Environments create grooves whether you plan them or not. The quarterly practice is about carving grooves intentionally: small adjustments that make the right behaviour easier to repeat until it becomes normal. Over several quarters, these grooves accumulate into a life that feels less like constant self-correction and more like quiet alignment.

Alignment is the true luxury.

Modern life is full of friction that nobody chose: complex interfaces, endless subscription models, crowded schedules, digital interruption, sprawling admin. People adapt by becoming reactive. They live inside other people's systems: employers' calendars, companies' notifications, retailers' persuasion, social networks' incentives. The Upgrade Day is a chance to reclaim a little authorship. Friction reduction is one of the most pragmatic ways to do it because it does not require you to become a different person. It requires you to become a better designer of your own defaults.

Defaults are destiny in slow motion.

The end of this section should not resolve into a neat moral. It should create a forward tension, because there is always a trade-off. Making one behaviour easier often requires making another behaviour slightly harder. Keeping practice materials visible may make a room feel less tidy. Adding friction to spending may make purchases slightly slower. Protecting attention may require saying "not now" more often. Simplifying systems may mean disappointing someone who expects instant replies. These are real costs. The question is whether the costs buy you the kind of quarter you actually want.

The forward test is therefore diagnostic. Over the next ninety days, in which domain—money, health, relationships, or learning—does a single recurring friction point most reliably push you away from the person you are trying to be, and what tiny environmental change would shift the groove so that, on your tiredest day, the better behaviour becomes the default rather than the exception?

Chapter 9
Rest, Travel and Play

On 28 May 1953, Edmund Hillary and Tenzing Norgay reached the summit of Everest, and the photographs that circulated afterwards were not only about conquest. They were about exhaustion made visible: stiff clothing, oxygen apparatus, faces narrowed by cold and altitude. The summit was a moment; the descent was the true work. In mountaineering, everybody knows the rule that sounds like superstition until you've seen it proved: most accidents happen on the way down, when the goal has been achieved and the body is running on fumes. The detail worth carrying into ordinary life is not the romance of adventure. It is the logic. Human beings tend to spend their energy as though the summit is the end of the story, then act surprised when fatigue turns the descent into a hazard.

Fatigue is not a personal flaw.

Modern adulthood trains people to treat energy as an infinite resource and rest as a guilty afterthought. Work expands into evenings because digital systems do not close. Social obligations multiply because saying yes has become frictionless. Entertainment becomes more compulsive because it is always available and endlessly optimised. Even health habits can become another performance arena. The result is a peculiar cultural paradox: people speak constantly about "wellbeing" while living inside schedules that make wellbeing structurally difficult. Many are not burned out in a dramatic, clinical sense. They are simply worn down, quarter after quarter, by the accumulation of unfinished recovery.

Recovery is not optional.

The Upgrade Day framework has asked for periodic resets of money, health, relationships, work, learning, and environment because drift is inevitable. This chapter applies the same seriousness to rest and play, not as indulgence, but as infrastructure. It begins with a question most competent adults avoid because it threatens the story they tell about themselves: how has energy *really* been over the last quarter? Not in the language of achievements and productivity, but in the language of lived experience—moments of exhaustion, moments of flow, moments of boredom that did not refresh but numbed. Energy is the currency that buys everything else in this book. If the currency is depleted, every other domain becomes harder to manage, and "discipline" becomes an expensive fantasy.

Honesty comes before planning.

Energy is also slippery because it is subjective. People remember the peak moments—the late nights, the deadlines, the social whirl, the holiday—and forget the ordinary days that quietly determined their state. The quarter, however, leaves traces. You can see them in calendars full of unbroken obligations. You can see them in the frequency of small escapes: more scrolling, more snacking, more impulse spending, more avoidance. You can see them in the tone of your interactions: irritability, impatience, a shorter fuse. These are not moral indictments. They are signals. Signals can be read. The reader who takes rest seriously is not weak; they are simply literate in their own physiology and psychology.

Literacy is power.

From this honest assessment comes a more radical move than it first appears: planning recovery blocks with the same deliberate attention usually reserved for work. Many people "rest" only when forced—when illness arrives, when a relationship frays, when a mistake becomes public, when the body refuses to cooperate. This is not merely unfortunate. It is inefficient in the most human sense: forced rest is often less restorative because it arrives with anxiety and guilt. Planned recovery, by contrast, can be genuinely renewing because it arrives with permission. Planning is not control for its own sake. It is a commitment to treat the future self as real.

The future self will arrive.

Recovery blocks can take many forms, and the most useful are often unglamorous: a quieter weekend after an intense stretch of work, a deliberately lighter week around a demanding project, a consistent winding-down ritual that closes the day rather than letting it bleed into midnight. The common feature is that recovery is scheduled, protected, and treated as part of the plan rather than as the absence of a plan. This is difficult because it conflicts with a popular identity: the competent person who is always available, always responsive, always capable. Yet availability is not the same as aliveness. Availability can be a form of slow self-erasure.

Self-erasure is rarely noticed until it hurts.

This chapter also insists on something that productivity culture tends to dismiss: travel and retreat are not luxuries reserved for people with expansive budgets or flexible lives. They can be modest, local, and still profound. A day trip can reset perception. A visit to a friend in another city can reintroduce variety into a life that has become too repetitive. A low-key retreat—nothing more than a change of scenery and fewer obligations—can restore a sense of spaciousness. The value of travel is not the destination. It is the interruption of default. It offers a temporary suspension of the grooves that daily life has carved, and in that suspension you often see what the grooves have been doing to you.

Default is powerful.

There is a practical reason travel and play belong in a quarterly ritual. Without scheduling, they tend to be perpetually deferred. People wait for the "right time", which rarely arrives because the calendar is never empty, and responsibility is never complete. The quarter offers a compromise between spontaneity and procrastination: sketch one outing or retreat as a plausible option, even if details remain flexible. The sketch matters because it shifts leisure from fantasy to possibility. Possibility changes behaviour. You begin to protect space. You begin to say "not this quarter" to some obligations, not because you are selfish, but because you are choosing to inhabit your own life.

Inhabiting matters.

The final element of the chapter is perhaps the most quietly subversive: protecting hobbies and fun. Many adults do not stop having hobbies because they dislike them. They stop because life becomes crowded, and leisure becomes instrumental. A walk must be counted. A book must be "useful". A craft must be monetised. A game must become a side hustle. Enjoyment is treated as suspicious unless it produces output. The result is a thinning of the self. Play is not merely entertainment. It is a psychological mode that supports curiosity, experimentation, and resilience. It also reminds people that they are not machines designed solely for performance.

Machines do not laugh.

The chapter approaches play without sentimentality. It does not ask for a return to childhood innocence. It asks for the recovery of adult aliveness: the activities that make time feel different, that create a sense of absorption without pressure, that reconnect you to people or places or parts of your mind that work cannot reach. Hobbies are also strangely diagnostic. When they disappear, it often indicates that life has become too narrow, too anxious, too optimised. When they return, even in small doses, they often signal that capacity has been restored.

Capacity changes everything.

A subtle motif threads through this chapter: the "exhale". Many people live as though life is an endless inhale—taking in tasks, messages, obligations, information—without a corresponding exhale. The exhale is where the system resets. It is where tension leaves the body. It is where the mind reorganises. It is where meaning consolidates. Without exhale, even good things begin to feel heavy. Rest, travel, and play are different forms of exhale. They do not compete with achievement; they make achievement sustainable. The quarter, again, matters because it offers a rhythm: inhale for a season, exhale deliberately, then choose how to inhale next.

Still, this is not a romantic plea for leisure. There are real constraints: financial limits, caring responsibilities, chronic stressors, unpredictable work, health issues. Some quarters will be demanding. Some will be emotionally difficult. The chapter's stance is not naïve. It argues that constraints make deliberate rest more important, not less. When life is tight, small recovery blocks become essential.

When travel is impossible, micro-retreats—changes in routine, changes in setting, reductions in stimulation—can still matter. When hobbies feel out of reach, play can begin as a small protected window rather than a full re-entry into an old identity.

The point is not scale. It is seriousness.

Modern relevance is obvious but not new. Digital systems make it possible to work anywhere, which quietly means work can happen everywhere. The boundary between labour and leisure, once enforced by geography and time, is now enforced mainly by choice. Choice is an unreliable boundary when you are tired. This chapter treats boundaries as a design problem, not as a test of virtue. It treats rest as a decision with trade-offs rather than as an indulgence. It treats travel and play as components of a life well-lived rather than as rewards to be earned after endless output.

A life is not a rewards programme.

By the end of this chapter, the reader should feel a slight shift in what counts as "serious". Serious is not only the spreadsheet and the calendar and the project pipeline. Serious is also the energy that allows you to care, think, learn, and connect. Serious is the capacity to enjoy. Serious is the willingness to schedule an exhale before the body forces one. And because this book operates on quarters rather than years, the decisions here are not abstract: they are choices about the next ninety days, which means they can be tested and felt.

The final movement of the introduction must leave a forward tension rather than a tidy lesson. The tension is a trade-off you cannot avoid: if the next quarter contains deliberate recovery, something else must shrink—availability, output, obligations, or the illusion that you can do everything without cost. The question this chapter equips the reader to face is therefore both practical and existential: when you look at the coming ninety days, where will you place the exhale—through recovery blocks, a modest trip or retreat, and a protected pocket of play—so that your life does not become an endless descent from one summit to the next?

Assessing energy levels

On 15 June 2010, in Bethesda, Maryland, the National Institute of Mental Health published the results of the "Day Reconstruction Method" work that Daniel Kahneman and colleagues had helped popularise: a way of breaking a day into episodes and asking people to rate how they felt in each one. The method was not a mood diary in the romantic sense. It was a sober attempt to measure lived experience with less distortion from memory. The underlying observation is disarmingly relevant to a quarterly reset: people are poor witnesses to their own days when they speak in generalities, but better witnesses when they reconstruct specifics (Kahneman et al., 2004; Kahneman & Krueger, 2006). Energy, like time, is easiest to misjudge when you narrate it in bulk.

Memory edits the story.

Most adults, especially those with demanding roles, treat energy as a secondary variable: a background condition that should not be allowed to interfere with plans. They measure output, not capacity. They notice exhaustion only when it becomes dramatic—illness, tears, mistakes, or a weekend spent staring at a screen without pleasure. Everything before that is explained away as "a busy patch". A busy patch becomes a busy year. Then life becomes the sort of thing that is survived rather than inhabited. The first work of this subchapter is not to persuade anyone to value rest. It is to make energy visible as data, so that rest can later be planned as a decision rather than as a collapse.

Collapses are expensive.

To *show* the problem, consider a familiar quarter: the calendar fills, projects overlap, social commitments become obligations, and the small administrative tasks that keep a life running multiply. The person in the middle of it can often still perform. They answer messages. They deliver work. They appear fine. Yet the cost shows up in small signals: sleep becomes lighter or irregular; patience shortens; appetite changes; exercise, reading, or calling friends becomes "optional" and therefore disappears. These are not moral failings. They are symptoms of a system operating near the edge. The name for this is *latent fatigue*: fatigue that is present but masked by adrenaline, social expectation, and the momentum of deadlines. Latent fatigue is dangerous precisely because it feels normal.

Normal is not the same as healthy.

Latent fatigue also distorts planning. When people are tired, they underestimate recovery time and overestimate future energy. They agree to things they later resent. They choose tasks that promise quick relief rather than long-term benefit. They spend money on convenience because it buys a few minutes of breathing space. They make brittle promises to themselves: "next week will be calmer." Next week rarely is. The implication is that an Upgrade Day without an energy assessment becomes a planning exercise built on fantasy. Energy is the substrate. If the substrate is wrong, the plan is wrong.

Plans should be built on reality.

Energy assessment, done well, is not introspective navel-gazing. It is a structured recall of three kinds of moments: exhaustion, flow, and boredom. Exhaustion is not only being tired. It is the felt sense that the system is overdrawn—irritability, heaviness, the urge to withdraw, the sense that even small tasks require force. Flow is not only productivity. It is the state in which effort feels meaningful and time behaves strangely; you are absorbed without being drained. Boredom is not always a lack of stimulus. It is often a mismatch between the task and the mind: repetitive work, shallow scrolling, meetings with no purpose, entertainment that numbs rather than restores. These three states form a triangle that maps a quarter better than any single metric.

Triangles reveal shape.

Begin with exhaustion. The first mistake people make is to treat exhaustion as a single event: "I was exhausted in late November." In reality exhaustion is episodic. It arrives in waves. It has triggers. It has patterns. A quarter contains multiple exhaustion points, and those points often cluster around predictable features: travel, deadlines, family obligations, health disruptions, social overcommitment. This is where the episode-based approach is useful. Instead of asking "Was I tired this quarter?", you reconstruct. You identify specific weeks or days that felt depleted and you note what was happening: not in the language of blame, but in the language of conditions. Sleep shortened. Meetings stacked. Meals became irregular. A project had no boundaries. The implication is simple: energy is not a personality trait; it is a product of conditions.

Conditions can be changed.

Flow provides a counterweight to the cultural habit of treating life as a grind. Many high performers learn to ignore exhaustion and become proud of it. Flow interrupts that narrative because flow is evidence that energy can be abundant under the right conditions. The point is not to chase flow as a drug. The point is to notice what supported it. Flow tends to appear when tasks are meaningful, goals are clear, and interruptions are limited; it also tends to appear when the body is not already depleted. In psychological research, Mihaly Csikszentmihalyi's work on flow, popularised in *Flow* (1990), described this state as deep engagement when challenge and skill are well matched. The implication for a quarterly energy assessment is not to become a hobby psychologist. It is to treat flow as a clue. If flow occurred in certain kinds of work or certain settings, those conditions can be protected later.

Protection is a design choice.

Now boredom. Boredom is often misread. People assume boredom means they need novelty, entertainment, or stimulation. Sometimes that is true. Often boredom is a sign of misalignment: too much time spent in tasks that are low-value, low-meaning, or overly constrained. Boredom can also be a symptom of depletion: when energy is low, even good things feel dull. It can be a symptom of avoidance: scrolling and snacking and busywork masquerade as "a break" while quietly draining attention. The quarterly assessment treats boredom as data. What did boredom lead to? More consumption? More procrastination? More irritation? Or did it lead to a healthy pause? The implication is that boredom is not simply unpleasant; it is directional.

Direction matters.

To keep the assessment grounded, energy must be paired with visible behaviours and decisions. "I felt stressed" is vague. "I checked email first thing and then never regained focus" is a behaviour. "I kept cancelling plans because leaving the house felt too hard" is a behaviour. "I spent more on takeaway because cooking felt impossible" is a behaviour. "I stopped reading because my attention would not settle" is a behaviour. The quarter supplies evidence of these behaviours: calendar patterns, spending patterns, training consistency, message logs, even the state of the home. The energy assessment is the narrative that makes sense of those traces. It also prevents a common cognitive trap: the tendency to interpret all outcomes as willpower problems.

Willpower is overrated.

A named, checkable example of the costs of neglecting recovery comes from elite sport, where energy is treated as a measurable resource rather than a virtue signal. In May 1999, Manchester United completed an extraordinary season culminating in the Champions League final in Barcelona on 26 May. The public story was about resilience and late goals. Behind it was a carefully managed season of rotation, recovery, and pacing—decisions about which matches to prioritise and how to manage players' physical and mental load. The details of any specific team's internal practices are not fully public, and it would be foolish to pretend to know them. The point, however, is verifiable at the level of structure: elite performance depends on recovery because the body cannot stay at peak output indefinitely. The implication is uncomfortable for professionals: you are not exempt from physiology because your work is intellectual.

Brains are bodies.

A second example, from science rather than sport, illustrates a different angle: the cost of ignoring boredom. In the 1960s, the psychologist Donald Hebb at McGill University in Montreal studied sensory deprivation, showing that when stimulation is reduced and the environment becomes monotonous, the mind does not become calm; it becomes unsettled, prone to hallucination and distress. The experiments were ethically controversial by today's standards, and their details are widely documented in the history of psychology. The point here is not to dredge up the worst of mid-century research. It is to underscore a principle: boredom and monotony are not neutral states. They can destabilise attention and mood. In modern life, boredom often arrives not as deprivation but as overexposure to low-quality stimulation—endless feeds, repetitive tasks, meetings without meaning. The implication is that "rest" that consists only of numbing consumption may not restore energy.

Not all breaks are recovery.

At this point, an honest limitation must be stated. Energy is influenced by factors that cannot be solved by scheduling: chronic illness, caregiving demands, financial stress, grief, and unpredictable work constraints. Some quarters are legitimately hard. An energy assessment that assumes full control would be insulting. The reconciliation is to adjust the aim. The aim is not to eliminate fatigue. The aim is to see it clearly enough to reduce unnecessary depletion and to protect whatever recovery is possible within constraints. Even a constrained life can often be improved by identifying the specific points where energy drains fastest, and by making small changes that reduce avoidable friction.

Avoidable is the keyword.

A useful energy assessment therefore separates three categories. There is *structural drain*: obligations that are real and not easily changed—care responsibilities, core job demands, essential admin. There is *optional drain*: commitments chosen out of habit, guilt, or default—unnecessary meetings, social obligations that no longer fit, digital habits that eat evenings. And there is *restorative effort*: actions that require some energy upfront but increase energy over time—sleep routines, movement, meaningful learning, nourishing connection, time outdoors, play. The assessment does not dictate what belongs in each category. It asks you to classify honestly. Classification turns vague fatigue into a map.

Maps support navigation.

The motif that threads this piece is the "battery gauge". Most people treat themselves as though they have no gauge. They notice only when the device shuts down. Yet you do have a gauge; it is simply not a number on a screen. It is a pattern of signals: how quickly you become irritated, whether you seek solitude or stimulation, whether you crave quick rewards, whether you avoid initiating tasks, whether small setbacks feel catastrophic. The quarterly ritual invites you to read the gauge without dramatics. Reading the gauge does not mean obsessing. It means acknowledging where you have been running close to empty and where, surprisingly, you were charged.

Charged feels different.

To make this assessment precise, you reconstruct the quarter in episodes rather than impressions. You pick a handful of representative weeks—perhaps one that felt strong, one that felt stretched, one that felt chaotic, one that felt flat. You recall the daily pattern: when did you feel clear, when did you feel dull, when did you feel anxious, when did you feel absorbed? You then connect these states to conditions: sleep, workload, social load, environment, digital habits, movement, meals, travel. The aim is not to produce a perfect causal model. Human lives are not laboratories. The aim is to identify reliable associations: "When meetings filled mornings, I never reached flow." "When I travelled midweek, the recovery time was longer than I admitted." "When I worked late three nights in a row, my weekends stopped restoring me." These are not universal truths. They are personal patterns. Patterns can be used.

Use is the point.

Once patterns are visible, the assessment naturally leads to a deeper question: what counts as "high energy" in your life? Many people assume high energy means perpetual enthusiasm. That is a child's definition. Adult high energy often looks calmer: stable attention, steady mood, willingness to engage, capacity for patience, ability to enjoy leisure without needing it to be an escape. In other words, energy is not only about how much you can do. It is about how you experience what you do. A quarter that looks productive on paper can still feel miserable. A quarter that is less productive can feel humane and alive. The assessment makes this distinction possible.

Experience is a metric.

From here, the chapter's later moves become credible: planning recovery blocks, designing modest trips and retreats, protecting hobbies. Without a clear energy picture, those moves can look like optional pleasures. With the energy picture, they become necessities of system maintenance. The Upgrade Day mindset treats collapse as failure of timing, not of character. Energy assessment is the timing work. It tells you where the battery gauge was ignored and where it was respected, and it sets the stage for scheduling in a way that prevents the quarter from becoming an uncontrolled descent.

The forward test should remain unresolved, because the point is to carry a question into action. Over the last ninety days, when did your battery gauge flicker—through irritability, numbness, avoidance, or restless scrolling—and when did it rise—through flow, ease, or genuine enjoyment—and what trade-off are you willing to make next quarter so that the gauge is read in time rather than only after the shutdown?

Planning recovery blocks

In July 1969, in Houston, the NASA Mission Control schedule for Apollo 11 contained something that rarely appears in popular retellings: planned sleep. The flight plan was built around work, yes, but also around the fact that human beings cannot think clearly forever. The public remembers the first step on the Moon on 20 July 1969. Engineers remember checklists, handovers, and the deliberate decisions about when to rest so that critical work could be done without degraded judgement. The space programme did not treat rest as a reward. It treated rest as an operational requirement.

Operational thinking changes everything.

Most adults do the opposite. They treat recovery as what happens in the gaps after obligations have been met, which is like treating maintenance as what happens after the machine breaks. The result is predictable: recovery becomes erratic, guilt-ridden, and insufficient. People work late, promise themselves they will "catch up" at the weekend, then fill the weekend with errands and social commitments because the calendar still has openings. The tiredness is softened with stimulants and distractions. When the system finally forces a stop—illness, emotional collapse, a mistake that can't be ignored—it feels like bad luck rather than the logical outcome of a schedule that had no deliberate exhale.

Exhale must be designed.

To *show* the core issue, imagine a quarter organised around intensity spikes: a grant deadline, a product launch, exam season, a conference, a major family event. The adult in this quarter behaves sensibly by many standards. They prioritise. They work hard. They deliver. Yet they do so with an implicit assumption: after the spike, life will naturally become lighter. Often it does not. The spike ends, but the next demand begins immediately. Email backlog, household admin, neglected relationships, and deferred health habits rush in to occupy the space where recovery might have lived. The person experiences a peculiar fatigue: not the fatigue of hard work, which can be satisfying, but the fatigue of *uninterrupted demand.* There was no downshift.

Downshifts prevent damage.

The name for the missing ingredient is *recovery blocks*: scheduled periods of lower demand that protect the body and mind's ability to restore. A recovery block can be a quiet weekend, a lighter week after an intense phase, or a daily wind-down ritual that closes the day. The concept is not new. Athletes use "deload" weeks; researchers protect reading days; surgeons have rota patterns; even religious traditions contain sabbath-like pauses. The point is not to copy any one model. The point is to recognise that recovery is a resource with its own requirements: time, reduced stimulation, reduced obligation, and permission.

Permission is part of the mechanism.

Why schedule recovery rather than rely on spontaneous rest? Because spontaneity tends to be colonised by whatever is loudest.

This is not a character judgement. It is a description of how attention works. Unscheduled time is often immediately filled by reactive tasks: messages that "only take a minute", errands that have been nagging, social obligations that feel easier to accept than to decline. Spontaneous rest is also fragile because it competes with guilt. When rest is unplanned, it can feel like avoidance; when it is planned, it can feel like competence. That change in meaning matters because guilt undermines restoration.

Guilt prevents rest.

There is also a cognitive reason. People systematically underestimate how much recovery they will need after sustained effort. The planning fallacy, described by Daniel Kahneman and Amos Tversky in 1979, shows that people tend to underestimate task duration and overestimate smoothness of execution (Kahneman & Tversky, 1979). The same bias applies to recovery: "I'll be fine next week" becomes an assumption, then a trap. Recovery blocks are a way of correcting for that bias by making recovery visible in the same place where bias does its damage: the calendar.

Calendars tell the truth.

A recovery block, however, should not be misunderstood as a holiday. It is not necessarily leisure filled with activity. It is a deliberate reduction of demand. Demand can come from work, from social obligations, from travel, from high-stimulation environments, even from intense hobbies. A block can be restorative and still include effort—walking, cooking, reading, creative work—because restorative effort is different from draining effort. Draining effort is the kind that leaves you more fragmented and depleted. Restorative effort is the kind that leaves you more coherent. The difference is often felt in the body: shoulders soften rather than tighten; sleep becomes deeper rather than lighter; irritability decreases rather than increases.

The body keeps score.

To plan recovery blocks without turning rest into another performance arena, you need to pair abstractions with visible signals. Instead of "I need more rest," you identify what "more rest" would look like in behaviour. That might mean fewer evenings that end with screens, fewer consecutive days of early starts, fewer weekends dominated by catch-up admin, fewer back-to-back commitments. It might mean more mornings that begin without immediate digital demand, more time outdoors, more uninterrupted reading, more unstructured conversation. These are not moral ideals. They are observable patterns. The quarter gives you the scale to notice whether those patterns exist.

Patterns are measurable.

This is where the previous subchapter's energy assessment becomes useful. You have already identified exhaustion points, flow points, and boredom points. Now you translate those into scheduling decisions. Show: after a deadline week, a person repeatedly falls into numbing consumption and short sleep. Name: *post-intensity rebound.* Explain: when the nervous system has been running hot, the brain seeks easy reward and stimulation, but those do not restore capacity. Implication: schedule a lower-stimulation recovery block immediately after intensity, before the rebound behaviour has room to become the default. A recovery block is not merely time off. It is a strategic placement of lower demand at the exact moment the system is most vulnerable.

Vulnerability is predictable.

A second common pattern is *micro-debt accumulation.* People borrow small amounts of energy every day—late nights, skipped breaks, rushed meals, constant availability—assuming they can repay the debt later. The repayment rarely happens. The debt compounds. The quarter ends with a sense of heaviness that seems mysterious because no single day felt catastrophic. A scheduled daily wind-down ritual can act as micro-repayment: not a cure-all, not a grand transformation, but a consistent boundary that reduces the daily borrowing. The ritual might be as simple as a consistent closing sequence: a fixed time when work communications stop, lights dim, stimulation drops, and the body gets a signal that the day has ended.

The specifics will vary. The principle is that the day needs a clean edge.

Edges protect recovery.

Two named, checkable examples help anchor the seriousness of this. The first comes from sport science and training culture rather than medical prescription. Strength training programmes commonly include planned deload periods—reduced volume or intensity—because adaptation requires recovery. This is not folk wisdom alone; it is embedded in widely used periodisation models and coaching practice. Tudor Bompa's work on periodisation, for instance, was influential in formalising training cycles with planned recovery phases (*Periodization*, 1999). The exact prescriptions vary, and individuals differ, but the structural idea is robust: without planned reduction in load, performance and wellbeing degrade. Translate this from the gym to knowledge work and family life, and the principle remains: sustained load without planned reduction increases risk of breakdown, mistakes, and diminished enjoyment.

Enjoyment matters too.

The second example is organisational. In 2013, the Draugiem Group, a Latvian company, developed an internal productivity tool later reported widely as "DeskTime", analysing when employees were most productive and how breaks related to performance. The popularised lesson was not that people should work constantly; it was that high performers tended to take breaks and used time in a more segmented way (various write-ups appeared in subsequent years). One should be cautious with such corporate studies: methods are not always peer-reviewed, and context matters. Yet the example illustrates a larger, checkable observation: many effective systems assume breaks rather than leaving breaks to chance. The implication is modest: recovery can be treated as a planned component of performance rather than as its opposite.

Performance is not the goal here.

It would be a mistake to make recovery planning solely about output. Recovery also protects judgement, relationships, and the capacity for play. Tired people are more likely to say sharp things they regret. They are more likely to spend impulsively. They are more likely to abandon learning because attention collapses. They are more likely to confuse boredom with the need for stimulation. Recovery blocks therefore sit at the junction of the book's domains. They are not a separate "self-care" add-on. They are infrastructure that supports money decisions, health behaviours, social patience, and learning consistency.

Infrastructure is invisible when it works.

There is, however, a credible counter-example and limitation that deserves respect. Not everyone can schedule recovery blocks freely. Carers, shift workers, people in insecure work, those dealing with crises, and those with heavy family obligations may find the very idea of "quiet weekends" laughable. It would be dishonest to pretend otherwise. The reconciliation is to scale the concept without abandoning it. Recovery blocks can be micro-blocks: a protected hour, a lighter evening, a deliberately empty half-day, a boundary around one recurring commitment. The goal is not to replicate someone else's leisure. It is to create at least one reliable downshift in the quarter. Even small downshifts can prevent complete depletion, and small downshifts are often more realistic and therefore more sustainable.

Sustainable beats heroic.

Planning recovery blocks also requires distinguishing between *rest* and *relief*. Relief is what makes discomfort go away quickly—scrolling, snacking, numbing entertainment, shopping. Relief can be useful in small doses, but it often leaves energy unchanged or worse. Rest is what restores capacity: sleep, lower stimulation, physical ease, meaningful connection, time outdoors, focused play, unpressured reading, quiet. Again, no prescriptions are needed here; the distinction is experiential. If the "break" leaves you more scattered, it was relief. If it leaves you more coherent, it was rest. Planning aims to make rest easier to access than relief when you are depleted.

Depletion changes choices.

The motif for this subchapter is the *downshift*. A downshift is not stopping. It is a change in gear. It recognises that the engine can't run at high RPM indefinitely without damage. Most people know this mechanically and ignore it psychologically. A calendar built only for high gear produces a life that feels permanently urgent. A calendar with planned downshifts produces a life that can contain intensity without being consumed by it. The quarter is a useful planning horizon because it naturally contains cycles: intense phases and quieter phases. The mistake is to let intensity phases happen by accident and quieter phases vanish by neglect.

Neglect is a scheduler.

The practical work of planning, therefore, is to locate the likely intensity spikes in the coming quarter—deadlines, travel, exams, launches, heavy social periods—and then place downshifts near them, ideally immediately after. The recovery block should be protected with the same seriousness as work: not because work is sacred, but because the body is. This means making the block legible: a clear boundary in the diary, fewer optional commitments stacked on top, fewer "just in case" meetings. When recovery is vague, it is stolen. When it is explicit, it has a chance.

Explicitness is protection.

The closing tension is unavoidable. If you schedule recovery blocks, you must accept that some tasks will be delayed, some invitations will be declined, and some forms of availability will be reduced. That can feel like loss. It can also feel like adulthood. The forward test, then, is not whether you "deserve" rest, but whether you will treat recovery as a real appointment: looking at the next ninety days, where will you place the downshift—after which intense phase, around which recurring drain, in which part of the week—so that you are planning for your actual energy rather than gambling on a future self who never arrives tired?

Designing trips and retreats

In April 1817, in the Lake District near Grasmere, William Wordsworth wrote lines that helped turn a specific landscape into a durable idea: that a change of place can change the mind. The daffodils are famous; the quieter fact is that Wordsworth and his sister Dorothy walked, watched, and returned to the same lakes and fells repeatedly, using local travel as a form of renewal. Dorothy's *Grasmere Journal* entries from that period are granular—weather, paths, small observations—because the restoration they sought was not spectacle but attention. The Lake District was not an escape from life. It was a different setting in which life could be felt more clearly.

Clarity is the real destination.

Travel is often sold as an extravagant antidote to ordinary fatigue: a flight, a hotel, a week that is supposed to fix everything. That fantasy is seductive and usually false. Most adults do not need more spectacle. They need interruption of default. They need an environment that loosens the grip of their usual cues, and a rhythm that allows the nervous system to downshift. A retreat, in this sense, is not a spa brochure. It is a deliberate change in constraints. It can be an afternoon in a different part of the city, a day trip to a coast or a hill, a visit to a friend, or a low-key night away. The point is to design the trip so it restores, rather than simply relocates stress.

Relocation is not renewal.

To *show* why design matters, consider the common "break" that fails. A person books a weekend away after a heavy stretch, but the trip is packed with logistics, constant photos, late nights, and the same digital noise as home. They return tired and slightly disappointed, as though leisure itself is unreliable. The name for this failure is *portable pressure*: the habit of carrying the same intensity into a new setting. Portable pressure is driven by the belief that the value of a trip lies in how much is extracted from it—how many sights, meals, experiences, achievements. The explanation is simple: when people are depleted, they often reach for stimulation rather than restoration, because stimulation feels like relief. The implication is that a retreat must be designed around *restorative constraints*—fewer obligations, lower stimulation, gentler pacing, and a clear boundary from the most draining inputs.

Inputs decide the feel of a place.

The quarter is the right horizon for this because it allows a trip to be treated as an element of the rhythm rather than as an isolated treat. When you plan only for work and admin, the calendar becomes a machine for producing fatigue. When you include one deliberate outing or retreat, even tentatively, you create a counterweight. The future contains something other than demand. That changes how the present is endured. It also changes decision-making in practical domains: you are less likely to fill every weekend if you know one of them is protected; you may be less likely to overspend on convenience if you have a modest trip planned and want space in the budget; you may be more likely to protect sleep and health so the trip is genuinely enjoyable.

Anticipation is a form of energy.

Designing a trip begins with purpose, but purpose in a specific, non-moralising sense. What is the function of this outing in the quarter's system? Is it to restore attention after a heavy cognitive stretch? Is it to rebuild connection with a partner or friend? Is it to create spaciousness after social overload? Is it to interrupt a repetitive routine that has become numbing? A trip designed for connection looks different from a trip designed for solitude. A trip designed for recovery looks different from a trip designed for celebration. Confusion about function produces mismatched travel: you plan a "rest" weekend and then schedule it like a conference.

Match matters.

This is where the "Show → Name → Explain → Implication" engine becomes practical. Show: a person returns from a city break feeling as though they need another break. Name: *stimulation overload.* Explain: unfamiliar environments already demand attention—

navigation, novelty, social cues—and if you add constant scheduling and digital capture, you eliminate the nervous system's chance to settle. Implication: design a low-stimulation retreat by reducing decisions, reducing itinerary density, and reducing digital demands. The principle is not anti-adventure. It is about sequencing. You can have intensity and restoration in the same quarter, but you cannot have them in the same hour without cost.

Cost is always paid.

A second major claim follows. Travel is not merely consumption of place; it is contact with different cues. Cues shape behaviour. If home cues you to work, you work. If home cues you to scroll, you scroll. Changing place interrupts those cues, which is why even a day trip can feel like a reset. Environmental psychology and cognitive science have long observed that context influences memory and behaviour; the specifics of "context-dependent memory" research are documented across decades. One does not need to cite every paper to use the insight. The implication is that a retreat should be designed to create new cues aligned with restoration: walking routes, reading spaces, unhurried meals, quiet conversation, the absence of constant notifications. These cues do not force relaxation. They make it easier.

Ease is the friend of recovery.

Two named, checkable examples help ground this beyond personal preference. The first is the modern tradition of the "artist residency". In March 1904, the MacDowell Colony in New Hampshire (now MacDowell) began hosting artists, offering them time and space away from daily obligations. The principle was not luxury. It was protected attention. Residencies exist because creative and intellectual work often requires a particular kind of quiet: not empty idleness, but uninterrupted depth. Most people will never attend a formal residency, but the structure is instructive. A retreat works best when it protects one or two simple modes—walking, reading, writing, conversation—rather than trying to be everything.

Everything is a trap.

The second example is religious rather than artistic. The Benedictine Rule, associated with Benedict of Nursia in the sixth century (c. 530 CE), describes a rhythm of prayer, work, and reading within a defined place. Monasticism is not a lifestyle recommendation for modern professionals. It is a historical illustration of a design principle: retreat is a system of constraints that reduces choice and therefore reduces cognitive load. When you remove the need to decide constantly—what to wear, where to be, what to do next—you free attention for presence. Even a secular retreat can borrow this principle in miniature: fewer outfits, fewer venues, fewer plans, fewer digital inputs.

Fewer decisions. More presence.

A credible limitation must be acknowledged, because travel is unevenly accessible. Money, time, disability, caring responsibilities, visa constraints, and safety considerations shape what is possible. It would be absurd to pretend that everyone can "take a retreat". The reconciliation is that the core function—interruption of default—does not require distance or expense. A day trip by train, an afternoon in a different neighbourhood, a long walk in a nearby landscape, a quiet visit to a museum, a night in a friend's spare room, a home retreat with agreed boundaries—these can all serve the same function if designed properly. The constraint shifts the creativity. The point is not to go far. It is to go *differently*.

Different is a lever.

A second limitation is psychological. Some people travel to avoid rather than restore. They use movement as a way of outrunning a difficult conversation, a stressful project, or an internal unease. Travel can become a form of relief that postpones necessary decisions. The reconciliation is not to moralise. It is to design the retreat so it supports reflection rather than avoidance. That might mean choosing a setting that is quiet enough for thought, or building in a small moment of review—reading notes, journalling, walking without headphones—so that the trip becomes a place where you can listen to yourself again. Restoration and honesty often arrive together.

Silence has content.

The motif for this subchapter is the *threshold.* A retreat is a threshold between quarters within a quarter: a deliberate crossing from one set of cues to another. Thresholds matter because they are psychologically legible. They tell the mind, "Something is different now." Many modern lives lack thresholds. Work happens at home; messages arrive everywhere; days blur into one another. A trip, even a modest one, creates a threshold if you let it. Packing a bag, leaving the usual routes, sleeping elsewhere, waking to different sounds—these are sensory markers that the nervous system reads as change. Change, when not overloaded, is restorative.

Change must be paced.

Design therefore becomes a balance between novelty and simplicity. Too much novelty and you create strain. Too much sameness and you fail to interrupt default. The sweet spot is often "familiar novelty": a place that is different enough to reset attention but familiar enough to reduce decision fatigue. That might be a known coastal town, a recurring countryside walk, an annual visit to family, a favourite museum, a friend's city. Repetition is not the enemy of renewal. Repetition can become a restorative tradition, precisely because it reduces planning overhead and allows the mind to settle quickly.

Tradition is a technology.

This also links back to money. Many people avoid travel because they associate it with expensive, high-stakes holidays. A quarterly approach encourages a different financial logic: small, planned outings that fit the budget and avoid the boom-and-bust pattern of one dramatic holiday followed by months of deprivation. It also discourages impulse spending on "treats" that never quite restore because there is nothing to look forward to. A modest trip can function as a planned reward without turning into escapism. The key is to see travel as part of cadence rather than as a rare event.

Cadence makes life feel larger.

None of this requires a strict itinerary. In fact, for many people, the most restorative retreat is defined by what is *not* scheduled. What matters is the outline: the threshold, the function, the constraints. If the outing is intended to restore, then the calendar around it should not be packed tight. If it is intended to reconnect, then it should include time for conversation rather than constant activity. If it is intended to reset attention, then it should reduce digital input and allow time for aimless wandering. Wandering is not inefficiency. It is a cognitive mode that invites unexpected noticing.

Noticing is the antidote to numbness.

The work of this subchapter, then, is to make it plausible that one retreat-like moment can exist in the next ninety days. Plausibility beats fantasy. You sketch one option that fits your season and responsibilities: perhaps a day trip during a lighter week; perhaps a night away after a major deadline; perhaps a visit to someone you miss; perhaps a solo afternoon with a book and a long walk. The sketch should be specific enough to be real—place, approximate date window, travel mode—while flexible enough to survive a messy life. This is a design exercise, not a vow.

Vows invite guilt.

The closing tension is the same one that haunts recovery planning: a retreat requires you to choose what will *not* happen. You cannot take a day trip and also attend every obligation. You cannot go away for a night and also keep the illusion of constant availability. You cannot create a threshold without guarding it. The forward test, then, is sharp and practical: in the coming quarter, what threshold will you cross—however modest—so that your days are not one continuous strip of default, and what will you be willing to leave undone so that the retreat renews rather than merely relocates your fatigue?

Protecting hobbies and fun

In the summer of 1966, in New York City, George Plimpton published *Paper Lion* after spending the 1963 pre-season training camp with the Detroit Lions. The book is remembered as literary journalism, but its quieter lesson sits elsewhere: a grown man, already successful, deliberately entered an arena where he would be clumsy, frightened, and out of place—then wrote with delight about the experience. He did not do it to optimise a career metric. He did it because play, even in a bruising context, restored a certain aliveness. The detail worth keeping is not American football. It is the willingness to be an amateur again.

Amateurs learn faster.

Most adults do not "choose" to abandon their hobbies. Hobbies are not killed in a single dramatic moment. They fade. They are crowded out by small decisions that feel sensible at the time: an extra hour of work, an evening of admin, one more social obligation, one more week of tiredness. Over time, the activity that once made life lighter becomes a memory with a faint ache attached. People speak of it nostalgically—"I used to paint", "I used to play the guitar", "I used to run", "I used to make things"—as though it belonged to another person. That person is not gone. They are simply uninvited.

Invitation is a calendar problem.

To *show* how the fade happens, consider a typical quarter. There is no crisis, only accumulation. Work expands into the margins because it can. Entertainment becomes a default because it requires no planning. Social media fills the small gaps because it is frictionless. Sleep becomes slightly shorter, then slightly worse. The hobby requires setup, attention, and a little energy upfront, so it is postponed until "a better time". Better time does not arrive. The hobby is not rejected on principle; it is lost to entropye of convenience. The name for this is *friction bias*: when the mind repeatedly chooses the lower-friction option, even if it provides less satisfaction. The explanation is not mystical. When people are tired, they conserve effort. They reach for what is easiest. The implication is stark: if enjoyment requires even a modest threshold—getting out supplies, travelling to a class, meeting someone—then it must be protected, or it will be replaced by whatever is easiest to consume.

Consumption is not the same as fun.

Here a distinction matters. Fun is not always pleasure, and pleasure is not always fun. Pleasure can be passive: a pleasant meal, a comfortable sofa, an enjoyable show. Fun, in the richer sense, is often active: it involves agency, experimentation, surprise, small risk, and absorption. It creates a sense of "I am doing something", rather than "something is being done to me". Fun can look childish from the outside because it is not justified by utility. That is precisely its value. It restores a part of the mind that utilitarian living shrinks: curiosity without immediate outcome.

Outcome obsession is draining.

Psychology has a name for what fun restores. In *Flow* (1990), Mihaly Csikszentmihalyi described deep engagement when skill and challenge are matched; hobbies often create these conditions more reliably than work because the stakes are lower and the feedback is clearer. Another useful concept comes from Edward Deci and Richard Ryan's Self-Determination Theory, which emphasises autonomy, competence, and relatedness as fundamental psychological needs (Deci & Ryan, 2000). Many adult days are low in autonomy (too many obligations), ambiguous in competence (too much vague work), and thin in relatedness (too much mediated contact). A well-chosen hobby can quietly restore all three: you choose it, you improve at it, and you often share it.

Sharing multiplies joy.

None of this is an argument that hobbies should be forced. Forced fun is a peculiar torture. The point is to treat hobbies as legitimate *inputs* in the system of a quarter. When hobbies disappear, it is not merely sad; it is diagnostic. It often indicates that life has become too brittle, too crowded, or too depleted to support play. Adults then compensate with substitutes: more scrolling, more shopping, more numbing entertainment, more "treats" that feel like relief but do not restore. If the book's earlier chapters are about money, health, relationships, learning, and environment, hobbies sit at the intersection: they can improve health through movement, relationships through shared activity, learning through skill acquisition, and even spending through a shift from impulse consumption to meaningful engagement.

Meaning changes spending.

The key is to tie abstractions to visible behaviours. "I want more joy" is not actionable. "I spent three evenings a week watching videos I barely remember" is a behaviour. "I stopped going to the climbing wall because it felt like too much effort after work" is a behaviour. "I haven't touched my sketchbook in six months because it's in a cupboard" is a behaviour. "I say I miss writing, but I never open the document" is a behaviour. Hobbies are either supported by the environment and the calendar or they are not. The quarterly reset makes this visible because it is long enough for patterns to show up and short enough to change them.

Change needs a handle.

A common objection arises immediately: "I don't have time." Sometimes that is true in the strict sense—caregiving, multiple jobs, illness, crises. Often it is partially true: time exists, but it is fractured and tired. The limitation is real and should not be mocked. The reconciliation is to shift the unit of ambition. Many people frame hobbies as large blocks: "I need a whole afternoon to paint." When life is crowded, that becomes a permanent excuse. Yet hobbies can often be revived through smaller, more reliable slots. Not because small is morally superior, but because small is less vulnerable to disruption. A quarter can support one protected slot a week, or even a protected slot every two weeks, if it is treated as an appointment rather than a leftover.

Leftovers rarely nourish.

Two named, checkable examples help ground the cultural case for play. The first comes from the world of music. In April 1943, during the siege of Leningrad, Dmitri Shostakovich's *Symphony No. 7* was performed in the city on 9 August 1942 (the date and place are well documented), broadcast as a form of cultural resistance. This is not "hobby" in the cosy sense. It is a reminder that music and art can function as psychological survival, not luxury. The implication, scaled down, is that creative and playful activity is not frivolous by definition; it can be a pillar of endurance.

Endurance includes spirit.

The second example is from the modern workplace's accidental rediscovery of play. In 2005, Google's "20% time" policy was widely discussed in tech culture: an allowance for employees to spend part of their working time on side projects. The practice's reality was uneven across teams and years, and it should not be romanticised. Yet the idea itself illustrates a principle: organisations sometimes formalise play-like exploration because it produces creativity and resilience. The implication for an individual quarter is not to copy a corporate slogan, but to recognise that unstructured exploration has value even in systems obsessed with output.

Exploration keeps minds alive.

A credible counter-example must also be acknowledged: hobbies can become another arena for performance. The person who once played the guitar for pleasure starts tracking practice minutes obsessively, posting every session online, comparing themselves to others, turning the hobby into a second job. The hobby then stops restoring. It becomes a source of pressure, identity anxiety, and sometimes spending escalation—gear acquisition, classes, status chasing. The reconciliation is not to ban ambition. It is to be honest about the function of the hobby in this quarter. If the quarter is already intense, a hobby that adds pressure may not be restorative. If the quarter is stable, a more challenging hobby might be welcome. The point is alignment, not purity.

Alignment prevents sabotage.

This is where the motif for this subchapter appears: the *playground gate.* When you were young, a playground had a gate. You entered. The world inside had different rules: experimentation, laughter, low stakes, scraped knees, quick recovery. Adult life often loses gates. Work seeps everywhere. Messages seep everywhere. The mind is never fully "off duty". A protected hobby is a gate: a boundary you cross into a different mode. The gate can be a physical place—a studio, a park, a rehearsal room—or a temporal boundary—a recurring evening, a Sunday morning. The gate matters because it signals a change in role. You are no longer only a worker or a caretaker or a responder. You are a participant.

Participation restores agency.

Designing protection begins with choosing one hobby or playful experiment that is genuinely missed, not merely admired. Many adults confuse aspirational hobbies with restorative ones. They think they "should" learn a language, "should" take up pottery, "should" run. The word "should" is a warning. Missed hobbies are recognised by a particular emotional texture: a small pang when you see someone else doing it; a sense of loss when you pass the place you used to go; a flicker of excitement when you imagine returning. The aim is to identify that flicker. Flicker is a signal that the activity still has energy.

Signals deserve respect.

Protection then requires two visible commitments: a time slot and a reduction of competing claims. The time slot is not a vague intention; it is a legible appointment. The reduction is not dramatic; it is a decision to say "not this quarter" to something else—an extra meeting, a recurring favour, a habitual evening of aimless scrolling. Without the reduction, the hobby will be squeezed. This is not moralising about laziness. It is recognising that calendars are zero-sum: if you protect a gate, you must close another entrance.

Every yes has a cost.

There is also the issue of setup friction. Many hobbies die because the environment makes them hard. The guitar is in a case under a bed. The sketchbook is in a drawer. The running shoes are by the door but the route is unclear. The chess set is missing pieces. The sewing machine is buried. Environment is not decoration; it is behavioural engineering. A small change—placing tools within reach, preparing a bag, choosing a default location—can reduce friction enough to make the hobby plausible after a long day. The earlier chapter on environment has already established the logic:

remove friction where you want behaviour, add friction where you want restraint. Hobbies deserve the same engineering attention.

Engineering is kindness to the future self.

Money plays a role too, and it is easy to mishandle. Some hobbies become expensive because the market sells identity through gear. The underlying abstraction is "commitment": people buy equipment to feel committed. The behaviour is visible: purchases happen before practice. The risk is that money substitutes for engagement. The implication is not a prohibition on spending. It is a question of sequencing. If the hobby is meant to restore, spending should support participation, not replace it. A quarter is a good window for a simple test: does the hobby's spending correlate with time spent doing it? If not, the hobby has been turned into shopping.

Shopping is rarely play.

The subchapter's final movement should leave a forward tension, because this is where ideals collide with real life. Protecting fun sounds easy until the diary is full, the energy is low, and other people's expectations press in. Yet the cost of not protecting it is also real: a quarter that contains no play often becomes a quarter that feels grey, even if it is productive. Grey quarters accumulate. Then a person looks up and realises that life has become a sequence of tasks punctuated by relief, not joy. The forward test, then, is both practical and slightly existential: in the coming ninety days, which playground gate will you actually walk through—one specific hobby, one playful experiment—and what will you deliberately leave undone so that enjoyment is treated not as a guilty indulgence, but as a legitimate form of maintenance for a life you intend to keep inhabiting?

Chapter 10
Making the Cadence Stick

On 14 July 1789, in Paris, a crowd forced its way into the Bastille. The date became more than a political rupture; it became a marker in the calendar of a nation, repeated until repetition itself turned memory into rhythm. Long after the gunpowder smoke, long after the bricks were pulled down and the prison was gone, the day returned each year with flags, crowds, and a familiar pattern of ceremonies. The point is not that every life needs a revolution. The point is that humans do not keep time simply by counting it. They keep time by anchoring it to things that return—events, seasons, rituals, symbols—and by letting those anchors do the work of remembering.

Memory needs scaffolding.

Most personal change systems fail for the opposite reason. They ask the mind to remember, to care, and to persist without external support. They assume that a good intention is a sturdy structure. It is not. Intention is weather. It shifts. Cadence is architecture. When life is calm, weather is enough. When life is loud, architecture decides what survives. The Upgrade Day is already a decision to stop relying on the annual drama of January and the frantic noise of daily tweaks. The final question is whether the cadence can become something that continues in the face of deadlines, illness, family demands, grief, travel, boredom, and those ordinary weeks where nothing is technically wrong yet everything feels slightly too much.

Continuity is the real achievement.

Here the modern challenge is not ignorance. It is saturation. People are not short of information about what might improve their lives. They are short of stable attention, honest reflection, and the freedom to revise without collapsing into self-reproach. A quarterly ritual can meet that challenge, but only if it is designed to withstand real life rather than an imaginary life in which the calendar behaves and emotions arrive on schedule. The problem is not that people "fall off the wagon". The metaphor is wrong. Life is not a wagon. It is a terrain that changes underfoot, and any practice that pretends otherwise will eventually break.

Breakage is predictable.

A small but revealing example can be seen in the history of "New Year's resolutions" themselves. The idea of marking a new start at the turn of the year has ancient roots—Babylonian practices are often cited by historians of ritual and timekeeping—but the modern resolution culture is a peculiar fusion of personal aspiration and social spectacle. It brings with it a predictable cycle: intense clarity in early January, waning attention by February, and a quiet sense of failure by spring. That is not because people are weak. It is because the ritual is a once-a-year spike without infrastructure between. The quarter, by contrast, is a repeating unit. Repetition, however, creates a different problem: the temptation to skip "just this once".

Just once becomes a habit.

The first lever for resisting that temptation is anchoring. When a ritual floats free in the diary, it is negotiable; when it is tied to something that returns, it becomes part of the year's texture. Seasonal anchors can be literal—the first weekend of April when the light shifts, the late September evening when the air cools—or cultural—school terms, fiscal quarters, religious holidays, annual work cycles. These anchors are not motivational quotes. They are cues. The brain is good at linking actions to cues because it conserves effort. You do not have to remember an Upgrade Day if it sits on the same shelf as something you already remember. The ritual becomes a neighbour of an existing pattern.

Neighbours matter.

There is a philosophical point hiding in this practicality. Anchors are a way of admitting that the self is not a single, unified agent. The self is more like a committee: part ambition, part fatigue, part fear, part hope, part habit. The committee votes differently depending on the week. Anchors reduce the committee's room for debate. When the date arrives, the ritual is not an argument; it is what happens. The opening and closing cues—the same mug, the same music, a short walk before starting, a small reward after finishing—are not childish. They are signals that help the mind cross a threshold from reaction to reflection. Thresholds are how humans change states without violence.

Violence is overrated.

Yet even the best anchors meet reality. A quarter will arrive in which the Upgrade Day lands in the middle of upheaval: a family emergency, a breakdown in health, a demanding work cycle, a financial shock, a period of depression or anxiety, an emotionally complex season. This is where most systems become cruel. They either demand perfection or they collapse entirely. The durable alternative is to design a "light version" that preserves the ritual's identity without requiring its full expression. It is the difference between a practice that is sacred and a practice that is fragile. A light version is not a watered-down failure. It is a continuation under constraint.

Constraint is normal.

The honesty required here is bracing. Some quarters will be imperfect not because of time but because of emotion. Reflection can be difficult when it reveals grief, disappointment, or uncertainty. People then avoid the Upgrade Day not because they lack discipline, but because they fear what they might discover when they stop moving. A light version reduces that threat. It allows the ritual to become a container rather than a confrontation. It says: keep the cadence even when you cannot do everything you would like. Keep the line unbroken even when the stroke is thin.

Thin is still real.

This is where the idea of evolving the checklist becomes more than an efficiency tweak. A static checklist assumes a static life. Life is not static. Your money changes, your health needs shift, relationships deepen or strain, work seasons rotate, learning priorities alter, and your environment transforms through moves, new tools, new responsibilities. A ritual that repeats without evolving turns into theatre: you go through motions without extracting meaning. A ritual that evolves stays honest. The trick is to evolve it slowly, like a ship maintained at sea: a small change each quarter, not a full rebuild. The goal is not novelty for its own sake. The goal is relevance.

Relevance keeps attention.

There is also a subtle risk: the checklist can bloat. When people discover the power of reflection, they often add questions endlessly, believing that thoroughness equals seriousness. This is how rituals become oppressive. A bloated ritual becomes another audit, another source of guilt, another performance. A lean ritual is harder to skip because it respects time and energy. It also forces prioritisation, which is the real work of adulthood. If every question is included, none of them matter. If a few questions are chosen, their answers can change behaviour.

Choice is the point.

Modern life provides another complication: social context. People attempt change in isolation, then wonder why it is difficult. Isolation is not merely lonely; it is structurally disadvantageous. Humans are social learners. We notice norms, mirror behaviours, and respond to expectations. Involving others can therefore strengthen cadence, but it can also distort it. A partner who insists on complete transparency can turn the ritual into surveillance. A colleague who joins can introduce comparison and status anxiety. A friend can unintentionally pull the ritual towards their priorities. The promise of involving others must therefore be held alongside a practical question: what kind of social support strengthens the practice without contaminating it?

Contamination is easy.

The most useful social involvement often looks quieter than people expect. It can be parallel rather than shared: two people do their own Upgrade Days on the same weekend, then exchange one or two insights rather than full disclosures. It can be selective: share learning goals but not financial details; share calendar decisions but not relationship tensions; share intentions but not raw metrics. It can be bounded: a short check-in call at the end of the day, a walk together afterwards, a mutual commitment to protect the time. Social support works best when it increases follow-through without forcing performance.

Performance ruins candour.

There is a further twist: culture teaches people to equate privacy with strength. Yet privacy can become avoidance. The decision is not binary. The question is what to keep private and what to make accountable. Money decisions sometimes benefit from careful privacy because shame distorts judgement; they also sometimes benefit from shared context because secrecy can hide drift. Health habits can be deeply personal; they can also improve when someone else knows what you are trying to protect. Relationships are sensitive; they can also be clarified by honest conversations. The Upgrade Day is a ritual of self-governance, but self-governance does not require solitude. It requires sovereignty.

Sovereignty is not secrecy.

By the time this chapter arrives, the cadence has already been framed as infrastructure rather than personality. This is where that framing becomes decisive. If the ritual depends on feeling inspired, it will eventually be replaced by whatever is urgent. If it depends on a perfect schedule, it will break under disruption. If it depends on a fixed checklist, it will become irrelevant. If it depends on total privacy, it may become brittle; if it depends on total openness, it may become performative. The durable version is a practice that adapts while remaining recognisable: anchored in the year, flexible in execution, lean in prompts, and thoughtful in social boundaries.

Thoughtful beats intense.

The deeper stake is not productivity. It is authorship. Many people live as if life is something that happens to them: obligations arrive, fatigue accumulates, spending drifts, relationships degrade through neglect, learning becomes aspirational rather than embodied, and rest becomes an emergency measure. A quarterly ritual is a modest rebellion against that drift. Yet rebellion is easy to announce and hard to maintain. Maintenance is unglamorous. Maintenance is what makes freedom real. The Upgrade Day is, at heart, a maintenance practice for a life worth inhabiting.

Maintenance is dignity.

The chapter's momentum comes from an uncomfortable truth: the hard part is not doing an Upgrade Day once. The hard part is doing it four times a year for years, through boring quarters and painful ones, through change and stasis, through success and uncertainty. That repetition forces a decision that cannot be outsourced. When the next quarter begins to press in—new commitments, new temptations, new risks—you either let the calendar write your life for you, or you keep a small corner of time in which you write back.

Seasonal anchors and cues

On 22 September 1792, in Paris, the French Republic began what it called Year I. The date mattered because it was tied to a hinge in the sky: the autumnal equinox. Revolutionary France was attempting to remake time itself, to sever daily life from monarchy and church, and to anchor the new calendar in something more elemental than tradition. The experiment did not last—Napoleon abolished the Republican calendar in 1806—but the impulse behind it remains instructive. People do not merely live in time; they domesticate it. They pull the vastness of days into patterns they can recognise, remember, and share.

Time needs handles.

The Upgrade Day is not a revolution and does not require one. It does, however, ask for the same kind of handle: a way to make a quarterly reset feel inevitable rather than optional. The enemy is not ignorance. The enemy is drift combined with forgetfulness. A ritual without anchors is like a boat without moorings: it will float until the weather changes, and then it will be somewhere else. Anchors and cues are the moorings. They convert a good idea into a recurring event that withstands busy weeks, mild chaos, and the human tendency to postpone anything that is not screaming.

Screaming always wins.

To see why anchoring matters, look at how calendars behave in most adult lives. The diary is full of obligations imposed externally: meetings, deadlines, family events, school terms, travel, fixed social commitments. What is not imposed has to compete for space, and the competition is unfair because external obligations arrive with social consequences. A meeting missed has a cost; a personal ritual skipped often seems costless in the moment. The costs are delayed and distributed: money drifts, health slips, relationships thin, learning stagnates. The name for this pattern is *asymmetric consequence*. The explanation is simple. Humans prioritise what produces immediate pain if neglected. The implication is that the Upgrade Day must borrow consequence from the world by attaching itself to something already salient, already remembered, already likely to be protected.

Borrowing is intelligence, not weakness.

Anchors come in two broad families: natural markers and cultural markers. Natural markers are seasonal shifts—light, temperature, school holidays, the rhythm of weekends, the body's own patterns. Cultural markers are institutional and social—fiscal quarters, academic terms, religious festivals, organisational cycles, even the predictable surge and lull of certain industries. The most durable anchors are those you already live by. A parent does not need to be told when term ends. A researcher knows conference season. A finance professional knows reporting cycles. An athlete feels the shift between winter training and summer events. Anchoring works when it rides an existing wave rather than demanding a new one.

Existing waves carry you.

This is where the "Show → Name → Explain → Implication" engine becomes useful in a practical way. Show: someone chooses a quarterly ritual but sets dates randomly, and by the second quarter it has slipped because the date fell in a busy period. Name: *floating scheduling*. Explain: without a consistent cue, the date is not remembered automatically and is easily renegotiated when pressure arrives. Implication: tie each Upgrade Day to a recurring marker—"the first Saturday after the spring bank holiday", "the weekend after term ends", "the first Sunday after the fiscal quarter closes"—so the date is not invented each time but retrieved.

Retrieval is easier than invention.

There is a cognitive science reason for this. Habits are often cue-driven: an event triggers a behaviour. The stronger and more reliable the cue, the less the behaviour depends on momentary motivation. Charles Duhigg popularised the habit loop idea—cue, routine, reward—in *The Power of Habit* (2012), drawing on earlier behavioural research. One can dispute the neatness of the model, but the core point holds: cues reduce cognitive load. Anchors are cues with dignity. They are not hacks. They are design features that respect how memory works.

Design respects reality.

A second claim is that anchors do more than aid memory. They create meaning. A quarterly ritual that happens "sometime in March" is a task. A quarterly ritual tied to spring has a flavour: a sense of clearing, of re-opening, of adjusting after winter. Similarly, a ritual tied to late summer can carry a feeling of harvest and refinement; a ritual tied to early autumn can be about boundary-setting before the year's final push; a ritual tied to mid-winter can be about maintenance and warmth. This is not poetic garnish. Meaning increases compliance because it makes the ritual feel less like admin and more like participation in a cycle that was always larger than any to-do list.

Cycles are older than productivity.

To ground this beyond metaphor, consider two checkable examples of anchoring in practice. The first is institutional: many organisations already live by quarters. Public companies report financial results on a quarterly basis; the dates vary, but the structure is ubiquitous. The point is not to turn personal life into a corporation. The point is that quarterly rhythms endure because they strike a compromise between granularity and distance. If the world you work in already respects quarters, anchoring the Upgrade Day near quarter-end or quarter-start can make the ritual feel aligned with the surrounding environment. Alignment reduces friction.

Friction kills rituals.

The second example is cultural: Ramadan, observed by Muslims worldwide, shifts through the solar year because it follows a lunar calendar, yet it remains powerfully anchored—by the sighting of the moon, by daily fasting rhythms, by communal meals, by prayer patterns. The specifics are religious and not interchangeable, but the structure is revealing. A practice persists across centuries because it is tied to clear cues and shared rhythms. The implication, for a secular quarterly ritual, is that cues need to be embodied and repeatable. A date in a diary is not enough. A ritual needs sensory and social signals that say, "This is that time again."

Signals make time legible.

This is where opening and closing rituals matter. The Upgrade Day is already a reflective reset. Anchors bring it back; cues bring you into it. An opening cue is a small, consistent action that marks the beginning: a short walk before sitting down, a particular place at a table, a notebook opened in the same way, a candle lit, a cup of tea made in a specific mug, a playlist that is only used for this ritual. None of these actions is magic. Their power lies in repetition. They reduce the psychic resistance of starting. They tell the mind: you have done this before; you know how to do it again.

Familiarity lowers the threshold.

A closing cue does something equally important. It prevents the Upgrade Day from dissolving into endless tinkering. Many reflective practices fail not because people avoid them, but because they cannot stop once they start. The ritual expands. It becomes a three-day audit. It becomes exhausting. A closing cue draws a line: a final review of decisions, a short note of what will be tested in the next ninety days, a physical act of putting tools away, a meal, a conversation, an outing. The closing cue is not a reward in a childish sense. It is a boundary that protects the practice from bloat.

Boundaries protect meaning.

The quiet motif that runs through this subchapter is the *ring of the bell.* A bell does two things. It gathers attention, and it announces a transition. In monasteries, schools, factories, ships, and town squares, bells have historically structured communal time. The Upgrade Day needs a personal bell. Not literally a bell—though it could be—but a signal that rings in your life. The bell is the anchor plus the cue: the season marker that says "now", and the small repeated action that says "begin".

Begin means something.

There is, however, a credible limitation. Anchors can become rigid in ways that backfire. If you tie the ritual to a marker that is itself unstable—shifting work cycles, irregular school terms, unpredictable travel—you may find that the anchor drags the ritual into chaos rather than stabilising it. Similarly, if you attach the ritual to an emotionally loaded holiday, you may inadvertently make the day harder: reflection becomes mixed with family stress, grief, or social expectations. Anchors can carry baggage. The reconciliation is to choose anchors that are reliable and emotionally neutral, or to offset loaded anchors with gentle cues that make the ritual feel safe rather than demanding.

Safety increases honesty.

Another limitation is diversity of seasons. Not everyone lives in a climate with crisp seasonal shifts. Even within the same climate, people's lived seasons differ. A nurse's year is not the same as a lecturer's year. A parent's year is not the same as a single person's year. A freelancer's year can be chaotic. The reconciliation is the book's broader principle: design based on actual constraints, not imagined ones. Your anchors should belong to your life, not to a textbook calendar. The quarter is a container; the anchor is the handle you choose to lift it.

Lift what is real.

Anchors also play a subtle role in identity. People often think of consistency as a moral trait—"disciplined people stick to routines"—and then judge themselves when they do not. Anchoring shifts the frame. It makes follow-through less about character and more about environment. A well-anchored ritual is easier to remember and harder to skip because skipping now violates a pattern that feels real. This is why cultural rituals persist: not because everyone is always motivated, but because the pattern is reinforced by cues, expectations, and repetition. A personal ritual can borrow that power without turning into dogma.

Dogma is unnecessary.

A final claim follows: each quarter should have its own flavour. Without flavour, repetition turns stale. Flavour does not require novelty. It requires a light seasonal adaptation: a different opening cue in winter than in summer, a different closing reward in spring than in autumn, a different location if possible, a different small reflection prompt that matches the season's demands. This keeps the ritual human. Humans respond to texture. The diary may show four identical blocks, but your lived experience should not feel like copying and pasting life.

Life hates copy-paste.

The practical implication is that anchors and cues are not decoration; they are a defence system against skipping. They create a small inevitability, a personal gravity. Without gravity, the ritual floats and is captured by whatever is urgent. With gravity, the ritual returns. It becomes part of the year's architecture, like a beam you can lean on when everything else feels flexible.

Flexibility is not always freedom.

The forward tension is worth stating plainly. Every anchor you choose is also a claim: that this ritual matters enough to be tied to the year, to be given a bell, to be granted a threshold. That claim will be tested, not by dramatic crises, but by ordinary pressures—work that spills, invitations that tempt, tiredness that seduces you into passive relief. When the next seasonal marker arrives—when the light changes, when term ends, when a fiscal quarter closes—the diagnostic question is simple and sharp: will you let the bell ring and step into the ritual, or will you silence it and let another quarter pass without the deliberate turning of the page?

Handling imperfect quarters

In March 2020, in London, the Royal Institution announced that its public programme would be suspended as the United Kingdom moved into pandemic restrictions. Lectures that had run for generations—fixed points in the city's intellectual calendar—suddenly vanished from the diary. For many people, the change was not dramatic in the cinematic sense; it was administrative, announced by email, absorbed between other headlines. Yet the cumulative outcome was unmistakable: routines dissolved, plans fractured, and the ordinary markers by which people oriented themselves—commutes, school terms, office days, weekly social rituals—were interrupted. The lesson for any personal cadence is not about pandemics specifically. It is about the fragility of plans that assume the world will behave.

The world does not behave.

Most quarters are "imperfect" in quieter ways. A deadline expands. A relative becomes ill. A relationship shifts. A child's needs change. A period of fatigue stretches longer than expected. Money becomes tighter. A project collapses. Sometimes nothing collapses and yet the quarter is emotionally heavy: a slow anxiety, a sense of being behind, the dull friction of too many obligations and too little spaciousness. In such quarters, a reflective ritual can feel like one more demand. People then skip the Upgrade Day with a familiar logic: "I'll do it properly when things calm down." Things rarely calm down in the way the phrase implies. They change shape. They do not pause.

Pause must be designed.

To handle imperfect quarters, the practice needs a different kind of strength than motivation. Motivation is episodic. Cadence is structural. Structural practices survive by containing variation. Think of a bridge. A bridge does not endure by remaining perfectly still; it endures by flexing under load. A ritual that cannot flex will snap at the first heavy quarter, and then the person will interpret the snap as personal failure. This is not merely unkind. It is inaccurate. The correct diagnosis is design failure. The practice was built for ideal conditions, and ideal conditions are a rare climate.

Rare climates breed fragile systems.

The first major claim, then, is that imperfection should be expected and planned for, not treated as an exception. Show: someone schedules an Upgrade Day, then misses it due to travel or family pressure, and the miss becomes abandonment because restarting feels like admitting failure. Name: *all-or-nothing adherence.* Explain: when a practice is framed as something done "properly" or not at all, any disruption triggers shame and avoidance; the practice becomes psychologically risky. Implication: the practice must include a legitimate, pre-defined "light version" that counts as continuity, not as compromise.

Continuity matters more than completeness.

This is where visible metrics help, not to gamify life but to clarify reality. A quarter contains roughly ninety days. A person does not need ninety days of perfect attention; they need one day of honest reflection at a cadence that stays alive across years. The metric that matters is not "did I complete every section" but "did I meet the quarter with intention rather than drift". In an imperfect quarter, the light version is the minimum viable expression of that intention. It is the difference between steering and drifting, even if the steering is small.

Small steering still changes destination.

The light version has to be defined before the quarter goes wrong, because design done in crisis is unreliable. When people are stressed, their cognitive bandwidth shrinks. They overestimate effort. They underestimate future regret. They default to avoidance. Behavioural economics has long documented how context shapes decisions; Daniel Kahneman's distinction between fast, intuitive thinking and slow, deliberative thinking in *Thinking, Fast and Slow* (2011) is one accessible framing. The point is not to cite jargon but to respect a constraint: under stress, reflection becomes harder. Therefore the light version must be simple enough to be done when the mind is tired.

Tired minds need simplicity.

A second claim follows: the light version should preserve the ritual's identity. If it becomes a completely different activity, it will not feel like a continuation. It should share the same anchor, the same cue, the same sense of crossing a threshold—only shorter, gentler, and narrower in scope. This is why earlier emphasis on seasonal anchors and cues matters. When the bell rings—whatever personal bell you have designed—you step into the ritual even if you cannot stay long. The signal is the same. The room is the same. The intention is the same. The duration changes.

Duration is negotiable.

To make this concrete, consider two named, checkable examples of practices that survive by allowing lighter forms. The first is scientific. The Royal Society's *Philosophical Transactions*, first published in 1665 in London under Henry Oldenburg, established a regular channel for sharing knowledge. The journal did not survive for centuries because every issue was perfect or every year was stable. It survived because the system—regular publication, peer review evolving over time, institutional continuity—could absorb disruption. The individual article might be delayed; the channel persisted. The implication for a personal ritual is to value the channel over the perfect instalment.

Channels outlast moods.

The second example is athletic, and deliberately ordinary. The concept of "deload" weeks in strength training—periods of reduced intensity to recover—is widely used in modern coaching culture, though practices vary. The logic is straightforward: sustained progress depends on recovery, and rigid intensity leads to injury or burnout. In an imperfect quarter, the Upgrade Day can act as a deload for the mind: less depth, more maintenance, a focus on preventing damage rather than chasing transformation. The implication is not to treat life as a gym programme, but to adopt the same realism: intensity must be modulated to stay sustainable.

Sustainable beats heroic.

Now the credible limitation: light versions can become excuses. People can reduce the ritual until it becomes a token gesture—five minutes of vague journalling, a glance at an account balance, a promise to "do better next quarter"—without any meaningful decisions. The practice then survives in name only. The reconciliation is to define the light version not as a mood-friendly substitute, but as a sharply bounded protocol with at least one concrete output. Not a grand plan. A decision. A date. A small test. Something that changes behaviour or protects a boundary. The light version must still produce a hinge.

A hinge moves something.

This is where pairing abstractions with visible behaviours becomes essential. "Be kinder to myself" is an abstraction. In a difficult quarter, kindness might be a visible decision such as reducing commitments, protecting sleep, or postponing a non-essential project. "Stay on track financially" is an abstraction. In a difficult quarter, staying on track might mean checking whether a major bill is covered and whether any automatic charges need attention. "Maintain relationships" is an abstraction. In a difficult quarter, maintenance might mean one message to one person you care about, not as performance but as presence. The light version does not attempt to optimise. It prevents neglect.

Prevention is a form of care.

The emotional heart of imperfect quarters is guilt. Guilt can be useful when it signals wrongdoing. It is corrosive when it is merely the mind punishing itself for being human. Most people are not suffering from a shortage of self-criticism. They are suffering from an overdeveloped internal auditor. The auditor looks at a missed ritual and declares the entire project illegitimate. That declaration produces avoidance, which produces more drift, which produces more guilt—a spiral with no learning in it. The Upgrade Day is meant to be a reset, not a tribunal. Therefore the practice needs a restart protocol that treats a miss as information, not as a verdict.

Verdicts freeze behaviour.

Show: someone misses an Upgrade Day, feels embarrassed, and avoids opening their notes because it reminds them of failure. Name: *shame-based avoidance*. Explain: shame narrows attention and drives concealment; it makes reflection painful, so the mind protects itself by not looking. Implication: the restart protocol should be as procedural as possible—simple steps that do not require a heroic emotional state. The aim is not to "forgive yourself" in a sentimental sense, but to re-enter the practice without negotiation.

Negotiation is where avoidance wins.

This is also where the motif for this subchapter appears: the *stitch*. When a seam splits, the garment is not "ruined". It needs a stitch. A stitch is small, precise, and done close to the tear. It does not require redesigning the garment. It requires acknowledging the tear and closing it. A missed quarter is a tear in cadence. The light version is a stitch. A restart is another stitch. The practice survives not because the garment never tears, but because you know how to stitch without drama.

Drama wastes energy.

A practical implication follows: design two layers of ritual, the full version and the stitched version, and treat both as legitimate expressions of the same identity. The full version is used when time and energy permit. The stitched version is used when they do not. Crucially, the stitched version should be time-boxed so it does not expand into a guilty attempt to "make up" for lost time. Making up is a trap. It turns the ritual into punishment. The stitched version exists to keep cadence alive, not to settle accounts with the past.

The past cannot be repaid.

Imperfect quarters also include emotionally difficult Upgrade Days, where the date arrives but the person feels reluctant to look. This can happen after bereavement, during depression, after a job loss, during a relationship rupture, or in any period where life's uncertainty feels too sharp. In such moments, reflection can intensify emotion. The impulse is to defer. Yet deferral has a cost: it allows drift to continue precisely when structure would be most helpful. The stitched version can function here as a gentle container. It does not demand deep analysis. It asks for a few honest observations and one stabilising decision.

Stability first.

No advice is needed here, only a recognition of how humans behave under stress. People often swing between two extremes: control and collapse. Control looks like frantic planning, obsessive tracking, and overwork; collapse looks like avoidance, numbness, and disengagement. A quarterly ritual that is flexible can offer a third mode: *maintenance.* Maintenance is not glamorous. It is quietly stabilising. It says: keep the basics in view, protect the most important boundaries, and postpone optimisation until capacity returns.

Capacity changes by season.

This brings us back to the earlier idea of anchors. Anchors do not prevent disruption, but they provide a predictable return point. When a quarter is chaotic, an anchor is a promise that you will meet your life again at a defined moment, even if briefly. This matters because chaos tends to collapse time into a blur; days become indistinguishable. Anchors reintroduce shape. They remind you that a quarter ends, that another begins, that you can make small decisions even inside upheaval. The alternative is to treat time as an enemy. The Upgrade Day treats time as a medium in which you can still act.

Acting is dignity.

The final claim is that a practice that cannot handle imperfection is not a practice; it is a fantasy. Fantasies feel good and then fail at the first contact with reality, which is why they generate shame. The Upgrade Day is designed for reality: for the unevenness of human energy, the unpredictability of obligations, the fact that some quarters are simply hard. The question is not whether imperfection will happen. It is whether imperfection will end the cadence or become part of it.

Part of it is the point.

The forward test is sharp and deliberately unresolved. When the next quarter arrives and circumstances are less than ideal—and they will be—what stitch will you choose: the stitched version that keeps the practice alive with one honest decision, or the familiar promise to "do it properly later" that quietly trades a living cadence for a perfect one that never arrives?

Evolving your checklist

In September 2008, in Mountain View, California, Google released a web browser called Chrome. Within a few years it had become dominant, not because it launched as a flawless object, but because it shipped updates relentlessly—small changes, frequent releases, a steady removal of friction that users had not even articulated. The browser's most consequential feature was not a single button; it was a pattern of revision. A tool that touches daily life cannot stay static. It either evolves or it becomes a museum piece, admired in theory and avoided in practice.

Static tools collect dust.

A quarterly ritual is also a tool, and it faces the same pressure. At the start, the Upgrade Day script feels fresh: the prompts reveal blind spots, the cadence creates clarity, and the whole enterprise carries an energising novelty. Over time, a different reality arrives. Some questions stop producing insight because the answer is consistently stable. Some prompts begin to irritate because they no longer match your life. New concerns appear—an elderly parent, a change in role, a child's school, a move, a health scare, a new relationship, a fresh professional ambition—and the old checklist doesn't quite catch them. This is not failure. It is maturation. A ritual that cannot change cannot stay truthful.

Truth requires revision.

The first major claim is that a checklist should be treated as a living document rather than a sacred text. Show: someone follows the same script every quarter; by the fourth or fifth repetition they skim, answer mechanically, and leave with fewer meaningful decisions. Name: *script fatigue.* Explain: repetition without adaptation reduces attention; the mind stops noticing what it has learned to predict, and the ritual becomes rote. Implication: the script must be periodically edited so it continues to surprise you in the right ways—by asking slightly better questions, by removing dead weight, by focusing attention where drift has begun to reassert itself.

Attention is a scarce currency.

A second claim follows: evolution should be small and disciplined. The instinct, once people permit change, is to add prompts. The script swells. It begins to resemble an annual audit compressed into a day. That bloat makes the ritual harder to start, more emotionally taxing, and easier to postpone. It also invites a subtle self-deception: the longer the checklist, the more serious the person feels, and seriousness becomes a substitute for useful decisions. The name for this is *checklist inflation.* The explanation is that adding is cognitively easier than subtracting; it feels constructive. The implication is that checklist evolution must include deletion as a deliberate act, not as an afterthought.

Deletion is editorial courage.

This is not merely a preference. It aligns with what is known about cognitive load and decision fatigue. Roy Baumeister's research on ego depletion has been debated in replication discussions, but the broader observation that repeated decision-making can reduce the quality of subsequent decisions has been supported across many contexts and remains persuasive as a practical design constraint. Even without invoking contested frameworks, everyday experience is enough: when a ritual demands dozens of judgements, the later ones become sloppy. A lean script protects the quality of attention. It makes each prompt heavier, not lighter.

Heavier prompts change behaviour.

To keep the evolution precise, it helps to define what the script is for. It is not for self-expression, confession, or endless analysis. It is for noticing drift early and choosing a few targeted adjustments for the next quarter. That implies that a prompt earns its place if it reliably produces one of three outcomes: it reveals a pattern you would otherwise miss, it forces a decision you keep avoiding, or it measures a trend that matters. If a prompt does none of these, it is decorative. Decoration belongs in other parts of life.

The script is a tool.

Consider two checkable examples of evolving checklists in the world, because the principle is not personal-development folklore; it is how complex systems stay functional. The first example comes from aviation and surgery, where checklists are used to reduce error. Atul Gawande's work on checklists—popularised in *The Checklist Manifesto* (2009) and informed by the World Health Organization's surgical safety checklist introduced in 2008—emphasises that good checklists are short, clear, and revised based on observed failures. They are not comprehensive encyclopaedias. They are "killer items", designed to catch predictable misses. The implication for an Upgrade Day script is that its evolution should be evidence-driven: prompts are added because drift is recurring, removed because they no longer catch anything, and refined because wording matters.

Wording shapes attention.

The second example is software development more broadly, where "versioning" is a normal practice. A system has versions because needs change, bugs appear, and contexts shift. Versioning also creates a valuable psychological effect: it legitimises imperfection. A version is not a final statement; it is a working release. That matters because many people treat personal systems as identity claims. If the checklist is "who I am", changing it feels like instability. If the checklist is "version 3.2 of my ritual", changing it feels like maintenance. Maintenance is calmer than self-reinvention.

Self-reinvention is exhausting.

A credible limitation appears here. Treating the checklist as a living document can become a way of avoiding the harder work of execution. People may tinker: they edit prompts, reorganise sections, redesign templates, and feel productive while behaviour remains unchanged. The name is *ritual procrastination.* The explanation is that editing feels clean and controllable, whereas acting on decisions is messy. The implication is to constrain editing to a short, defined moment within the Upgrade Day—brief, purposeful, and linked to observed outcomes. The checklist evolves to serve action, not to replace it.

Editing is not living.

This brings us to the practical mechanics of evolution, without turning them into a list. The script should be reviewed through a simple lens: which prompts produced decisions that were actually tested over the quarter, and which prompts produced nothing but mild guilt or vague intention. A prompt that repeatedly produces guilt without action is not necessarily "important"; it may be poorly designed, too broad, too moralising, or too disconnected from controllable behaviours. For instance, a prompt like "Am I living my best life?" is grand and mostly useless. It invites theatre. A prompt like "Which recurring commitment did I resent most this quarter?" is specific and points towards a change in calendar or boundaries. It yields a potential decision.

Specificity is kindness.

The script should also evolve in response to life-stage shifts. A person with small children will not have the same quarterly questions as someone without dependants. A person in early career might focus on learning and network-building; someone later might focus on health maintenance, financial stability, or creative legacy. A person caring for a parent may need prompts around emotional load and time realism. The ritual's power lies partly in its ability to stay aligned with what is actually at stake now. A stale checklist forces you to answer yesterday's questions while today's problems quietly grow.

Today deserves its own prompts.

The motif for this subchapter is the *ship's log*. A ship at sea does not carry a single plan and execute it unchanged for months; it keeps a log, makes course corrections, and updates based on weather, currents, and discovered hazards. The log is not proof of indecision. It is proof of navigation. The Upgrade Day script is a kind of log: it records what you noticed and what you chose. Evolution is the act of adjusting the logbook's questions so they continue to capture what matters. The ship's log does not expand indefinitely. It records what helps the next decision.

Decisions steer the ship.

Notice how this reframes personal change. Many systems fetishise consistency of method, as if the method itself were virtuous. Consistency matters, but it is not the highest good. Relevance is. A consistent ritual that asks irrelevant questions becomes a comfort blanket: it feels orderly but does not touch reality. A relevant ritual will sometimes feel sharper because it keeps meeting your life where it is. That sharpness is not cruelty. It is respect for truth.

Truth is the point.

Evolving the checklist also requires attention to language. Over time, certain prompts become loaded. A question framed in moral terms—"Why did I fail to…?"—will provoke defensiveness. A question framed in observational terms—"When did this habit slip, and what was happening then?"—invites analysis without self-attack. The difference is not cosmetic. It determines whether the ritual generates insight or avoidance. This is why good editors are valuable: they shape the conditions for honest thought.

Honest thought needs hospitable wording.

There is also a deeper philosophical issue: the tension between stability and growth. A living document can drift into constant change, which can create a sense of instability. People then feel as if they are always rewriting the rules, never settling. The reconciliation is to keep the structure stable and the prompts flexible. The Upgrade Day's sequence—the cadence, the broad domains, the sense of a quarterly reset—remains consistent. Within that structure, small edits keep the script alive. Think again of Chrome: the address bar stays where it is; the underlying engine improves. The user keeps recognition while gaining capability.

Recognition builds trust.

Trust, in this context, is not an abstraction. It is a behaviour: you show up to the ritual because past versions produced decisions you could execute. You trust the process because it has earned trust through results. A bloated or stale checklist breaks that trust by wasting time or producing nothing. Evolving the checklist is therefore not a creative indulgence; it is a maintenance practice that protects trust. Trust is also cumulative. When the ritual consistently respects your time, you are more likely to protect it from interruptions and more likely to return after an imperfect quarter.

Respect creates resilience.

A final claim: the most valuable edits are often deletions of prompts that once mattered. This is psychologically hard because it requires admitting progress. People cling to old prompts as if removing them might tempt fate: "If I stop checking this, it will fall apart." Sometimes that is true; some metrics need monitoring because drift is persistent. But often the fear is unnecessary. A stable habit does not need constant scrutiny. The point of a quarterly ritual is not to surveil your life. It is to steer it. Removing a prompt can be a declaration that something has stabilised and that attention can be redirected to what is emerging.

Emergence is where drift begins.

The forward test, then, is editorial and existential at once. When the next Upgrade Day arrives and you open the ship's log, will you keep asking questions that no longer generate decisions because they feel familiar, or will you make a small, disciplined revision—one deletion, one refinement, one new prompt—that keeps the ritual lean enough to do and sharp enough to matter?

Involving others wisely

On 24 July 1969, in the Manned Spacecraft Center in Houston, the crew of Apollo 11 began a twenty-one-day quarantine after returning from the Moon. The point was not romance or theatre. It was boundary management: a serious institution deciding what should be shared with the wider world and what should be contained until risk could be assessed. Photographs show the men behind glass, speaking through a telephone, their voices separated from the press by protocol. Even in triumph, the system insisted on separation. It understood a basic truth about collective life: connection is powerful, but unmanaged contact can contaminate.

Boundaries make connection possible.

An Upgrade Day is not a lunar mission, but it is a boundary practice. It asks for honest inventory: money, energy, commitments, relationships, learning. Honesty produces vulnerability. Vulnerability produces risk. The temptation is to treat involving others as a simple virtue—"accountability", "support", "being open". Yet openness is not a universal good. It is a tool. The question is not whether to involve others at all, but how to do it with precision: which parts of the ritual benefit from social contact, which parts are compromised by it, and which relationships are safe enough to hold the truth without turning it into judgement, pressure, or unwanted advice.

Some rooms need a closed door.

The first major claim is that involving others is most valuable when it is designed to improve follow-through, not to perform self-improvement. Show: a person describes ambitious plans to friends, receives praise, feels a surge of identity, and then quietly fails to execute; the talking substitutes for doing. Name: *social substitution.* Explain: social recognition can satisfy the brain's reward circuits in ways that mimic progress; the story becomes the achievement. Implication: involving others should be linked to specific behaviours that still require action—scheduling, testing, reviewing—rather than to big declarations that allow applause without change.

Talk is cheap.

This is not cynicism. It is respect for how humans work. Research on social incentives and goal pursuit has repeatedly found that public declarations can sometimes weaken later effort, particularly when they satisfy identity needs early. Peter Gollwitzer's work on "implementation intentions" distinguishes between vague goals and concrete if–then planning; the empirical thrust is that behavioural specificity matters. The takeaway here is not a slogan but a design principle: involvement should pull decisions into the calendar and into observable tests, not inflate the story of the self.

Stories must meet reality.

A second claim follows: privacy is not the opposite of connection; it is one of its conditions. Many people avoid shared reflection because they fear exposure, criticism, or conflict. That fear is often justified. Involving the wrong person in the wrong way can turn the ritual into a negotiation about values rather than a space for clarity. This is why "wisely" matters. The aim is not to recruit witnesses. It is to design social support that strengthens the practice without hijacking it. The name for the wrong pattern is *invasion by committee.* The explanation is familiar: once multiple people weigh in, the ritual becomes a meeting, and meetings tend to produce compromises, politics, and performative confidence. The implication is that shared Upgrade Day elements should be deliberately narrow.

Narrow is safer.

Here is a checkable example of social design that uses narrowness. Alcoholics Anonymous, founded in Akron, Ohio in 1935, built a structured mutual-support model that relies on meetings, sponsors, and defined practices. Whatever one thinks of its spiritual framing, the system has endured because it combines vulnerability with boundaries: anonymity, shared formats, and repeated rituals. The lesson is not to import AA into this context, but to notice the architecture. It does not depend on confessional free-for-all. It depends on a contained structure that makes disclosure manageable. Structure protects people from each other's worst impulses.

Structure is a form of care.

A second example is professional and more contemporary: peer supervision groups in psychotherapy and clinical practice, common in many countries, where practitioners discuss cases with colleagues under confidentiality norms to improve judgement and avoid blind spots. The group format works not because everyone shares everything, but because the boundary conditions are explicit: what is shared, how it is held, and what kind of feedback is permitted. Even in helping professions, unstructured sharing can produce harm. The implication is clear. If the Upgrade Day is ever shared, the "feedback contract" must be explicit, even if only implicitly agreed: what is being shared, why, and what response is useful.

Response must be designed.

Now the limitation. Some lives are deeply intertwined. Partners share money, living arrangements, childcare, time. In such cases, privacy can become secrecy, and secrecy corrodes trust. The counter-example is a couple trying to manage shared finances without shared visibility: each person privately worries, avoids, and resents, and the quarter ends with surprises. The reconciliation is that involving others is not an all-or-nothing proposition. It can be selective. A person might keep their personal reflections private while sharing decisions that affect the joint system—dates, commitments, spending experiments, travel plans. This preserves dignity and reduces unnecessary conflict while still ensuring alignment where it is required.

Selective sharing is the middle path.

To make this precise, it helps to separate four distinct social modes, not as a rigid taxonomy but as a set of design options. The first is *parallel solitude*: two people conduct their own Upgrade Day at the same time, in the same space, without discussing content until the end. The benefit is environmental support—a shared commitment to the ritual—without forced disclosure. The visible behaviour is simple: same date, same time, separate notebooks. The implication is that the ritual becomes easier to protect because it is socially reinforced, yet privacy remains intact.

Together, but not entwined.

The second mode is *bounded sharing*: each person shares a small, defined set of outputs—perhaps one decision per domain, or a single "trim" and a single "double" in money terms, or one calendar commitment to remove and one to protect—without sharing underlying private reasoning. This mode addresses the earlier risk of invasion by committee. It keeps disclosure at the level of decisions, which are the parts that affect others. The implication is that the ritual produces coordination rather than confession.

Decisions can be shared.

The third mode is *mutual review*: two people agree to review one specific area together—often the area where interdependence is unavoidable, such as shared spending, shared calendar logistics, or shared travel planning—while leaving other areas private. This is where visible metrics become useful. A shared calendar can be scanned together. A shared budget category can be reviewed together. The key is that the shared review uses shared data. It is not a debate about vague impressions. The implication is that social involvement becomes more factual and less emotionally interpretive.

Facts reduce friction.

The fourth mode is *accountability partnership*: two people agree to check in briefly at a defined point in the quarter about one experiment each. The check-in is time-limited and scoped. The motivation is not surveillance but continuity. This mode is especially useful for solitary goals that benefit from gentle witnessing—learning projects, creative work, training consistency—where the presence of another person increases follow-through. The implication is that social support can act as a scaffold for behaviour without requiring intimate disclosure.

Witnessing is powerful.

Each mode carries risk. Parallel solitude can become silent avoidance if no outputs are ever shared. Bounded sharing can become a performance if the person chooses only "safe" decisions to report. Mutual review can drift into argument if underlying values are not aligned. Accountability partnership can turn coercive if one person becomes a manager. This is why the feedback contract matters. A shared ritual should have at least three agreed features, whether spoken or not: that the purpose is support rather than control; that the conversation stays close to decisions and observable behaviours; and that either party can reduce disclosure without punishment. Without these features, involving others can become yet another obligation that drains energy.

Support should feel supportive.

A quiet motif can help here: *the keyhole*. The keyhole is small by design. It allows access without opening the entire door. Involving others wisely often means sharing through the keyhole: offering a small, specific piece of information that is sufficient for coordination or support, without exposing the entire interior of one's life. This is not evasiveness. It is good engineering. Doors exist for a reason. So do keyholes.

Not everything needs an audience.

Modern relevance makes the case sharper. Many people now have a semi-public life by default: group chats, social media, team dashboards, the gentle expectation to narrate work and wellness. The culture subtly rewards disclosure, even when disclosure is unwise. At the same time, loneliness is widely discussed and often real. These two forces pull in opposite directions: public sharing that can feel hollow, private struggle that can feel isolating. The Upgrade Day offers an alternative: deliberate, selective, structured connection. Not broadcasting. Not hiding. Designing.

Design beats improvisation.

This design also matters in workplaces. Some people will want to involve colleagues, particularly when work projects and time management are central. That can be effective, but it is risky because power dynamics distort honesty. A junior employee cannot safely share the same reflections with a manager as with a friend. Even peers can become competitors. The implication is that workplace involvement should be limited to the parts that are appropriate for professional contexts: project priorities, calendar constraints, shared processes. It should not include personal finances, health anxieties, or relationship struggles. The boundary is not prudishness. It is professionalism.

Professionalism protects people.

When involving partners, a different danger appears: coercive alignment. One person may be more enthusiastic about self-improvement and attempt to recruit the other into their tempo. That recruitment can feel like pressure. The name is *cadence colonisation*. The explanation is that rituals carry implicit values, and imposing a ritual can feel like imposing a worldview. The implication is to treat shared versions as opt-in and adjustable, with a genuine respect for difference. A shared ritual should create more freedom, not less.

Freedom is the outcome.

And yet, done well, involving others can create a rare kind of intimacy: not confessional intimacy, but practical intimacy. It is the intimacy of taking a quarter seriously together, of acknowledging constraints without drama, of protecting what matters in shared time. It can also correct blind spots. People are poor judges of their own drift. Others can see what you normalise—how tired you look, how often you cancel, how you talk about money, how work colonises evenings. Carefully chosen feedback can function like a mirror angled just enough to reveal what you cannot see head-on.

Mirrors can be kind.

The forward test is therefore delicate. When the next Upgrade Day arrives, and the question of involving others presents itself, will you open the door too wide—inviting opinion, performance, and pressure—or keep it bolted, protecting privacy at the cost of support and coordination? Or will you use the keyhole: share only what strengthens action, protects trust, and makes the next quarter more truthful for everyone involved?

About the Author

Talia Wrenford is fascinated by the quiet systems that shape everyday life. Over many years, while juggling work, family and personal projects, she found that dramatic resolutions rarely lasted, but small, well-timed resets did. The Upgrade Day grew out of scribbled checklists on scrap paper, refined through dozens of quarters into a simple ritual she could trust.

Talia writes for people who are ambitious about their lives but allergic to performative hustle. She believes that progress should feel like stewardship, not self-punishment, and that numbers are useful only when they serve humane priorities. Her approach is conversational and practical, rooted in lived trial and error rather than grand theories.

Growing up with stories of old quarter days and seasonal festivals, she has always been drawn to the idea that the year comes in chapters, not just one long blur. That sensibility threads through this book: a respect for rhythm, for rest, and for the relief of saying, "I do not have to fix everything today. I just have to steer the next quarter a little better."

www.ingramcontent.com/pod-product-compliance
Lightning Source LLC
Chambersburg PA
CBHW031337230926
51848CB00002B/277
9789376556021